Becoming Parents

Pamela L. Jordan
Scott M. Stanley
Howard J. Markman

Becoming
Parents

How to Strengthen Your Marriage
as Your Family Grows

Jossey-Bass Publishers
San Francisco

The "Re-Romanticing Exercise" in Chapter Twelve (pp. 203–205) is from Hendrix, H., & Hunt, H. (1994). *The couples companion: Meditations and exercises for getting the love you want*. New York: Pocket Books. The exercise is reprinted herein with kind permission of Harville Hendrix and Helen Hunt.

Excerpts and paraphrases of SAVE content incorporated throughout Chapter Fourteen are adapted from Markman, H., Stanley, S., Neidig, P., Leber, D., Blumberg, S., & Holtzworth-Munroe, A. (Aug. 1994). *PREP/SAVE leader's manual*. Denver, CO: PREP Educational Products, Inc., and from Markman, H., Stanley, S., Neidig, P., Leber, D., Blumberg, S., & Holtzworth-Munroe, A. (1993). *Couple's manual*. Stony Brook, NY: Behavioral Sciences Associates, Inc. These materials are reprinted herein with permission of PREP Educational Products, Inc., and Behavioral Sciences Associates, Inc.

Text concerning negotiating household duties in Chapter Sixteen (pp. 267–272) is adapted from Ashery, R. S., & Basen, M. M. (1983). *The parents with careers workbook*. Washington, DC: Acropolis. This material is reprinted herein with permission from Acropolis Books, Inc.

Jossey-Bass books and products are available through most bookstores. To contact Jossey-Bass directly, call (888) 378-2537, fax to (800) 605-2665, or visit our website at www.josseybass.com.

Substantial discounts on bulk quantities of Jossey-Bass books are available to corporations, professional associations, and other organizations. For details and discount information, contact the special sales department at Jossey-Bass.

 Manufactured in the United States of America on Lyons Falls Turin Book. This paper is acid-free and 100 percent totally chlorine-free.

Library of Congress Cataloging-in-Publication Data

Becoming parents: how to strengthen your marriage as your family
    grows/Pamela L. Jordan . . . [et al.].—1st ed.
        p.   cm.
    Includes bibliographical references.
    ISBN 0-7879-4767-9 (alk. paper)
    1. Parenthood. 2. Marriage. I. Jordan, Pamela L., date.
HQ755.8.B435   1999
306.874—dc21   99-24493
                                                     CIP

FIRST EDITION
HB Printing   10 9 8 7 6 5 4 3 2 1

Contents

Acknowledgments

The information in this book is based on the work of many experts on marriage, the family, the transition to parenthood, and health promotion. The work of numerous researchers, theorists, and practitioners has been extremely important to us, including that of Kathryn Barnard, Don Baucom, Steven Beach, Jay Belsky, Susan Blumberg, Tom Bradbury, Andy Christensen, Mari Clements, Jane Cornman, Carolyn and Philip Cowan, Steven Duck, Norm Epstein, Frank Fincham, Frank Floyd, Peter Fraenkel, Mary Fry, John Gottman, Bernard Guerney, Kurt Hahlweg, Kim Halford, Amy Holtzworth-Monroe, Jill Hooely, Ted Huston, Ted Jacob, Neil Jacobson, Danielle Julian, Ralph La Rossa, Kris Lindahl, Gayla Margolin, Sherrod Miller, Peter Neidig, Pat Noller, Cliff Notarius, Dan O'Leary, Gerald Patterson, Lydia Prado, Caryl Rusbult, Cas Schaap, Gary Smalley, and Robert Weiss.

Over the years we have been assisted by a number of outstanding research assistants, consultants, and colleagues as we have developed and evaluated the PREP approach and the Becoming Parents Program. The list is now too long to include here, but we are greatly indebted to each of these people who have worked with us over the years.

We've also had the good fortune to connect with many people who have supported our work in meaningful ways. Two people stand out for their encouragement and assistance in meeting the needs of couples: Bill Coffin and his colleagues in the U.S. Navy and Diane Sollee of the Coalition for Marriage, Family, and Couples Education.

We also want to express our great appreciation for the wonderful staff at PREP, Inc., who help so many couples through their hard work: Natalie Jenkins, Veronica Johnson, Phyllis Lemons, Janelle Miller, Glenda Roslund, Jonathan Wade, and Caroline Bagdasarian.

The research studies underlying the content of this book have been supported by the National Institute of Nursing Research, the University of Washington School of Nursing, the John D. and Catherine T. MacArthur Transition from Early Childhood Network Risk and Prevention Group, the National Institute of Mental Health, the National Science Foundation, and the University of Denver. We are deeply grateful for this essential support that has made our work possible.

Alan Rinzler, our editor at Jossey-Bass, has been supportive and constructively critical throughout. He's been a major contributor to the quality of this book. We thank Alan and the staff at Jossey-Bass for their vital role in bringing this book to life.

Finally, we want to express our deepest gratitude to the individuals, couples, and families who have shared their lives with us in our various research studies. They have opened their hearts and their relationships to our questionnaires, interviewers, and video cameras. The knowledge presented in this book comes from all they have taught us. We also thank our clients and seminar participants who have further shaped our ideas.

The support and assistance of everyone we have mentioned here form the foundation of the book you are about to read. We share a common desire for you to use the knowledge we've gained through years of research to create the type of relationship you want.

April 1999

Pamela L. Jordan
Seattle, Washington

Scott M. Stanley
Denver, Colorado

Howard J. Markman
Boulder, Colorado

Introduction

If you are reading this book, you are probably considering or have already embarked on the most challenging and rewarding adventure of life: parenthood. Congratulations! And welcome to the journey.

Couples typically wonder, "What will become of the two of us as we become three?" This is a legitimate concern. You have probably heard that your relationship is destined to go downhill when you become parents, but parenthood often gets a bad rap that's undeserved. Having a child is a challenging transition for most couples, and there are risks to your relationship during this time of major change. But you can learn ways to protect your relationship and thrive as you move into parenting together. We want to help you make this one of the most wonderful times of your life as partners.

Becoming parents challenges you as individuals and as a couple. The demands of working together to care for a dependent infant or child bring you to a new level of knowing yourself and each other. You can view this time in your life as an opportunity to move your relationship to deeper levels of intimacy and friendship. Although the changes you are or will be going through can magnify any unresolved issues or problems in your relationship, we're here to teach you things that can help you take charge of your issues and your opportunities for lasting love and connection.

We have written this book to help you build and maintain the special and wonderful aspects of your relationship—the two of you!—to create a strong foundation for your family as you become parents and become three—or more. This book is based on the latest research on couple communication and commitment and the experiences of men and women as they become parents for the first time. We will provide you with specific knowledge and survival skills for nourishing your couple relationship, taking care of your self, and dealing with the many ways becoming parents affects your life.

Your marriage is the foundation of your growing family. Just as learning such skills as how to change a diaper or feed a baby will help you care for your new child, learning specific skills to maintain or strengthen your marriage and take care of your self will help you deal better with the many feelings, decisions, and challenges of becoming parents and moving through life together as a couple. Your marriage forms the environment in which your child will grow. Making the effort to have a healthy marriage is one of the most important things you can control that can help your child develop well.

RISKY BUSINESS

Both marriage and parenthood are risky business and have some rather dismal statistics. Although most people marry intending to keep their vows, four out of ten young couples marrying today for the first time will get divorced. And many other couples who do stay together do so despite being unhappy.

Despite the risks associated with marriage, an estimated 90 percent of couples who marry will become parents. Research indicates that at least half of new-parent couples become less satisfied as partners as they become parents; one-third to one-half of them experience as much distress in their marriage as couples who are already in marital counseling. However, some of the latest studies suggest that couples who don't have children experience similar declines in satisfaction over these years of marriage. The decline in marital satisfaction may therefore be more related to the neglect of or damage to the good things between partners rather than to whether or not the partners are parents. Nevertheless, having a child is a major change that many couples don't handle as well as they could.

In the short run, having a baby increases your odds of experiencing depression. One-third or more of both mothers and fathers experience significant depression as they become parents. Depression affects not only the individual but also the marriage and the parent-child relationship. Marital problems are another top cause of depression, and depression is the most common mental health problem in our society.

Despite these startling statistics, the typical preparation for parenthood is really only preparation for labor and birth. Childbirth preparation classes focus primarily on the events of labor and birth, which constitute approximately twenty-four hours in parents' lives, and address the experience and needs of the mother while placing the father in the role of support person. During labor and birth—or the adoption process should you become parents through that route—parents are surrounded by more lay and professional support than they are likely to experience again, unless they are faced with a life-threatening illness. But childbirth preparation classes do little to prepare mothers and fathers for the many life changes that accompany the addition of a first child to the family or their lifetime of parenting—approximately 157,248 hours just until the child reaches eighteen—especially in terms of the effect on their relationship. Although parenthood is the most difficult job anyone could ever have, most of us become parents with little or no preparation.

WHY THIS BOOK?

"When you have a baby, you set off an explosion in your marriage, and when the dust settles, your marriage is different. Not better, necessarily; not worse, necessarily; but different" (writer Nora Ephron). There is great potential during this major life transition—potential for damage, yes, but even greater potential to really thrive in your relationship together. Our intent in writing this book is to focus on the positives and teach information and skills that will help you make your marriage and parenting together all you ever hoped they could be.

We want to help you stay on the positive side of the statistics: healthy individuals forming a couple that stays together for the long run, is happy, continues to grow, and soars to the heights of friendship, intimacy, and teamwork that parenting together can bring. But that will take some work. When it comes to marriage and parenting there's a lot of knowledge about what works and doesn't work, but too often that information doesn't get to the folks in the front lines—you! It's as though you're the first couple to be married or to become parents together!

Our approach is based on the Prevention and Relationship Enhancement Program (PREP®), a program developed by clinical psychologists and marital researchers Dr. Howard Markman, Dr. Scott Stanley, Dr. Susan Blumberg, and various colleagues at the University of Denver. PREP is designed to help couples beat the odds and have happy, healthy, long-lasting marriages. Because of its roots in solid research, its demonstrated effectiveness, and its straightforward approach, PREP has received a great deal of attention from couples across the country, professionals in the field of marital counseling, and the media. PREP workshops use specific steps and exercises to teach couples the skills and attitudes associated with good relationships. Thousands of couples report that their relationships have benefited from the PREP approach. The PREP program comprises Chapters One through Twelve of this book. Those chapters are adapted from the book *Fighting for Your Marriage* (Jossey-Bass, 1994), by Markman, Stanley, and Blumberg.

Although PREP has been used for a number of years around the United States and the world with a variety of engaged and married couples, it wasn't adapted and expanded for use with first-time expectant and new parents until Dr. Pamela Jordan and her colleagues developed the Becoming Parents Program a few years ago. This book consists of the majority of the Becoming Parents Program. Also included is information from the Stop Anger and Violence Escalation (SAVE™) program, which was developed by Dr. Peter Neidig and colleagues to teach couples techniques to effectively manage stress and anger and prevent aggression.

The techniques and strategies in this book are based on the most up-to-date research on marriage and the transition to parenthood. We base our suggestions on solid research rather than pop-psychology speculation; that is, we don't just make assumptions about what may help couples but use research and testing to see what really works. Although we'll discuss problems, patterns, and challenges that can destroy the relationships of couples becoming parents, this book is less about what goes wrong and more about specific things you can do to achieve and maintain a successful, satisfying relationship so that you can parent together as a team.

WHO IS THIS BOOK FOR?

Although any couple can use these techniques, this book is specifically focused on couples who are becoming parents for the first time. There are unique aspects to every journey into parenthood. Some couples become parents by accident, whereas others go to great lengths and costs to become parents through assisted reproductive technology or adoption. Even if you are only considering becoming parents or have already become parents, you can benefit from the information and techniques in this book.

HOW ARE THINGS GOING FOR YOU?

The following quiz is based on a number of marriage studies. Although it was not developed specifically for partners becoming parents, it covers many of the best predictors of marital distress and divorce and can give you a rough idea of how your relationship is doing. If you answer "true" to many of these statements, consider it a warning sign that your relationship needs help.

1. Little arguments escalate into ugly fights with accusations, criticisms, name-calling, or bringing up of past hurts.

2. My partner criticizes or belittles my opinions, feelings, or desires.

3. My partner seems to view my words or actions more negatively than I mean them to be.

4. When we have a problem to solve, it's like we're on opposite teams.

5. I hold back from telling my partner what I really think and feel.

6. I think seriously about what it would be like to be in a relationship with someone else.

7. I feel lonely in this relationship.

8. When we argue, one of us withdraws—that is, doesn't want to talk about it anymore or leaves the scene.

As you read through this book, you will understand not only why these statements are important but also what you as a couple can do to build and maintain the healthy patterns associated with satisfying and lasting relationships.

HOW TO GET THE
MOST OUT OF THIS BOOK

Ideally, you should work through this book with your partner. This means reading each chapter together or individually, then meeting together to discuss it, work through the exercises at the end of the chapter, and practice the skills or techniques being taught. You can gain a great deal, though, by reading and working through this book alone. If even one person applies the information and uses the skills, he or she creates a chain reaction that can be beneficial to both partners.

Often one partner will buy our book and hope to get the other interested. If this is your situation, we have a couple of suggestions. First, be enthusiastic about wanting to work through the book together. Make the point that this is something you want to do for "us"—your marriage—and for your child. Reluctant partners typically respond poorly to pressure.

Second, suggest that your partner leaf through the book to get a feel for it. Most books about becoming parents focus only on the mother and assign the father the role of support person. This book addresses both partners as they become parents. And rather than preaching a particular way to do things, we teach information and skills that will help you decide what's best for you as two unique individuals forming a unique couple and a unique family.

Many people avoid reading self-help books out of a concern that the material will be more of the latest hype from the "guru of the month" club. If this is a concern, you'll find this book refreshing for the no-nonsense, commonsense, research-based ideas it presents. The techniques and recommendations aren't just someone's idea of a "swell thing." They are based on years of research that has shown they work!

A lot of self-help books help people understand themselves or their partner better but do little to help change behavior patterns. All the insight and good intentions won't help if your relationship doesn't change. That's why we give homework in our workshops. In this book, you should do the exercises at the end of each chapter. There's no more effective way to get the most out of the ideas we present.

OVERVIEW OF THE BOOK

The material presented in this book is organized into four parts, each with a number of chapters. These parts represent the following steps related to your becoming parents:

1. How to communicate and handle conflict well
2. How to adopt the attitudes and actions of strong relationships
3. How to preserve and deepen the positive bond between you
4. How to take good care of yourselves and your relationship as you become parents

In Part One, we'll introduce a number of very effective skills for handling conflict and disagreements. These include the following:

- How to talk so your partner will listen

- How to listen so your partner will talk

- How to work through problem solving in an organized and effective way

- How to establish basic rules and procedures for your relationship

These skills will suggest behaviors that may be very different from how you might normally do things, but that's the point. Although these techniques aren't really difficult to understand, they'll take work to master as a couple. Like any new skill, they'll become easier with practice. You will be asked to complete exercises and practice a number of new skills together. We believe it will be worth your effort to make what you learn here a part of your relationship.

In Part Two, we'll concentrate on the ways successful couples think about and view their relationships. Whereas Part One focuses primarily on behavior, Part Two focuses more on thinking patterns and motivation. It emphasizes your individual responsibility to think and act in ways that promote the health of your relationship. You'll be asked to think about

- How hidden issues affect your couple relationship and how to identify and deal with them

- The role of expectations in your satisfaction or dissatisfaction in your couple relationship

- Where core values and beliefs come from and how they affect you and your couple relationship

- The role of commitment in your couple relationship

- The importance of forgiveness to the restoration of couple intimacy

As in the rest of the book, our goal is to help you consider these important dimensions in a useful, straightforward manner that can strongly affect your relationship for the better.

Part Three will help you explore a number of important dimensions related to the reasons people get married in the first place: how to keep friendship, fun, and intimacy alive and well in your couple relationship and protect them from the effects of stress and conflict. Although doing this is difficult in any marriage, the challenge tends to be far greater for parents.

It's difficult to have a healthy and happy couple relationship if you aren't taking good care of your self. And with the added demands of parenting, many people move themselves to the bottom of their priority list. In Part Four, you'll learn strategies to create a healthy lifestyle by managing fatigue, managing stress at work and at home, creating a support network that works for you, balancing work and family responsibilities, and determining who does what at home.

A FEW WORDS ABOUT FATHERS

Women have an advantage in the parenting arena. Because they have the privilege of being pregnant, giving birth, and breast-feeding, mothers tend to be thought of as the *real* parents. Men tend to be thought of as providers and as the protectors of the family. Mothers, therefore, hold a great deal of control over the degree to which fathers are brought into the pregnancy or are involved in parenting. Just as a mother really can't escape the reality of pregnancy, the father can only experience pregnancy vicariously through his mate.

Consequently, for many fathers, the pregnancy and child are not really real until the baby is four to six months old and perceived as a unique human being—a functional, capable, independent, responsive, and interactive person, complete with imperfections. What some mothers see as a lack of interest on the part of their mates is really just the fathers' traveling on a different time line into parenthood.

We believe mothers need to invite their partners into the experience of pregnancy by sharing what they are feeling and thinking. This doesn't mean their just taking the opportunity to complain about the discomforts and inconveniences of pregnancy—though sharing their fears and discomforts would be a natural part of being in it together. Pregnancy is a privilege many men would like to experience. In addition to sharing their experience, mothers need to encourage their partners to share *their* thoughts and feelings. Many men are hesitant to share with their pregnant mate for fear of stressing her and thereby hurting her or the baby. This hesitancy can lead to distance between you and your partner.

If you have shared the miracle of the conception of this child and are going to share parenting, you need to begin by sharing your individual experiences of the pregnancy and your journey into parenthood. Even if you are becoming parents through adoption and neither of you has the advantage of being pregnant, mothers need to invite their partners into parenthood. Although most men want to actively parent their children with their partners, doing so can involve swimming against the current of some strong stereotypes about what being a man is all about.

If men are to be recognized as parents, recognition needs to begin in the couple relationship. Fathers lack the support and role modeling that mothers often take for granted. Even parents, relatives, and friends cast fathers in a supporting role. Again, we are not advocating any particular division of labor in your couple relationship. We just want to provide a warning: if you don't work together to make things the way the two of you prefer them to be, you are likely to get stuck in patterns defined more by others or by rigid stereotypes than by what is best for the two of you and your baby. We want to help you and your partner take charge of this wonderful period of your life together.

Again, congratulations on your growing family! We hope you'll find the information and techniques presented in this book helpful as you make the journey into parenthood. This is a perfect time to rededicate yourselves to each other and your marriage.

Your baby will need immunizations to prevent a number of serious and potentially life-threatening illnesses. The techniques in this book can immunize your couple relationship to prevent problems that can threaten your happiness or even your future together.

Give your baby the best birthday present of all: two parents who love each other and are committed to a healthy and happy marriage and to parenting together as a team. Now, let's begin with Chapter One, where you'll learn more about how couples handle conflict and how we think you can best begin to strengthen your marriage as your family grows.

Becoming Parents

Part I

Handling Conflict
Protecting Your Marriage

M ost couples don't have good skills or techniques for protecting all the wonderful aspects of marriage from the conflicts
and disagreements that will inevitably arise as they become parents.
Conflicts tend to multiply and intensify when a baby joins the family because of all the changes, increased stress, and fatigue. The
majority of Part One focuses on how you can handle the difficult
issues well so as to protect your relationship and family from mishandled conflict.

You will learn specific skills and techniques to deal with issues
and problems as you become parents. These will be essential tools
to use as you work to build a parenting partnership and a marriage
that is all you want it to be. Your relationship forms the core of the
world you live in—the environment for you, your partner, and your
child. One of the most important things you can do to be a great
parent is to work to make your relationship with your partner the
best it can be. A healthy marriage goes a long way toward creating
healthy adults and healthy children.

Four Key Patterns That Can Harm a Relationship

Researchers who study married couples have found that the way couples handle conflict is an important predictor of their chances of divorce. One of the most powerful things you can do to protect your couple relationship as you become parents is learn constructive ways to handle conflicts and disagreements, which will undoubtedly increase when a baby enters the family. In this chapter, we'll focus on four specific patterns that couples often fall into when they are in conflict that usually lead to or indicate relationship problems:

1. Escalation
2. Invalidation
3. Negative interpretations
4. Withdrawal and avoidance

Once you understand these patterns, you can prevent them from taking over in your relationship. We will not only describe these patterns but also teach you, throughout this book, specific constructive skills and techniques to use instead.

SOME RESEARCH FINDINGS

Researchers have identified many of the factors that put marriages at risk. In fact, in some studies, researchers have classified with

90 percent accuracy who will break up and who will stay together, solely by observing premarital or early marital interaction. Some of the factors that increase the likelihood that a relationship won't last are parents' divorce, young age at time of marriage, living together before marriage, differences in religious background, and particular personality traits. It's helpful to know about these factors, but you can't necessarily change them. How couples communicate, especially how couples interact during conflict, is probably the best predictor of relationship problems, and this is something you *can* do something about. All couples have problems and experience conflict as they become parents. How you handle these challenges is what counts most for the future of your family.

We want you to be aware of how destructive these patterns are. Some researchers estimate that one negative interaction can wipe out the effect of up to twenty positive ones! If you have some of these patterns in your relationship, don't despair. We'll teach you more constructive ways of interacting with each other. If you don't have any of these patterns, you still need to be aware of them so that they don't creep into your relationship as you face the challenges of parenthood.

❧ ESCALATION: WHAT GOES AROUND COMES AROUND

Escalation occurs when one partner says or does something negative, the other responds with something negative, and off the two go into a real battle. Couples who are happy now and likely to stay that way are less prone to escalation; and if they do start to escalate, they are able to stop the negative process before it erupts into a full-blown, nasty fight.

As an example of escalation, let's look at Ted, a construction worker, and Wendy, who runs a catering business out of their home.

Ted and Wendy have been married for eight years and recently had a baby. Like many couples, their fights start over small things.

TED: *(sarcastically)* You'd think you could put the diaper cream back where it belongs.

WENDY: *(equally sarcastically)* Oh, like you never forget to put it back.

TED: As a matter of fact, I always put it back.

WENDY: Oh, I forgot just how compulsive you are. You're right, of course!

TED: I don't even know why I put up with you. You're so negative.

WENDY: You could leave. No one's barring the door.

TED: Maybe I will, and I'll take my son with me.

One of the most damaging things about escalating arguments like this is that partners say things that threaten the very lifeblood of the relationship. As frustration and hostility mount, which happens easily with exhausted parents, partners often try to hurt each other with verbal, and sometimes even physical, attacks.

You may be thinking, "But we don't fight like cats and dogs—how does this apply to us?" Escalation can actually be very subtle. Voices don't have to be raised for you to get into a pattern of returning negative for negative. Research shows that even subtle escalation can lead to divorce.

Consider the following conversation between new parents Max and Deanna.

MAX: Did you pay the hospital bill on time?

DEANNA: That was going to be your job. I've got my hands full with the baby.

MAX: You were supposed to do it.

DEANNA: No, you were.

MAX: Did it get done?

DEANNA: No. And I'm not going to, either.

MAX: *(muttering)* Great. Just great.

Deanna and Max are happy with their marriage. Imagine, how-ever, years of small arguments like this taking a toll on their mar-riage by eroding the positive things they now share.

It's very important for the future health of your relationship to learn to counteract any tendency you have for your arguments to escalate. If you don't escalate much, great! Your goal is to learn to keep things that way. If you do escalate a lot, your goal is to recog-nize this pattern and stop it.

Short-Circuiting Escalation

From time to time all couples have arguments that escalate, but some couples steer out of the pattern more quickly and more posi-tively. Compare Ted and Wendy's argument, earlier, with Maria and Hector's. Maria, a sales clerk for a jewelry store, and Hector, an attorney for the Department of Justice, recently adopted a baby boy. Like most couples, many of their arguments are about everyday events.

MARIA: *(annoyed)* You left the formula out again.

HECTOR: *(irritated)* Why are little things so important to you? Just put it back in the refrigerator.

MARIA: *(softening her tone)* But it might be spoiled, and I don't want to take any chances with the baby. Is that so bad?

HECTOR: *(calmer)* I guess not. Sorry I was snotty.

Notice the difference. Like Ted and Wendy, Hector and Maria began to escalate, but they quickly steered out of it. When escala-tion is short-circuited, it's usually because one partner backs off and says something to deescalate the argument, breaking the negative cycle. Here, Maria softens her tone, and Hector avoids getting defensive.

You can avoid, or at least interrupt, many conflicts by using a more gentle approach. As we go on, we'll be teaching you a number of ways to prevent escalation or keep it in check.

☻ INVALIDATION: PAINFUL PUT-DOWNS

Invalidation occurs when you subtly or directly put down the thoughts, feelings, actions, value, or character of your partner. Invalidation includes belittling or disregarding what's important to your partner out of insensitivity or outright contempt. Let's take a closer look at this pattern.

Here are two other arguments between Ted and Wendy and between Maria and Hector.

WENDY: *(very angrily)* You missed your doctor's appointment again! You are so irresponsible. I can see you dying and leaving me and the baby, just like your father.

TED: *(bruised)* Thanks a lot. You know I'm nothing like my father.

WENDY: He was irresponsible, and so are you.

TED: *(dripping with sarcasm)* I'm sorry. I forgot my good fortune to be married to the responsibility poster child.

WENDY: At least I'm not so obsessive about stupid little things.

TED: You are so arrogant.

MARIA: *(with a tear)* You know, I'm really frustrated by the hatchet job Bob did on my evaluation at work.

HECTOR: I don't think he was all that critical. I'd be happy to have an evaluation like that from Fred.

MARIA: *(with a sigh and turning away)* You don't get it. It might mean I won't have a job when my maternity leave ends.

HECTOR: I think you're overreacting.

These examples are as different as night and day. Although both show invalidation, the first example is much more caustic and damaging to the relationship. With Ted and Wendy, the argument has disintegrated into an attack on character.

Although Maria and Hector don't show such contempt, Hector is putting Maria down for the way she's feeling. He may think he's being supportive, but his statement is invalidating. Maria feels hurt because, in effect, her husband has said her concerns are inappropriate. The invalidation displayed by Ted and Wendy in the first example is more destructive than Hector's more subtle form of invalidation.

Another subtle form of invalidation occurs when you're expecting praise for something positive you've done, and your partner ignores the positive and blows out of proportion something minor and negative. For example, suppose you worked hard all morning taking care of the baby and doing the laundry, and your partner came home and complained about the breakfast dishes still being on the counter. You would probably feel pretty invalidated. You were pleased with what you had accomplished, and all your partner could focus on was what you *didn't* do.

Invalidation hurts. People naturally cover up their innermost thoughts and feelings when they believe they will be put down. Invalidation is one of the best predictors of future relationship problems and divorce.

Preventing Invalidation

In the arguments illustrated earlier, both couples would have been better off if each partner had acknowledged and shown respect for the other's viewpoint. See how these conversations could have gone instead.

WENDY: *(very angry)* I'm really angry you missed your doctor's appointment again. I worry about you being around for me and the baby in the future.

TED: *(bruised)* It really upset you, didn't it?

WENDY: Yes! I want to know you're going to be here for us, and when you miss an appointment that I'm anxious about, I really worry about our future as a family.

TED: I understand why it would make you worried when I don't take care of myself.

MARIA: *(with a tear)* You know, I'm really frustrated by the hatchet job Bob did on my evaluation at work.

HECTOR: That must really tick you off.

MARIA: Yeah, it does. I'm afraid I won't have a job when my maternity leave ends. How would we manage without my income?

HECTOR: I didn't know you were so worried about losing your job. Tell me more about how you're feeling.

In these examples, we've replayed the issues with very different outcomes for both couples. Now there is ownership of feelings, respect for each other's character, and an emphasis on validation. By *validation* we mean that the person raising the concern is respected and heard. Validation is a powerful tool you can use to build intimacy and reduce anger and resentment.

You don't have to agree with your partner to validate his or her feelings. It takes discipline to use validation rather than invalidation, especially when you're exhausted, frustrated, or angry, or when the baby is screaming. In later chapters we'll teach you some effective ways to enhance validation.

● NEGATIVE INTERPRETATIONS: WHEN PERCEPTION IS WORSE THAN REALITY

Negative interpretations occur when you interpret your partner's behavior much more negatively than your partner intended or when one partner consistently thinks the motives of the other are more negative than they really are. This can be very destructive and will make it more difficult to deal constructively with any conflict or disagreement.

You can get an idea of the effects of negative interpretations from the following dialogues. Michelle and David have been married six years and are generally happy with their relationship. Yet their discussions have been plagued by a specific negative interpretation. Michelle believes David dislikes her parents when in fact he is quite fond of them. She has this mistaken belief because of a few incidents early in the marriage that David has long forgotten. Here's part of their discussion about taking the baby to meet Michelle's parents.

MICHELLE: The baby is three months old, and my parents still haven't met her. I think we should go see them over the holiday next month.

DAVID: (*thinking how tight the budget is*) I wonder whether we can really afford to make the trip.

MICHELLE: (*in anger*) It's really important they meet their first grandchild. I'm going.

DAVID: I'd like to go. Really. I just don't see how we can afford a thousand dollars in plane tickets. And I think it would be a lot easier if your parents came here rather than our having to travel with the baby.

MICHELLE: You just can't be honest and admit you don't like my parents.

DAVID: There's nothing to admit. I do like your parents. I'm thinking about money here, and what's easiest with the baby.

MICHELLE: That's a convenient excuse. (*storms out of the room*)

If a negative interpretation is strong enough, nothing will change it. David addresses the decision from the perspective of the budget and what will be easiest with the baby. But Michelle's interpretation prevents her from appreciating this and will block effective communication and a solution that would satisfy them both. Fortunately, such negative interpretation is not a consistent pattern in their marriage.

In more troubled marriages, negative interpretations can mount and create an environment of hopelessness and demoralization. Graham and Susan were high school sweethearts, have been married ten years, have two-month-old twin girls, and have been very unhappy in their marriage for more than five years—in part due to the corrosive effect of strong, negative interpretations. Almost nothing either one does is perceived positively by the other, as seen in this recent conversation about parking the car.

GRAHAM: You left the car out again.

SUSAN: Oh. I guess I forgot to put it in when I came home from the pediatrician's.

GRAHAM: *(with a bit of a sneer)* I guess you did. You know how much that irritates me.

SUSAN: *(exasperated)* Look, I forgot. Do you think I leave it out just to irritate you?

GRAHAM: *(coldly)* Actually, that's exactly what I think. I've told you so many times I want the car in the garage at night.

SUSAN: Yes, you have. But I don't leave it out just to tick you off. I just forget. I'm a bit distracted with two little babies.

GRAHAM: If you cared what I thought about things, you'd remember.

SUSAN: You know I put the car in nine times out of ten.

GRAHAM: More like half the time, and that's when I leave the garage door open for you.

SUSAN: It doesn't matter what reality is. You'll see it your way.

This argument may sound minor, but it's not. It is evidence of Graham's long-standing tendency to interpret Susan's behavior in the most negative way possible.

Negative interpretations are a good example of *mind reading*. Mind reading occurs when you assume you know what your partner is thinking or why he or she did something. When your mind reading is positive—when you bring home your partner's favorite ice cream, for example—it doesn't cause damage. But when mind reading includes negative judgments about your partner's thoughts and motives, your relationship is in real danger.

Negative interpretations are so destructive, in part, because they are hard to detect and counteract. We all have a strong tendency to see what we expect to see in others and in situations. We can be wrong, but once we've formed beliefs and expectations about our partner's motives and behaviors, it's difficult to see them more positively.

For example, if you believe your partner only asks you about your parenting techniques to be critical and competitive, you'll never appreciate that your partner respects your abilities and wants to learn from your example. No one is immune to looking for information to confirm his or her expectations about others. In distressed relationships, there is a tendency for partners to discount the positive things they see, believing they happened by chance rather than because of their partner's good intentions.

Battling Negative Interpretations

Merely wishing your partner would change negative behaviors won't make it happen. Negative interpretations are something you have to confront within yourself. Only *you* can control how you interpret your partner's behavior. You need to ask yourself whether there's a chance you might be interpreting your partner's behaviors more negatively than they were intended. Then, although it is difficult to do, you must push yourself to look for evidence against your typical negative interpretation.

As you work through this book and learn techniques to strengthen your relationship, be sure to give your partner the benefit of the doubt. Assume you are both working to change your relationship for the better—to be the best partners and parents you can be. Don't allow negative interpretations to sabotage your efforts.

●WITHDRAWAL AND AVOIDANCE: HIDE AND SEEK

Withdrawal and avoidance are different faces of a pattern in which one partner shows an unwillingness to get into or stay with important discussions. *Withdrawal* can be as obvious as getting up and leaving the room or as subtle as tuning out during an argument. The withdrawer may get quiet during an argument or quickly agree to some suggestion—with no intention of following through—just to end the discussion.

Avoidance indicates the same reluctance to take part in certain discussions, but it involves trying to prevent the conversation in the first place. Someone prone to avoidance would prefer that the topic not come up at all, and if it does, he or she will withdraw. Let's look at this pattern in a discussion between Paula, a real estate agent, and Jeff, a loan officer. They have a three-month-old daughter, Tanya, whom they adore. Paula was concerned that Jeff's anger was putting Tanya in danger.

PAULA: When are we going to talk about how you're handling your anger?

JEFF: Can't this wait? I have to get these bills paid.

PAULA: No, it can't wait. I've brought this up at least five times!

JEFF: (*tensing*) What's to talk about? It's none of your business.

PAULA: (*frustrated and looking right at Jeff*) Tanya is my business. When you lose your temper, I'm afraid you might hurt her. Every time you get angry she starts crying, which makes you even more angry.

JEFF: (*turning away, looking out the window*) I love Tanya. There's no problem here.

PAULA: (*very angry now; Jeff goes into the next room and she follows*) You have to get some help. You can't just keep ignoring this.

JEFF: I'm not going to discuss anything with you when you're like this.

PAULA: Like what? It doesn't matter if I'm calm or frustrated—
you won't talk to me about anything important. You have to face
that you might hurt our baby. (*Jeff is quiet, tense, fidgeting.*) Well?

JEFF: (*going to closet and grabbing sweater*) I'm going out to get
some peace and quiet.

PAULA: (*voice raised, angry*) Talk to me. I'm tired of you leaving
when we're talking about something important.

JEFF: (*looking away from Paula, walking toward the door*) I'm not
talking, you are. Actually, you're yelling. See you later.

Many couples fall into this pattern when dealing with difficult
issues. When you're exhausted and feeling overwhelmed with a new
baby, it may seem easier to push or avoid issues than take the time
to deal with them constructively. One partner *pursues* dealing with
issues (Paula) and one *avoids* or *withdraws* from dealing with issues
(Jeff). This pattern is very common and very destructive to relationships. As with the other patterns we have looked at in this
chapter, it doesn't have to be this dramatic to lead to major relationship problems. Withdrawal and avoidance is one of the most
powerful predictors of relationship unhappiness and divorce.

Pursuing and Withdrawing Dynamics: The Gender Dance

The *pursuer* is the partner who most often brings up issues for discussion or identifies the need to make a decision about something.
The *withdrawer* is the person who tends to avoid or to pull away
from these discussions. Although studies show that men tend to
withdraw and women tend to pursue, there are relationships in
which this pattern is reversed and relationships in which partners
switch roles depending on the topic. Simply reverse the points we
make here if the patterns are reversed for you and your partner.

The partner who withdraws probably does so because it doesn't
feel safe to stay in the argument—meaning it's not emotionally
safe—or even fears the conflict may turn physical. Women with

withdrawing partners usually feel shut out and begin to believe that their partners don't care about the relationship. A lack of talking is interpreted as a lack of caring. Likewise, men complain that their pursuing partners get upset too often, griping about things and picking fights, as if their wives like to fight. Withdrawers want to avoid or stop conflict. Pursuers want to resolve issues. These are both admirable goals, but these patterns can't achieve them. Couples doing the best overall report the least amount of withdrawal, no matter who tends to be the one who pulls away.

It's important to learn how to stay out of this pursuer-withdrawer pattern. This takes working together. Stop yourself from making the most negative interpretation of your partner's behavior during conflict. Research suggests that couples who are happiest, most relaxed together, and most open are those who do the best job of avoiding this pursuer-withdrawer pattern. We'll provide tips for reducing pursuit and withdrawal and ways to avoid these destructive patterns as you become parents.

Avoiding Withdrawal

If you see this pattern in your relationship, realize it will probably get worse if you let it continue. You can't just avoid issues when you have to share responsibility for a baby. As pursuers pursue more, withdrawers withdraw more. And as withdrawers pull back, pursuers push harder. Trying to avoid dealing with important issues leads only to damaging consequences.

In the case of withdrawal and avoidance, you must first realize that your actions cause reactions. You will have greater success if you're working together to prevent or change negative patterns. Withdrawers aren't likely to withdraw less unless pursuers pursue less or more constructively. Pursuers find it difficult to pursue less unless withdrawers deal more directly with the issues at hand.

You need to keep the lines of communication between you open, but in a way in which neither of you feels the urge to withdraw. We will get more specific about how to combat these patterns in the next few chapters. For now, try to agree that if you are having trouble with pursuit, withdrawal, or both, you will work together to change the pattern.

✒ HOW POSITIVE FEELINGS ERODE IN MARRIAGE: THE LONG-TERM EFFECT OF DESTRUCTIVE PATTERNS

It's a myth that the positives in marriage slowly fade away for no particular reason or are wiped out by the addition of a baby to the family. We believe marriages fail at such an alarmingly high rate because couples handle conflict poorly, engaging in such patterns as those described in this chapter. Destructive patterns like these steadily erode all that's good in a relationship.

When partners regularly escalate in their discussions of issues, they may conclude it's just easier not to talk at all. They come to believe that talking always leads to conflict. When partners care more about getting their own way than resolving issues, invalidation becomes a convenient weapon. Eventually, no issue seems safe.

Many couples not only handle issues poorly but also typically have no time set aside to deal with issues nor agreement on how issues will be handled. Even the best relationships can fall victim to these destructive patterns.

Remember Jeff and Paula earlier in this chapter? They are a genuinely caring couple, but their inability to discuss the issue of his anger is damaging and may ultimately harm their child and destroy their relationship if nothing changes.

When negative patterns persist, real intimacy and a sense of connection die out, and couples settle for frustrated loneliness and isolation. A couple is headed for big trouble when one or both partners begin to associate being with the other with pain or the opportunity for a hassle. When your relationship becomes so frustrating, you might turn to the baby and away from your partner. If you want to keep your relationship strong or renew one that's struggling, learn to counteract the destructive patterns we have described. Fortunately, you can do it: you *can* prevent the erosion of happiness in your relationship.

In this chapter, we have described four patterns of handling conflict that predict future relationship dissatisfaction and divorce. We have explained that such patterns are particularly destructive to a relationship and that you are at higher risk of falling into these patterns with the stress and exhaustion of new parenthood. Later in this book, we'll suggest a specific set of agreed-on rules and techniques for handling conflict and difficult issues.

Most couples show some of these patterns to some degree. The following exercises are a first step toward protecting your relationship. In the next chapter, we'll teach you a powerful way to protect your communication against these destructive patterns.

EXERCISES

At the end of each chapter in this book, you will find exercises to help you think about and discuss different aspects of your couple relationship and practice skills to strengthen your marriage as you become parents. These exercises are adult couple work and need to be done when you aren't trying to take care of the baby at the same time. You will benefit most from these exercises if you can devote your full attention to them.

Relationship Danger Signs

Consider each of the questions that follow and jot your answers on a piece of paper. Then meet with your partner to talk about your perceptions. If this discussion raises conflict, put it off until you have worked through the next few chapters and learned more about how to talk safely.

Before getting into specific questions about the four negative patterns, consider the following question about your overall impression of how you and your partner handle conflict together: When you have a disagreement or argument, what usually happens? Think about the four patterns described in this chapter: escalation, invalidation, negative interpretations, and withdrawal and avoidance.

Escalation: What Goes Around Comes Around

Escalation occurs when one partner says or does something negative, the other responds with something negative, and off you go into a real battle.

1. How often do you escalate as a couple?
2. Do you get hostile with each other during escalation?
3. What or who usually brings an end to the fight?
4. Does one of you sometimes threaten to end the relationship when angry?
5. How do you feel when you are escalating as a couple? Do you feel tense, anxious, scared, angry, or something else?

Invalidation: Painful Put-Downs

Invalidation occurs when you subtly or directly put down the thoughts, feelings, actions, value, or character of your partner.

1. Do you often feel invalidated in your relationship? When and how does this happen?
2. What is the effect on you?
3. Do you often invalidate your partner? When and how does this happen?
4. What do you think the effect of invalidation is on your partner? On your relationship? What are you trying to accomplish when you do this? Do you accomplish that goal?

Negative Interpretations: When Perception Is Worse Than Reality

Negative interpretations occur when you interpret your partner's behavior much more negatively than your partner intended or when one partner consistently thinks the motives of the other are more negative than they really are. It's critical that you open yourself to the possibility that your view of your partner could be unfair in some areas. These questions will help you reflect on this possibility.

1. What are some areas in which you consistently see your partner's behavior as negative?

2. Is your negative view of your partner's behavior justified?

3. What are some areas in which you have a negative interpretation but are open to considering that you may be missing evidence to the contrary?

List at least two issues about which you're willing to consider the possibility that your partner has more positive motivations than you've been giving him or her credit for. Next, look for evidence that does *not* support your negative interpretation.

Withdrawal and Avoidance: Hide and Seek

Men and women typically deal differently with conflict in relationships. Men tend to withdraw and women tend to pursue discussion of issues in the relationship.

1. Is one of you more likely to pursue? Is one of you more likely to withdraw?

2. How does the withdrawer usually withdraw? How does the pursuer usually pursue? What happens then?

3. When are you most likely to fall into this pattern as a couple? Are there particular issues or situations that bring out this pattern?

4. How are you affected by this pattern?

5. For some couples, both tend to pursue or withdraw. Is this true for your relationship? Why do you think this happens?

6. What are you thinking while you withdraw or pursue? For example, the withdrawer might be thinking, "I really don't want to fight," while the pursuer might be thinking, "My partner doesn't love me."

You should now have a good understanding of these destructive patterns. This knowledge will help you know what patterns to counteract and replace with the positive behaviors and attitudes we will be teaching you.

2

Communicating Safely and Clearly
The Speaker-Listener Technique

Most couples' communication skills are put to the test when they've been up all night or the baby is screaming. As you learned in Chapter One, handling conflict well is critical to the future of your relationship and your family. And communicating well is critical to handling conflict. There are two keys to communicating well: making it clear and making it safe. In this chapter, you'll learn the Speaker-Listener Technique. When you use this technique, your communication is protected against destructive patterns, making clear and safe communication possible even under the stress and strain of parenting.

MAKING IT CLEAR:
THE PROBLEM OF FILTERS

Have you noticed how what you are trying to say can be very different from what your partner hears? You think you're being clear, but your partner just doesn't seem to "get it." Or you're sure you "know" what your partner said yesterday, yet today your partner says something that seems completely different. We've all experienced the frustration of being misunderstood.

Like the rest of us, Anne and Phillip can relate to this common problem. Anne is home with the baby while Phillip works as a counselor. They're both exhausted at the end of each day.

Driving home from work one Thursday night, Phillip thought it would be great to have a quiet dinner with his wife. He was thinking, "I'm wiped out, and I bet she is, too. I'd really like to go out to eat and have a quiet, relaxing dinner with Anne." Good idea, right? This is what happened.

PHILLIP: *(coming in the door)* Let's have a real dinner tonight.

ANNE: *(hears, "The meals you make aren't good enough")* I'd like to see *you* prepare a gourmet meal with a crying baby on your hip!

PHILLIP: *(hears her response as an attack and thinks, "Why is she always so negative?")* I made dinner once last week!

ANNE: *(The negative cycle continues, as Anne tends to feel she does everything around the house.)* Bringing home burgers and fries is *not* making dinner.

PHILLIP: *(With frustration mounting, he gives up.)* Just forget it. I didn't want to go out with you anyway.

ANNE: *(confused)* Who said anything about going out?

PHILLIP: *(feeling angry)* I did! I said we should go out to eat, and you got really nasty.

ANNE: I got nasty? You never said anything about going out.

PHILLIP: Did too!

ANNE: You're never wrong, are you?

Phillip had a great idea, yet conflict ruined the evening. Phillip wasn't as clear as he could have been in telling Anne what he was thinking. This lack of clarity left room for interpretation, and Anne assumed he was criticizing her cooking.

This kind of miscommunication happens all the time for parents. Many of the biggest arguments you'll have will begin when one partner fails to understand what the other is saying and does so in a way that fosters anger. What gets in the way?

Filters

Filters change what goes through them. Furnace filters take dust and dirt out of the air. Coffee filters let the flavor through and leave the gunk behind. As with any other filter, what goes into our "communication filters" is different from what comes out.

These communication filters are created from how we're feeling, what we think, what we've experienced in our life, and our family and cultural backgrounds, among other things. We emphasize five types of filters that can affect couples as they struggle for clear communication:

1. Inattention
2. Emotional states
3. Beliefs and expectations
4. Differences in style
5. Self-protection

Inattention

One's attention, or inattention, is a very basic kind of filter. Being able to give one's full attention is a big issue for parents, considering that life without distraction is often a thing of the past.

Internal factors also affect attention; these include exhaustion, thinking about something else, feeling bored, thinking about what you're going to say in response, and so forth. The key is to make sure you have each other's attention when it counts most. For important talks, wait until the baby is asleep, or at least quiet, and turn off the phone so you won't be disturbed. Make it easier to pay attention to one another, and try not to assume your partner is ready to listen just because you're ready to talk. Ask.

Emotional States

Your mood or emotional state can also be a filter. You've probably noticed that when your partner is in a foul mood you can get jumped on even for saying something nice. Research studies demonstrate that we tend to give people more benefit of the doubt when we are in a good mood and less when we're in a bad mood.

The best way to keep these kinds of filters from damaging your relationship is to acknowledge the filter when you are aware that one is operating. Here's an example. Both partners are tired after being up all night with a sick baby. Steve just came in the door from work, and Melissa is trying to cook dinner holding a fussy, sick baby.

STEVE: We've got to get that application for the new apartment finished tonight, or we'll never have more space.

MELISSA: (snapping with anger) I'm not the one who forgot to do it. Can't you see I have my hands full? Do something helpful.

STEVE: I'm sorry. I should have seen you were busy. Rough day?

MELISSA: Yes. I had a very frustrating day. I don't mean to snap at you, but the baby hasn't let me put her down all day, and I've had it up to here. If I'm touchy, it's nothing you've done.

STEVE: (takes the baby) Maybe we can talk about it after dinner.

MELISSA: Thanks.

Without using the term *filter*, Steve and Melissa are acknowledging that one is there. They could have let this conversation escalate into an argument, but Steve had the good sense to see he had raised an issue at the wrong time. He decided not to get defensive and chose to become gentle with Melissa in her frustration. Melissa responded by telling Steve she had a filter going—her bad mood. Knowing this helped him be less defensive.

Many kinds of emotional filters can exist inside a person. Being angry, worried, sad, or upset can color your interpretation of and response to what your partner says. Steve's response was helpful because it opened the door for Melissa to clarify her emotional filter and allowed them to deescalate and be clear with one another.

Beliefs and Expectations

Many important filters come from what you think and expect in your relationship. Research and experience tell us that people tend to see what they expect to see in others, which distorts communication. Studies also show that our expectations can influence the behavior of others. For example, if you believe your partner is upset with you, your partner may sound upset when talking with you, even if your partner isn't upset. We tend to "pull" from others the behavior we expect.

Enrique and Maricela were having problems deciding what to do for fun together. They hadn't had a date since their baby was born eight months ago. They were both frustrated by the lack of time for just the two of them. The following conversation was typical. Note how both acted as though they could read the other's mind.

ENRIQUE: (really wanting to go to a movie but thinking Maricela wasn't interested in going out) Your mother said she could watch the baby tonight. Maybe we should try to do something.

MARICELA: (thinking she'd like to get out but, hearing the tentativeness in his voice, thinking he really doesn't want to go out) Oh, I don't know. What do you think?

ENRIQUE: Well, we could go to a movie, but it's bargain night so we might not get in. Maybe we should just stay home and watch TV.

MARICELA: (thinking, "Aha, that's what he really wants to do") That sounds good to me. Let's make popcorn too.

ENRIQUE: (disappointed, thinking, "I knew it. She really doesn't want to leave the baby and go out and have some fun") Yeah, OK.

In this conversation, there was no escalation, invalidation, or withdrawal. Nevertheless the couple did not communicate well, due to the belief and expectation filters involved. Enrique's belief that Maricela didn't want to go out colored the entire conversation—so much so that the way he asked her to go out led her to think he wanted to stay home. He "knew" she really didn't want to leave the baby, which amounts to mind reading.

Enrique could only see that they stayed in again because that's what she wanted. His mental filter pulled the conversation in this direction and became a self-fulfilling prophecy. Maricela also did a good deal of mind reading. She assumed Enrique was tired and really wanted to stay home. The result was a distorted conversation in which neither said what he or she wanted. By the way, most mind reading that gets couples in trouble carries with it a negative interpretation. If they had been able to communicate clearly, without these filters, Enrique and Maricela might have had a long-overdue date.

Differences in Style

Everyone has a different style of communicating, and different styles can lead to filtering. Perhaps one of you is more expressive and the other more reserved. You may have some trouble understanding each other because you use such different styles. Styles are determined by many influences, including personality, culture, gender, and upbringing. Style differences rooted in family backgrounds can cause huge misunderstandings and become powerful filters that distort communication.

Sue and Trevor came from very different families. His was loud and emotionally expressive. Hers was quiet and reserved. A slightly raised voice in her family meant someone was really upset or angry, whereas it probably wouldn't even be noticed in his. Sue was often upset by Trevor's expressiveness, and Trevor commonly failed to notice when Sue was upset. It's very helpful to discuss your differing styles so that you can prevent misunderstandings with your partner.

Self-Protection

This last kind of filter comes from the fear of rejection, with which we all struggle. In self-protection, we don't say what we really want or feel, out of fear of rejection. Even something as simple as "Wouldn't you like to go see that new movie with me?" can reflect a self-protective stance. Instead of saying it directly, "I'd like to see that new movie. Want to go?" we often hide our desire because if we said it more clearly, it would reveal more of who we are and increase the risk of rejection.

This may not matter a lot when it comes to movies, but when it comes to the real issues of relationships—feelings, desires, and expectations—this tendency can lead to a lot of miscommunication. We'll say more about this when we discuss hidden issues in Chapter Five.

Filters and Memory: That's Not What You Heard

Some of the biggest arguments couples have are about what was said in the past. How often have you wished you had a recording of a previous conversation? These differences in memory typically occur because of the variety of filters operating in all relationships. Any of the filters discussed here can lead to differences and arguments about what was actually said or done in the past.

Read the conversation between Anne and Phillip again. Notice that they ended up arguing about what was said at the start of the conversation. He thought he had asked her out to dinner, but what he had said was vague. She thought he had criticized her cooking, which wasn't what he had said. Without a recording, no amount of arguing could get either one to back down from his or her version of the conversation.

We recommend two things to protect your relationship from such fruitless arguments about the past. First, accept that your memory isn't perfect. Accept that you both have filters and that there is plenty of room for things to be said or heard differently from what was intended.

Second, when you disagree about a memory, don't keep arguing about what was said in the past. We don't know of a single case where that helped a couple solve a problem or draw closer together. Deal with what you each think and feel in the present.

We all have filters, and they seem to become more prominent as you become parents. Either you can remain unaware of them, which can damage your relationship, or you can learn to spot them when conversations go awry. Try to get in the habit of announcing your filter when you are aware there might be one affecting your communication. For example: "I'm really upset about the baby cry-ing all day. I'm sorry I was abrupt. It has nothing to do with you."

We all have different moods, levels of attention, and beliefs. We also have differences in experience and upbringing that can result in filters to clear communication. After discussing the importance of safety in your relationship, we'll teach you a very effective com-munication technique for reducing the effect of filters on your important discussions.

MAKING IT SAFE: THE VALUE OF STRUCTURE

To have a great relationship, both of you must be able to express your beliefs, concerns, and preferences clearly, without damaging your relationship in the process. The patterns we discussed in Chap-ter One—escalation, invalidation, negative interpretation, and withdrawal—can make it unsafe to express what is most important to you. People generally don't share openly without there being some feeling of safety. Filters compound the problem, making it a wonder that couples can communicate about anything important—especially with a baby in the house.

Are relationships necessarily safe? No. Most people want the safe haven of a deep friendship, but many couples just don't get there. *Safe* doesn't necessarily mean *risk-free*. If you are going to share what you are concerned about, hurt by, or hoping for, you are going to take risks. On the one hand, you can't be accepted deeply without offering something deep for your partner to accept. On the other hand, you can take the risk, share deeply, and be rejected. This hurts a lot, because you've chosen to risk a deeper part of yourself in the relationship. If you take the risk and you are validated by your part-ner, you find a deep, soul-satisfying acceptance of who you are, warts and all.

When you disagree, or think you do, more is at stake and more can go wrong. For your relationship to grow through conflict, instead of being damaged by it, you'll need to work at preventing destructive behaviors like escalation, invalidation, negative interpretations, and withdrawal.

One way to avoid destructive behaviors is to use agreed-on techniques and rules to help you in important conversations. We call this adding structure to your conversation. With adequate structure, you can talk about important or difficult issues with less chance of damaging your relationship. When less is at stake or when you aren't in conflict, you don't need much structure. Just communicate the way you are most comfortable. But during the tough times, structure can get you through without damage and possibly lead to greater closeness.

THE SPEAKER-LISTENER TECHNIQUE

The Speaker-Listener Technique offers couples a way to communicate when issues are hot or sensitive or likely to get that way. Any conversation in which you want clarity and safety can benefit from this technique. Most couples can decide who will change the baby's diaper without this technique but can use help when dealing with emotionally sensitive issues like money, sex, or in-laws. It's the structure of the technique that makes it work. Here are the rules.

Rules for Both of You

1. *The Speaker has the floor.* Use a real object as the "floor." We hand out pieces of linoleum or carpet to use as the floor when giving workshops. You can use just about anything, though—a pen, the TV remote control, a diaper. If you don't have the floor, you are the Listener. The Speaker keeps the floor while the Listener paraphrases to keep the roles clear. Speaker and Listener follow the rules for their roles.

2. *Share the floor.* You share the floor over the course of a con-versation. One partner has it to start and may say a number of things. At some point you switch roles, and the floor changes hands. You continue going back and forth between roles.

3. *Don't engage in problem solving.* When using this technique you are going to focus on having good discussions, not on trying to come up with solutions. This is crucial to keeping the discussion on track.

Rules for the Speaker

1. *Speak for yourself. Don't read your partner's mind.* Talk about your thoughts, feelings, and concerns, not your perceptions of the Listener's point of view or motives. Use "I" statements and talk about your own point of view.

2. *Don't go on and on.* Talk in small chunks. You will have plenty of opportunity to say all you want to say, so you don't have to say it all at once. It's very important to limit what you say to manageable pieces in order to help the Listener actively listen. If you are in the habit of giving long monologues, remember that having the floor protects you from interruption, so you can afford to pause to be sure your partner understands you. A good general rule is to limit your statements to just a sentence or two, especially when first learning this technique.

3. *Stop and let the Listener paraphrase.* After saying a sentence or two, stop and allow the Listener to paraphrase what you just said. If the paraphrase isn't quite accurate, politely restate what was not heard as it was intended. Your goal is to help the Listener hear and understand your point of view.

Rules for the Listener

1. *Paraphrase what you hear.* To paraphrase, briefly repeat back what you heard the Speaker say, using your own words, to be sure you understood what was said. The key is to show your partner both that you were listening and that you heard the message he or she

was trying to send. If the paraphrase isn't quite right, which happens often, the Speaker should gently clarify the point being made. If you don't understand something, ask the Speaker to clarify, but you may not ask questions about any other aspect of the issue unless you have the floor.

2. *Don't rebut. Focus on the Speaker's message.* In the Listener role, you may not offer your opinions or thoughts. This is the hardest part of being a good Listener. If what your partner says upsets you, you need to withhold any response you may want to make so that you can continue to *pay attention* to what your partner is saying. You will have the opportunity to respond when you get the floor. As Listener, your job is to speak only in the service of understanding your partner. Any words or gestures that reveal your opinions are not allowed, including making faces. Your task is to understand. You don't have to agree with your partner or even believe that what your partner is saying is logical or reasonable. Your goal is to understand where your partner is coming from and why your partner might feel that way. You can express any disagreement when you have the floor.

Here are some ideas about what good paraphrases sound like. Suppose your partner says, "I really had a tough day, and Mom got on my case again about the baby sucking her thumb." Any of the following might be an excellent paraphrase:

"Sounds like you had a really tough day."

"So your mom's still critical of the baby sucking her thumb."

"Bad day, huh?"

Any of these responses conveys that you have listened and shows what you understood. A good paraphrase can be short or long, detailed or general. If you are uncertain how to get a paraphrase started, you might begin with, "What I hear you saying is . . ." Then fill in what you heard your partner say. Another way to begin a paraphrase is with the words, "Sounds like . . ." Merely repeating your partner's statements word for word does not communicate that you have understood.

When using the Speaker-Listener Technique, the Speaker is always the one who determines whether the Listener's paraphrase was on target. Only the Speaker knows what the intended message was. If the paraphrase wasn't quite accurate, it's important that the Speaker gently clarify or restate the point without responding angrily or critically. As the Listener, be sincere in your effort to show you are listening carefully. Even when you disagree with the point being made, your goal is to show respect for—and validation of—your partner's perspective. That means waiting your turn and not making faces or looking bored. Showing respect is the key. You can disagree completely and still show respect. Just wait until you have the floor to make your points.

There are three more important points: first, when using the Speaker-Listener Technique, it's important to stay on one topic at a time. Many issues are interwoven and can become involved in one conversation. You'll do better discussing important matters if you stick with one issue at a time. Second, don't try to problem-solve prematurely. Focus on having a good discussion to get all the issues on the table. This is the foundation of good problem solving. Third, nothing can help a couple communicate better if the partners' hearts aren't in it. Attitude counts a lot here. You will do best when you *sincerely* want to communicate better.

Using the Speaker-Listener Technique

Here is an example of how this technique can change a conversation that's going nowhere into an opportunity for real communication. Dana and Mark are new parents with a four-month-old baby, Zachary. For years they've had difficulty dealing with issues. Mark consistently avoids discussing problems, and if Dana corners him, he withdraws into himself. They know they need to communicate more clearly and safely on tough topics and have agreed that the structure of the Speaker-Listener Technique might help.

In this case, Dana and Mark have been locked in the pursuer-withdrawer cycle about the issue of Zach's day care as Dana prepares to return to work. However, they've been practicing the Speaker-Listener Technique and are ready to try something different. Let's see what happens.

DANA: We can't leave Zach's day-care situation up in the air any longer. I have to go back to work next month.

MARK: *(not looking up from the TV)* Oh?

DANA: *(walking over and standing in front of the TV)* Mark, we can't leave this decision hanging in the air. I've had it with you putting it off.

MARK: *(recognizing that this would be a wise time to act constructively and not withdraw)* Time out. I can tell we need to talk, but I've been avoiding it because it seems like talking just leads to fighting. Let's try that Speaker-Listener Technique we've been practicing.

The Speaker-Listener Technique is not a natural way to communicate, but it's a relatively safe way to communicate on difficult issues. Each partner gets to talk, each will be heard, and both will show commitment to discussing problems constructively.

If one of you tends to withdraw but starts moving constructively toward the pursuer in this positive way, the effect on the relationship is usually very positive. It contradicts the pursuer's belief that the withdrawer doesn't care about the relationship.

The conversation continues, with Mark turning off the TV and picking up a magnet they use for the "floor."

MARK (SPEAKER): I've been concerned, too. I'm not even sure Zach should go to day care this soon.

DANA (LISTENER): *(paraphrasing)* You're concerned too, and you're not sure he should go to day care yet.

MARK (SPEAKER): Yeah, that's it. These first few years are so important for his development. I'm not sure he should be with someone other than you or me unless the situation is just right.

Note how Mark acknowledges that Dana's summary is accurate before moving on to another point.

DANA (LISTENER): You're worried about him being in the best situation, right?

Dana isn't quite sure she has understood Mark's point, so she makes her paraphrase tentative.

MARK (SPEAKER): Well, partly, but I'm also not sure he's ready to be away from us. Of course, I realize your maternity leave is ending.

Note how Mark gently clarifies. He's moving forward in the conversation, rather than backward. In general, whenever the Listener feels clarification is needed, the Speaker can use the next statement to restate or expand on the intended message.

DANA (LISTENER): So you're feeling torn about Zach needing us a lot and my leave ending.

MARK (SPEAKER): That's right. Here, you take the floor. (*He hands Dana the magnet.*)

DANA (SPEAKER): Well, I appreciate what you're saying. I hadn't realized you'd thought much about it. I was worried you didn't care. (*As Speaker, Dana now validates Mark in the comments he has made.*)

MARK (LISTENER): Sounds like you're glad to hear I'm concerned.

DANA (SPEAKER): Yes. I agree this isn't an easy decision. If we do put him in day care next month, it has to be just the right place.

MARK (LISTENER): You're saying it would have to be just the right day care to do it so soon.

DANA (SPEAKER): Exactly. I think it might be worth trying if we could find a great environment for him. *(Dana feels good with Mark listening so carefully, and lets him know it.)*

MARK (LISTENER): So you would try it if we found just the right place.

DANA (SPEAKER): I might try it. I'm not sure I'm ready to leave Zach and go back to work.

MARK (LISTENER): Even with perfect day care you're not sure you're ready to go back to work.

DANA (SPEAKER): Right. Here, you take the floor again.

As you can tell, they've been practicing. They are both doing an excellent job of following the rules and showing concern and respect for each other's viewpoints. You can have discussions like this on difficult topics, even when you disagree. The key is to make it safe and show respect for your partner's thoughts, feelings, and opinions.

The Advantages of Using the Speaker-Listener Technique

The Speaker-Listener Technique has many advantages over unstructured conversation when couples are discussing difficult issues. Most important is the way it counteracts the destructive styles of communication described in Chapter One. This is crucial. A friend of ours, Gary Smalley, likens this kind of talking to "fast-food drive-through" communication.

"Welcome to WonderBurger. May I take your order?"

"Yes, I'd like a burger, fries, and a vanilla shake."

"That's a burger, fries, and a vanilla shake?"

"Yes."

When it's important to communicate clearly and accurately, you want to be sure to "get it right." It's not that this technique is the be-all and end-all of good communication. It's just a very simple way to be sure that you are sending clear messages and that your partner is hearing what you are saying.

You may be thinking, "But this feels really unnatural." Agreed. In fact, that's the reason it's so effective. What tends to come "naturally" when couples are dealing with difficult issues is often escalation, invalidation, withdrawal, and avoidance. Using the Speaker-Listener Technique slows down the conversation and ensures that the Speaker is heard and that the Listener is listening, and both partners get the opportunity to say what they have to say. When you choose to use the Speaker-Listener Technique, you are making the choice to control any destructive tendencies and give the discussion your best shot by using a caring and disciplined approach to understanding your partner.

The fact that these rules are simple doesn't mean that using the Speaker-Listener Technique is easy. Learning and using any new skill is difficult, especially when you are trying to overcome old habits. Practice is the key to learning any new skill. Also recognize that when you are very frustrated and upset with each other, it's unlikely that anything will work. At those times, it's far better to use Time Out, take a break, and try again when you've both calmed down. We will talk more about taking Time Out and cooling off in Chapter Four.

There are real benefits to agreeing to use the Speaker-Listener Technique for important discussions and tough issues. Using this technique limits a number of problems in communication.

1. *Escalation.* The structure of the technique makes it much harder to get into escalation. In fact, it's almost impossible to escalate if you both follow the rules and work at showing respect.

2. *Invalidation.* The simple process of paraphrasing prevents invalidation because the Speaker gets immediate feedback from the Listener on what was heard. You can strengthen the validation by saying, "I see what you mean" or "That makes sense" at the end of a paraphrase or when you get the floor. This doesn't mean you agree, just that you can see it from your partner's perspective.

3. *Pursuit and withdrawal.* For people who tend to withdraw from possible conflict, the structure makes it safer to remain in the conversation. With a clear sense that both of you are committed to keeping things from getting out of hand, there's less to be anxious about. For people who are usually in the pursuer role, structure in conversations ensures that you will be heard and issues addressed. This gets you both closer to a win-win situation and out of hopeless win-lose cycles. You can beat these common and destructive patterns by working together.

4. *Filters.* The Speaker-Listener Technique makes it much easier to identify filters as soon as they come up. They will be evident in the paraphrases. The Speaker will have a nonthreatening opportunity to say, "That's not quite what I said. I said . . . Could you paraphrase again, please?" All types of filters can be reduced using this technique, especially negative interpretations.

When you choose to use these skills, as well as the ground rules we will present in Chapter Four, you are choosing to protect your relationship from destructive conflict by using more structure. Practice is the key. With regular practice of the technique, you can bring about several positive changes. First, the technique will become easier and less artificial over time, so it will be readily available when you really need it.

Second, you'll find yourselves communicating better with each other, even when you're not using the rules. Your new skills will find their way into all your conversations. We can't overestimate the importance of this overall change in how your communicate. It's like the scaffolding you sometimes see being used to construct a building. After the scaffolding is gone, you only see the well-built building, but it was the scaffolding that helped the workers build it right. The Speaker-Listener Technique can have the same effect on your everyday, nonstructured communications.

Third, you'll be limiting damaging patterns and fostering great communication. We see many couples who work with this a while, practice it, then hardly ever need it because the practice completely changed the way they talk about important issues. They shift much more naturally into a better, more respectful communication pattern when issues arise.

∽

If you want to strengthen your couple relationship and reduce your chances of divorce, you need to learn to move toward each other and deal constructively with issues that have the potential to drive you apart. We'll cover many other important principles in this book, but none is more critical.

In the next chapter, you'll learn a structured model for solving problems. If you work at it, you'll find that using it in combination with the Speaker-Listener Technique can make a tremendous difference in your ability to deal with whatever issues you must face as a parenting couple.

EXERCISES

One of the most powerful ways we know to help couples change how they communicate on sensitive or conflictual topics and be able to communicate as a parenting team is by encouraging them to practice the Speaker-Listener Technique. This technique does not work miracles, but it does work well for couples who work on it together. To make something become part of your normal behavior, it must be practiced and practiced. At first it may feel awkward and uncomfortable, but as with anything new, it will become easier over time. Together you need to learn this technique so well that it becomes automatic when you have something difficult to discuss.

If you were just learning to play tennis, you wouldn't try to perfect your backhand on center court at Wimbledon. Instead you would hit backhands against a wall for hours to get it right. Allow yourselves to approach using the Speaker-Listener Technique in the same way—by tackling easy issues first before progressing to the hottest, most difficult issues.

Try to start practicing without the baby around—when the baby is sleeping, for instance. You will master new skills more quickly without distraction. Although we recommend you deal with the toughest issues without distraction, this may not always be possible. Work to master your new skills before you try them with your baby on your lap.

Remember, practicing the Speaker-Listener Technique can help you in two ways. First, you'll have the technique to use when things get rough. Second, practicing it regularly can change the way you talk together in general, even when you aren't formally using the rules.

Practice First with Nonconflictual Topics

Practice this technique *several* times a week for fifteen minutes or so each time, with each of you taking a turn as Speaker and Listener. If you don't set aside the time to practice, you'll never find this powerful technique very helpful.

For the first week, try the technique with only nonconflictual topics. Talk about anything of interest to either of you: your favorite vacation ever, news, sports, your dreams for the future, concerns you have at work, and so on. Try to stay away from topics you know are sensitive or hot. If issues around the baby are hot, postpone those discussions. Your goal here is to practice new skills.

Slowly Begin to Turn Up the Heat

After about three successful practice sessions with nonconflictual topics, choose low-conflict areas to discuss. Sometimes couples have difficulty knowing what will or won't trigger a fight. If the discussion gets heated on a topic you choose, drop it. It won't go away; you can deal with it when you've practiced more together.

Practice several discussions in which you both exchange some thoughts and feelings on these issues. For now don't try to solve problems, just have good discussions. Your goal is to understand each other's point of view as clearly and completely as possible. In the process you may solve some problems simply because all that was needed was to understand what the other person was thinking or feeling. That's OK, but don't set out to solve problems or intentionally try for solutions. You're focusing on good discussions right now. You'll learn and practice problem solving in the next chapter.

Gradually move on to tougher and tougher issues. As you do, remember to stick to the rules. The Speaker-Listener Technique will work if you work at it. As the technique becomes more comfortable, you'll be able to take full advantage of many other ideas presented in this book.

Share Your Experiences of Becoming Parents

Something you will want to discuss as you gain skill using the Speaker-Listener Technique is how you are each feeling about becoming parents or about parenting. If you are going to share parenting, you need to share your individual experiences with each other. Using the Speaker-Listener Technique will provide the structure and safety necessary to share your innermost feelings. You and your partner will benefit from periodically sharing your experiences throughout pregnancy and parenting.

3

Problem Solving

Parenthood brings countless decisions to make and problems to solve. We haven't addressed problem solving until now because most couples try to solve problems before they have really heard each other's views about them. Understanding, before solving, is crucial for maintaining respect and connection in your relationship. In this chapter, we present a straightforward approach to problem solving that can help you through those times when you really need practical, workable solutions.

THREE KEY ASSUMPTIONS

First we need to look at three important assumptions about problems and relationships over time. Couples who understand these assumptions are likely to do better than those who have never thought about these points. These key assumptions are as follows:

1. All parenting couples have problems.
2. Couples who are best at working through their problems work together as a team, not against each other as adversaries.
3. Most parenting couples rush to find quick solutions that don't take into account the real concerns of each partner, and therefore don't produce lasting solutions.

Let's explore each of these three points.

Assumption 1: All Parenting Couples Have Problems

Have you ever wondered why some couples seem to deal with the challenges of parenting so effectively? It's not that they don't have problems. Research shows that the key problems reported by couples change over the course of the relationship. Engaged couples reported that their main problem areas are jealousy and in-laws, which reflects their establishing boundaries with those outside their couple relationship. By the first year of marriage, couples reported communication and sex as more important, which reflects their learning to deal with each other.

Couples seem to shift from working on defining "Who is us and who is not us?" to dealing with "How are we treating one another?" No matter what stage of their relationship, most couples reported struggles with money. In fact, money starts more arguments than any other issue. That makes sense, considering that so many decisions in life revolve around money. Issues about children were second only to money as the most frequent argument starter.

Becoming parents is one of the most wonderful things in life but has the potential to intensify every one of the problems we have listed. Our key point is this: *it's not what your problems are but how you handle them that matters most in your relationship.*

Assumption 2: It's Best to Handle Problems as a Team

For some couples, mutual respect and skill combine to produce a powerful sense of teamwork as the partners work on solutions that will enhance their life together. You have a choice when dealing with a problem: work as a team against the problem or work against each other. Research shows that it's a bad sign when partners feel they are opponents.

Jeremy and Lisa are a couple who have the sense of teamwork flowing in their relationship. They were discussing how to handle feeding their four-month-old son, Brent, while Lisa is at work. Jeremy recently lost his job as a store manager.

LISA: I'm worried about breast-feeding.

JEREMY: What do you mean? Can't he do that when you're at home—with me giving him a bottle during your shift?

LISA: No. That's not going to work because I'll fill up with milk while I'm gone. I make milk whether or not he drinks it.

JEREMY: I had no idea that would be a problem. You mean you can't go through your shift without him nursing?

LISA: Not without being very uncomfortable.

JEREMY: Oh. What can we do to make this work out?

LISA: Well, either Brent nurses on my break or I need to pump.

JEREMY: What's better for you? I could help either way.

LISA: Would you be willing to bring him to work at lunchtime? If he'd nurse well then, that would carry me through the day, and if he needed to eat again before I got home, you could give him a bottle of breast milk.

JEREMY: Sure. I'd be glad to bring him over. That's no problem since I'm not working.

LISA: That would help a lot. I'd also get to see him during the day. Let's give it a try this week.

Notice how Jeremy and Lisa are working together. They're listening to each other, and there is a sense of respect and cooperation. Because they're able to handle this issue so well, there's no particular need to use a more structured approach, such as the Speaker-Listener Technique.

Contrast the tone of Jeremy and Lisa's discussion with that of Chandra and Eric, who have repeated arguments about housework, which generally go like this:

CHANDRA: (calmly) We need to do something about keeping the house looking better. It's such a mess most of the time . . . It's depressing to be here.

ERIC: (a bit annoyed) Look, that's your job. I have to work.

CHANDRA: (hurt and angered) Oh? Did you forget I have the full-time job of taking care of the baby? Besides, you don't even clean up after yourself!

ERIC: I'd do more around here if you earned some money.

CHANDRA: (*anger growing*) I work twenty-four hours a day taking care of our child. You need to do your share.

ERIC: We had a deal: I work and you take care of the baby and the house.

CHANDRA: What deal? When did I agree to do all the work around the house on top of caring for the baby?

ERIC: You said I wouldn't have to do any more work around here when my business picked up. That was the deal.

CHANDRA: (*looking him in the eye, and very angry*) That was when you used to do a lot more than you do now.

ERIC: (*He turns away, indicating that the conversation is over for him.*) I don't agree, and I'm not talking about it any more. A deal's a deal.

This discussion ends with Chandra feeling even more discouraged and with Eric annoyed that she brought up the problem. There is a definite lack of teamwork. All too often people approach problems as if their partner were the enemy to be conquered so that in the end there will be a winner and a loser. The good news is that you don't have to be locked into this pattern. *You can learn how to work as a team.*

Assumption 3: Rushed Solutions Are Poor Solutions

Many well-intended attempts at problem solving fail because couples don't take the time to understand the problem together, which prevents them from working out a solution they can both support. Two major factors cause couples to rush to solutions: time pressure and conflict avoidance.

Time Pressure

Life with a baby can seem like there's more to do than time to do it all. You try the quick fix because you don't believe you have the luxury of time for thorough discussions and thoughtful problem solving. But hasty decisions tend to be poor decisions, requiring you to take more time later to come up with a better solution. You must be committed to spending the time to hash things out thoroughly if you're going to make good decisions together.

Conflict Avoidance

This next example is fairly typical in describing how a couple can rush to a solution that is destined for failure, merely because the partners want to avoid further conflict. Peter and Julie have been married five years and have a two-week-old baby, Katie. It was difficult for Peter to go back to work at the end of last week. He really wanted to be home with "his girls," but this just wasn't possible financially. Each evening he has come home from work and found his mother-in-law there. Her intrusions into their lives have become an issue between Peter and Julie. The following is typical of their attempts to solve this problem.

PETER: *(after Grandma has left)* Your mom is here every night when I come home. *(Julie is tending to the baby and giving no indication that she is paying attention to Peter.)*

PETER: *(frustrated)* Did you hear me?

JULIE: Yes. Mom's being incredibly helpful.

PETER: Does she have to be here all the time? *(really annoyed now)*

JULIE: *(annoyed but calm)* She comes over to help. She's been doing the laundry and cleaning up. She takes care of the baby so I can get showered and dressed. Who do you think has been making dinner every day?

PETER: *(settling down a bit)* That's great, but I'm beginning to feel like an outsider in my own home.

JULIE: OK. I'll be sure she leaves before you come home.

PETER: Good.

End of discussion. The one good thing about this discussion is that they had it. However, it's unlikely that Julie and Peter came to any real resolution of the mother-in-law problem.

This example is typical of what couples do all the time: make quick agreements so that they can avoid conflict. Solutions arrived at this way rarely last, because all the important information isn't "on the table." Peter and Julie haven't addressed the ongoing issue of what Peter sees as the intrusion of Julie's mother into their life as a couple. And they haven't begun to touch the new issue of Peter's resentment of Julie being able to stay home with the baby or his feeling that the baby has replaced him in his wife's affections.

Peter and Julie aren't usually into quick fixes, but they do rush to solutions at times because they hate conflict. Finding a solution can be a relief when you and your partner are talking about an issue that causes distress. However, when you settle on a solution prematurely, the likely payback is more conflict later.

HOW TO HANDLE PROBLEMS WELL

We recommend a structured, step-by-step approach to problem solving. Although the steps are very straightforward, don't be misled by their simplicity. You must be willing to work together, be creative and flexible, and experiment with change. If you are, you'll be able to discover solutions to most of the problems you have to grapple with together as parents.

The steps of the Problem-Solving Process are as follows:

I.   Problem Discussion

II. Problem Solution

    A. Agenda setting

    B. Brainstorming

    C. Agreement and compromise

    D. Follow-up

We'll describe each step, then use a detailed example to help you understand them.

Problem Discussion

Problem Discussion is critical to handling problems well. In this step, you are laying the foundation for the Problem Solution to come. Although you may not agree about how to solve the problem, a good discussion can lead to a clear sense that you're working together and respecting each other.

Whether the problem is large or small, you shouldn't move on to Problem Solution until you both understand and feel understood by the other. This means you have each expressed your feelings and concerns on the topic, and you each believe the other has seen your point of view clearly, whether the other agrees or not.

We recommend you use the Speaker-Listener Technique for Problem Discussion. It's important to emphasize validation in this phase. Problem Solution can proceed much more smoothly in an atmosphere of mutual respect and support. When good discussions precede problem solving, problem solving as a team can go quickly and smoothly, even on the most difficult issues.

Constructive Griping

When you are discussing problems, it sometimes can be helpful to have a way to share gripes constructively. One way to do this is to use what Gottman, Notarius, Markman, and Gonso call an XYZ *statement* in their book, *A Couple's Guide to Communication* (Research Press, 1976). When you use an XYZ statement, you put your gripe or complaint into this format:

When you do X, in situation Y, I feel Z.

An XYZ statement gives your partner usable information: a description of the specific behavior (X), the context in which it occurs (Y), and how you feel when it happens (Z). This format gives your partner specific information about bothersome behavior rather than a vague complaint. It also encourages you to take responsibility for your feelings. Together, these increase the likelihood that the behavior might change.

For example, suppose you had a concern about the way your partner plays with the baby, which ends up costing you sleep. Which of the following statements do you think gives you a better shot at being heard: "You are so selfish," or "When you play so hard with the baby [X] at bedtime when she needs to be quieting down to go to sleep [Y], I feel really angry [Z]"?

It's pretty simple. Although no one likes to hear criticism, this simple technique can increase your chances of sharing it in a constructive way so it can be heard.

Just as using XYZ statements can help reduce the frequency of nasty conflicts, they can help you give each other positive feedback. For example, if you say, "I love you so much," your partner may have no idea what brought about the positive comment. But if instead you say, "When you surprised me by getting a baby-sitter and taking me out to dinner, I felt cared for and loved," your partner knows exactly what behavior you are appreciating, and you are much more likely to see it again.

The key point here is not to move from discussion to solution until you both agree the issue has been fully discussed. As much as 80 percent of the time you'll find that after an excellent discussion, there's really no problem solving to be done. Just having the good discussion and understanding where each of you is coming from are enough. As Mary Lou Casey said, "What people really need is a good listening to."

What most people want in their couple relationship is for their partner to be their friend: someone who listens, understands, and validates. This kind of listening and validation occurs in good problem discussions. Most of the time, what partners want when they are upset isn't agreement or even change but just to feel heard and understood. Nevertheless, many times your discussion of problems or issues will lead to the next step—working together to find specific solutions. The steps of the Problem Solution phase can help you get there.

Problem Solution

The following steps work well for couples, provided the work of Problem Discussion has been done first. As you follow the problem-solving steps here, we do *not* recommend you use the floor. Drop all the structure of the Speaker-Listener Technique and just follow the flow of these next steps.

Agenda Setting

The first step in the Problem Solution phase is to set the agenda. The key here is to be clear about what you are trying to solve at this time. The more specific the problem, the better your chances of coming to a workable solution. We recommend you state the agenda for problem solving in the form of a time-limited question, such as, "How are we going to handle getting the baby to bed earlier this week?" Instead of trying to solve a multifaceted problem all at once, you use agenda setting to help you identify a bite-size problem. Your solution will be focused and therefore easier to try and then evaluate.

At times, your Problem Discussion will have focused from start to finish on a specific problem. In this case, you won't have to define the agenda for problem solving. For example, you may be trying to decide what type of diapers to use on the baby. There may be no specific smaller piece of such a problem, so you will set the agenda to work on it as a whole: What type of diapers will we use for the baby for the first three months? Disposables, diaper service, or cloth laundered at home?

Brainstorming

There are several key points to brainstorming. First, let your creative juices flow. Write down all ideas, from the sublime to the ridiculous. Second, don't evaluate the ideas during this process—you need to control both your verbal and nonverbal responses. And third, have fun with this process; it will fuel your creativity.

The best thing about brainstorming is that it encourages creativity. Write down all the ideas you can. If you can resist the tendency to comment critically on the ideas, you will encourage each other to come up with some great suggestions. Wonderful solutions can come from considering some of the wildest ideas generated through brainstorming. Following these rules helps you resist the temptation to settle prematurely on a solution that isn't the best you can find.

Agreement and Compromise

The goal for this step is to come up with a specific solution or combination of solutions that you both agree to try. We emphasize the word *agree* because the solution is not likely to help unless you both agree to try it. We emphasize *specific* because the more specific you are about the solution, the more likely you will be to give it a try.

Although it's easy to see the value of agreement, some people have trouble with the idea of compromise. We've been criticized for using the term because to some, compromise sounds more like lose-lose than win-win. Compromise implies giving up something you wanted in order to reach an agreement. But we see compromise in a positive light. Many times, the best solution will be a blend of your ideas.

Follow-Up

An important step of the Problem-Solving Process that couples frequently overlook is follow-up. This step involves evaluating how the solution is working after a trial period. Typically solutions are not perfect and need to be tweaked a bit to work for the long term.

In addition, follow-up builds accountability because it requires you both to follow through with your solution and then evaluate it. When you decide on the solution you will try, you need to specify how long you will try it before you evaluate whether or not the solution is working. It also helps to specify "what it will look like" if the solution is working.

Lisa and Jeremy, from the example given earlier, decided to try their solution for one week before evaluating. They also decided that if their solution was working, Lisa would be maintaining her milk supply and wouldn't have breast engorgement, Brent would be fed when he was hungry, and Jeremy would be satisfied both with bringing Brent to Lisa during her lunch break and with feeding Brent bottles of breast milk as needed. When they evaluated after a week, the only change they needed to make was to have Lisa negotiate an earlier lunch hour to accommodate when Brent needed to eat.

Most people are so busy that they don't include the follow-up step, so the solution just doesn't happen or is never tweaked to be successful. This can lead to more dissatisfaction and a feeling of hopelessness about solving the problem. There is an old but true saying: "If you fail to plan, you plan to fail."

When you have found a solution that works well, we recommend you add another component to follow-up: reward. It's important to acknowledge the effort you put into using the Problem-Solving Process successfully and finding an effective solution to your problem. The solution in itself will be a reward, but we urge you to give yourselves another reward. After all, you are working to change how you do things as a couple to make your relationship better. Later in this book we will discuss having fun together, and the exercises for that chapter will provide ideas for rewards.

A DETAILED EXAMPLE: PETER AND JULIE

It didn't take Peter and Julie very long to realize that their problem solving about Julie's mother was not working. They decided to try the steps we are suggesting.

First, they set aside the time to work through the steps. Let's follow them through the process.

Problem Discussion with the Speaker-Listener Technique

PETER (SPEAKER): I appreciate your mom helping you out. I guess there's more to the problem than her being here when I come home.

JULIE (LISTENER): You think there's more to it than Mom being here every day when you come home.

PETER (SPEAKER): (letting Julie know she had accurately heard him) Yeah. I can't tell you how hard it is to force myself to leave you and Katie to go off to work each day. It was just so neat when the three of us were here together at first.

JULIE (LISTENER): You really liked it when it was the three of us together, and it's hard for you to leave us to go to work.

PETER (SPEAKER): We had so much time together, and we each had time with the baby. Now it seems like it's you and Katie and I'm just a visitor.

JULIE (LISTENER): Sounds like you're feeling left out. Is that it? (Here she thinks she understands but wants to be sure her interpretation is accurate.)

PETER (SPEAKER): Yeah. That's exactly what I'm feeling. Here, you take the floor, I want to know what you're thinking. (He hands Julie the floor.)

JULIE (SPEAKER): It really was great when we were all home together. It felt like we were a real family. Now you go off to work, and I feel kinda overwhelmed being totally responsible for the baby all day. I miss the predictable routine of going to work.

PETER (LISTENER): Things aren't great for you either. You miss us all being together as a family.

JULIE (SPEAKER): Right. I'm exhausted and frustrated. I'm still trying to figure out how to take care of Katie. I want to be a good mother, but it's hard. And I really miss you. It doesn't seem like we have any time together anymore.

PETER (LISTENER): Things are tough for you, too. And you miss our time together.

JULIE (SPEAKER): Yeah. I need more time with you and a break from Katie sometimes.

PETER (LISTENER): Me too . . . (*He catches himself interjecting his own opinion.*) Oh, I should paraphrase. You want more time with me and some time off from the baby.

JULIE (SPEAKER): Exactly! I want to work together so things can be better for both of us. There must be a way we can both be happier. (*letting him know she wants to work as a team*)

PETER (LISTENER): You want us to work together to make things better for both of us. (*Julie nods and hands Peter the floor.*)

PETER (SPEAKER): (*suggesting some alternatives*) Since you're with Katie all day, why don't I take her when I come home? She can be my responsibility in the evening until she goes to bed.

JULIE (LISTENER): You'll assume responsibility for Katie in the evening.

PETER (SPEAKER): Yes. Then you can have a break. Maybe we can have some couple time after she's asleep. At least we could have a little time before we both crash.

JULIE (LISTENER): Then we could have some time together after Katie's asleep.

PETER (SPEAKER): Exactly! Here's the floor.

JULIE (SPEAKER): Let's see if we can come up with more solutions together.

They discontinue the Speaker-Listener Technique.

PETER: OK.

JULIE: So, are we both feeling understood enough to move on to Problem Solution?

PETER: I am, how about you? (*Julie nods her head yes.*)

Here they are agreeing they've had a good discussion and are ready to try some problem solving. They are consciously turning this corner together to move into problem solving.

Problem Solution

Peter and Julie now go through the four steps of Problem Solution.

Agenda Setting

Here the important thing is for them to choose to solve a specific piece of the whole issue discussed. This focus increases their chances of finding a solution that will really work this time.

PETER: We should agree on the agenda. We should talk about how to have more time as a couple and how I can have more time with Katie. And then there's getting you some time off from Katie.

JULIE: Right. There are several different things here. Why don't we start with how you and I can have more time together first, and then we can talk about the other things. If we have some couple time, it will be a break from Katie for me.

PETER: OK. Let's brainstorm about how we can have more time together. We can talk about the other stuff at our couple meeting next week.

JULIE: So the question is, How can we have more time together this week?

Brainstorming

The key here is to generate ideas freely.

PETER: Why don't you write down the ideas while we brainstorm, since there's paper right next to you.

JULIE: OK . . . So we could have time together after Katie's asleep and before we crash.

PETER: Since your mom wants to help, maybe we could get her to stay with the baby Saturday night, and we could go out to dinner.

JULIE: We could sell Katie, make a profit, and go back to being footloose and childfree! Just kidding.

PETER: *(laughing)* On the weekend when Katie naps we could just relax and talk together or cuddle a little.

JULIE: Or we could get the girl next door to take Katie for a walk in the stroller. That would give us some time alone together, and we wouldn't have to leave the house.

PETER: This list is pretty good. Let's talk about what we'll try doing.

Agreement and Compromise

Now they sift through the ideas generated during brainstorming. The key is to find a solution they both can agree to.

JULIE: I know we're supposed to go through the pros and cons of each possible solution, but I like all these ideas—except selling Katie, that is. Why don't we really go for it and try to work in all these solutions this week?

PETER: I think that's a great idea. I'm up for the challenge. How 'bout starting tomorrow, we reserve one hour after Katie goes to bed as couple time.

JULIE: That would still leave time for other things that need to be taken care of before we go to bed.

PETER: If you would ask your mom to sit on Saturday evening, I'll make a reservation at that new restaurant we've been talking about.

JULIE: OK. Let's use one of Katie's naps on Saturday to be together. And I'll ask the girl next door to be available to take Katie for a walk on Sunday.

PETER: Yeah. Then maybe we could even cuddle!

JULIE: Are we clear on "the plan"? *(Peter nods.)* Let's schedule some time next week to see how things went and what we want to do for a long-term solution. We also need to remember to talk about ways I can get some time off from parenting.

PETER: Agreed.

They set a time to meet and follow up as planned.

Follow-Up

At their couple meeting the following week, Peter and Julie used most of the time to discuss how their plans had worked. They were both satisfied and agreed to repeat the plan for the next week. Because they had other issues to discuss, they scheduled an extra couple meeting two days later to discuss ideas for getting Julie some time off from Katie.

It felt good to take charge of a problem and manage it successfully. Peter and Julie realized this issue would need attention throughout their parenting career. The success of their solutions was a terrific reward for both of them. Because they had packed so much into the solution for one week, neither felt the need for any additional reward. Both felt that their relationship was being resurrected and had renewed hope that becoming parents didn't mean they had to sacrifice their couple relationship.

We'd like to tell you this model always works this well, but there are times when it doesn't. What do you do then?

WHEN IT IS NOT THAT EASY

In our experience, a few common dilemmas tend to come up when couples are dealing with problems. For example, friction is likely, and things can get heated. If things get so heated that you are resorting to negative behavior, it's time to take an extended Time Out, which we'll discuss later in this book. If you can get back on track by staying with the structure (for example, the Speaker-Listener Technique), great. If not, you need a break until you can continue constructively.

You can get bogged down and frustrated during any segment of the Problem Solution phase. Getting stuck can mean that you haven't talked through some key issues or that one or both of you aren't feeling validated in the process. If so, cycle back to Problem Discussion. In fact, feel free to cycle back to Problem Discussion *at any time* in the process if things heat up or you realize there's more to be dealt with before you can develop a good solution. It's better to slow things down than to continue to press for a solution that may not work.

Also keep in mind that the best solution you can reach may not always be the final solution. At times, you should set the agenda just to agree on the next steps needed to get to the best solution. For example, you might brainstorm about the kind of information you need to make your decision.

WHEN THERE IS NO SOLUTION

For some problems there are no solutions you are both going to feel good about. However, there are far fewer unresolvable problems than couples might think. Nevertheless, suppose you've worked together for some time using the structure, and no solution is forthcoming. You can let this difference damage the rest of your marriage, or you can plan for how to live with it. Sometimes couples allow the rest of a good marriage to be damaged by insisting there must be a solution to a specific unresolved conflict.

If you have a problem that seems unresolvable, you can go back through the problem-solving steps with this agenda: How are we going to protect the rest of our marriage from the fallout from this unresolved problem? This agenda rejoins the two of you in a common goal—protecting your marriage. You would literally be agreeing to disagree. Solutions that can move you forward come from both teamwork and tolerance. You can't always have your spouse be just the way you want him or her to be, but you can work as a team to deal with your differences.

Here we have given you a specific model that works well to help you preserve and enhance your teamwork. We wouldn't expect you to use such a structured approach for minor problems, but we believe you can benefit from using this model with more complex matters, especially those that could lead to unproductive conflict and the danger signs discussed in Chapter One. Using the Problem-Solving Process is one more way to add structure when you need it most and to preserve the best in your relationship. Although you can solve problems a variety of ways, this model will work well to help you preserve and enhance your teamwork in solving the problems you face when you are parents.

You may be thinking, "How can we take so much time to discuss and solve each problem? We'll be too busy with the baby to have such a luxury." Actually, taking the time for thorough problem discussion and structured problem solving saves time. You'll do a much better job and come up with solutions that will work for both of you. *If you don't take the time to do it well, you will come back to the same problem again and again because you either haven't thoroughly discussed the problem or have come up with a solution prematurely.* Invest the time now or deal with the problem again later, when it has probably fueled more conflict.

Before we leave this chapter, we have one more key point to make. Many couples' problems ebb and flow over time but continue to hover around the same issues. That's normal. Nevertheless, you can work on handling your issues as a team and in ways that don't damage the great things.

In the next chapter we conclude this part of the book, which has focused on handling conflict. We will build on the techniques presented so far to help you grow and thrive in your relationship together. The ground rules we present next will help you take control of the conflict in your relationship so that you don't allow it to take control of you.

EXERCISES

There are three exercises for this chapter. First, we would like you to practice using XYZ statements. Next you'll complete an exercise that will help you identify problem areas in your relationship. Third, and most important, you'll have a chance to practice the Problem-Solving Process you learned in this chapter. Learning good relationship skills won't help unless you both are motivated to practice and then use them when needed.

XYZ Statements: Constructive Griping and Constructive Praise

Think about things your partner has done or does regularly that bother you in some way. Write these concerns on a piece of paper as you would typically think about or state them. Once you have several "offenses" listed, rewrite them in the form of XYZ statements: "When you do X, in situation Y, I feel Z." If you run out of gripes about your partner, you can use gripes about others in order to practice enough to feel comfortable using XYZ statements. If you can be specific with your gripes, your partner might be able to understand what bothers you and may even change his or her behavior.

Now repeat the exercise but focus on things your partner has done or does regularly that please you. XYZ statements work just as well for giving specific positive feedback. For example, "When you came home with my favorite ice cream the other night, I felt loved." When you have finished this part of the exercise, share some of these positive thoughts with your partner. Being specific with your praise will increase the likelihood that you'll see the behavior again.

Identifying Problem Areas

The following is a simple measure of common problem areas in couple relationships. Originally developed by Knox in 1971, this technique has been used for years in couple research as a simple but accurate way to identify problem areas. Consider the following list of issues that all couples must face. Copy the list onto a separate piece of paper and add any additional issues there might be in your couple relationship. Now rate how much each issue is a problem in your relationship by writing a number between 0 (not at all a problem) and 100 (a severe problem) next to each issue. For example, if money is somewhat of a problem you might rate it 25. If money is not a problem at all, you would rate it 0, and if money is your major problem, you would rate it 100. Be sure to rate *all* the issues on your list.

Money	Friends	Communication
Recreation	Chores	Religion
Sex	In-laws	Careers
Alcohol/drugs	Jealousy	Other

Practice Problem Solving

When you practice the Problem-Solving Process, it's critical that you follow these instructions carefully. When you are dealing with real problems in your relationship, the possibility of conflict is great, and we want you to practice in a way that increases your chances of mastering these skills.

Once you have both completed your problem inventories, look them over together. Make a list of the issues you both rated as less serious, perhaps 25 and below. These are the issues to discuss as you are *learning* the Problem-Solving Process. Remember, you are learning a new skill, so you don't want to dive into the toughest issues until you both feel comfortable using the Problem-Solving Process. Practice with very specific, real problems and come up with specific and realistic solutions. This way, you will not only practice and become confident with this new skill but also make progress dealing with real issues in your relationship.

Set aside uninterrupted time to practice. This can be a challenge with a baby in the house. Thirty minutes or so should be enough time to use the Problem-Solving Process on some of your less serious issues. Practice the Problem-Solving Process at least three times a week for at least two weeks. This should give you enough time to master this new skill. Stick to the less serious problems at first and then, when you both agree you're ready, move to moderately serious problems. Be sure you and your partner *both* agree that Problem

Discussion is complete before you move into Problem Solution. We recommend you wait to discuss your most serious problems until you and your partner feel comfortable using *both* the Speaker-Listener Technique *and* the Problem-Solving Process. As you practice the Problem-Solving Process, keep this chapter open and refer to the specific steps of the process.

4

Ground Rules for Handling Conflict

A s you have seen in previous chapters, your marriage may be at risk if you don't learn to manage the conflicts and differences that certainly will arise as you become parents. If you do not have the skills to overcome negative patterns, the resulting anger can seriously damage your relationship. Now that you understand some powerful techniques for communicating and solving problems, we turn to our six ground rules for protecting your relationship from mishandled conflict.

We call these *ground rules* to highlight their importance for your marriage. If you use these ground rules properly, you can control difficult issues in your relationship rather than allow the issues to control you. We end Part One with this topic for two reasons. First, the ground rules sum up many of the key points we've made so far. Second, these rules will give you the opportunity to agree on how you want to change the ways you communicate and handle conflict together.

SIX KEY GROUND RULES

GROUND RULE 1: *When conflict begins to escalate, we will call a Time Out and either try talking again, using the Speaker-Listener Technique, or agree to talk about the issue later at a specified time, using the Speaker-Listener Technique.*

If we could get every couple to agree to just one change of behavior as they become parents, this would be it. It's that important! This one simple rule can protect and enhance relationships. Why? In general, it counteracts the negative escalation process that is so destructive to relationships, by giving you an agreed-on method of stopping unproductive arguments. We want you to approach this rule as something you are doing together for the good of your relationship.

You can call a Time Out when a discussion is getting off track, as well as when it is escalating. Time Out is called on the communication, *not* on a person. You call a Time Out in a productive way, by saying, for example, "I'm not sure we're really hearing each other right now. Let's try again after the baby's asleep," or "This is a really important issue, and I think we're getting off track. Let's stop and try it again using the Speaker-Listener Technique." Such statements include your partner, reinforcing that you are working together. When you use Time Out you're recognizing negative patterns and deciding to take a more constructive approach.

Time Out is not avoidance. Another key to this ground rule is that you are agreeing to continue, not avoid, the discussion—productively. You can either continue right now or in the near future, after a cooling-off period. If you are a pursuer, this part of the ground rule addresses your concern that a withdrawer could use Time Outs to prevent discussions about important issues. This ground rule is designed to stop unproductive arguments, not all dialogue on an issue. In agreeing to use the Speaker-Listener Technique when you come back to talking about an issue, you are agreeing to deal with the problem more effectively.

The Time Out itself can give withdrawers confidence that conflict won't get out of hand. Some withdrawers become better able to tolerate conflict, knowing they can stop it at any time. The Speaker-Listener Technique also makes it safer for withdrawers to deal with issues that come up, because it provides all-important structure. This ground rule will work without using the Speaker-Listener Technique, but we are convinced that using the Speaker-Listener Technique is the most effective way to structure talks about difficult issues.

When you decide to talk later, try to set a time right then, perhaps in an hour, or maybe at a specific time the next day. If things were already heated when you called the Time Out, you may find you can't even talk when you come back to the discussion. That's OK. You can set a time after things have calmed down between you. You can use the time while you're waiting to think about the parts of the problem that concern you. This is much better than planning how to "win" the argument.

Luke and Samantha have been married for ten years and have five-month-old twin sons. Before learning these techniques, the couple had frequent, intense arguments that ended with shouting and threats of ending the relationship. Both came from homes where open, intense conflict was common, so changing their pattern wasn't easy. As you'll see, they still escalate easily, but now they know how to stop and turn the discussion around.

SAMANTHA: (annoyed and showing it) You forgot to put the trash out in time for the garbage pickup. The cans are already full.

LUKE: (also annoyed, looking up from playing with the kids on the floor) It's no big deal. I'll just stuff it down more.

SAMANTHA: Yeah, right. The trash will be overflowing in the garage in two days. Where do you suggest I put the dirty diapers?

LUKE: (irritated) What do you want me to do? I forgot, so just leave it alone.

SAMANTHA: (very angry now, voice raised) You aren't getting a lot of things done around here that you're supposed to.

LUKE: This isn't getting us anywhere. Let's call a Time Out.

SAMANTHA: OK. When can we sit down and talk? After we get the kids to bed tonight?

LUKE: OK. As soon as they're asleep.

There is nothing magic here. This ground rule is quite simple, but its effect can be very powerful. Samantha and Luke used Time Out to stop an argument that was going to be destructive. Later, they sat down and talked, using the Speaker-Listener Technique, about Samantha's concern that Luke was not meeting his responsibilities at home. Then, using the Problem-Solving Process we presented in the previous chapter, they were able to come up with some ways to get the chores done as a team.

In this next example, another couple used this ground rule to save an important evening from potential disaster. Byron and Alexandra have been married for six years and have been trying to get pregnant for the last two. This has added plenty of strain to their marriage. They decided to take a weekend trip to a cottage in the mountains for a relaxing—perhaps romantic—couple of days together. For weeks each had been looking forward to this time together. This conversation took place as they got into bed together on their first night at the cottage.

ALEXANDRA: (*feeling romantic and snuggling up to Byron*) It's so nice to get away. No distractions. This feels great.

BYRON: (*likewise inclined, and beginning to caress her*) Yeah, should have done this months ago. Maybe a relaxed setting can help you get pregnant.

ALEXANDRA: (*bristling*) Help *me* get pregnant? That sounds like you think it's *my* fault we're not getting pregnant. Why did you have to bring that up?

BYRON: (*anxious and annoyed at himself for spoiling the moment*) I don't think it's your fault. We've been through that. I just meant . . .

ALEXANDRA: (*angry*) You just meant to say there's something wrong with me.

BYRON: Hold on. Let's take a Time Out. I'm sorry I mentioned pregnancy. Do you want to talk this through now, or set a time for later?

ALEXANDRA: *(softening)* If we don't talk about it a little bit, I think the rest of the evening will be shot.

BYRON: OK, you have the floor. *(He picks a book from the night-stand and hands it to her.)*

ALEXANDRA (SPEAKER): I got all tense when you brought up pregnancy, and I felt like you were blaming me for our infertility.

BYRON (LISTENER): So mentioning that subject raised unpleasant feelings, and more so because you felt blamed.

ALEXANDRA (SPEAKER): Yes. That whole thing has been just awful for us, and I was hoping to get away from it for the weekend.

BYRON (LISTENER): It's been really hard on you, and you wanted to forget about it this weekend.

ALEXANDRA (SPEAKER): And I wanted us to focus on rediscovering how to be romantic, like it used to be, before we had to start having sex on a schedule.

BYRON (LISTENER): Just you and me making love without a care.

ALEXANDRA (SPEAKER): *(feeling really listened to and cared for)* Yes. Your turn. *(hands Byron the floor)*

BYRON (SPEAKER): Boy, do I feel like a jerk! I didn't mean to mess up the moment, though I see how what I said affected you.

ALEXANDRA (LISTENER): You feel bad that you said anything. You didn't mean to mess things up between us tonight.

BYRON (SPEAKER): You got it. And I really don't think it's your fault we're not pregnant. Whatever isn't working right, I don't think of it as you or me messing up. When I said what I said about you getting pregnant, I think of "us" getting pregnant, but really, it's you that will actually be pregnant. That's all I meant.

ALEXANDRA (LISTENER): *(with a smile)* You didn't mean to be a jerk.

BYRON (SPEAKER): *(chuckling back)* That's kind of blunt, but yeah, that's what I'm saying. I think we should just avoid that whole topic for the weekend.

ALEXANDRA (LISTENER): You think we should make infertility an off-limits topic this weekend.

BYRON: Yes! (*He hands her the floor.*)

ALEXANDRA (SPEAKER): I agree. OK, where were we? (*tossing the book on the floor*)

BYRON: (*big smile*) You were calling me a jerk.

ALEXANDRA: (*playfully*) Oh, yeah. Come over here, jerk.

BYRON: (*moving closer to kiss her*) I'm all yours.

Notice how effectively they used Time Out to stop what could have turned into an awful fight and a weekend full of barriers and distance. Alexandra was too hurt to just shelve the issue. She needed to talk right then, and Byron agreed. Using the Speaker-Listener Technique to do so helped them diffuse the tension and come back together, and it saved their special weekend.

GROUND RULE 2: *When we are having trouble communicating, we will use the Speaker-Listener Technique.*

The goal of this ground rule is to ensure that you communicate safely and clearly when you really need to do it well. There are many times when you don't need to call a Time Out but still need to make the transition to a more effective method of communication. Using the Speaker-Listener Technique slows things down, ensures that each of you will have your say, guarantees you'll hear what your partner says so there are no misinterpretations, and makes it safe to talk about sensitive issues.

It's good to use this ground rule when you're planning to talk about a topic that's been hot for you in the past. For example, suppose you wanted to talk about how money is being spent. You know from your history that these talks usually get difficult. You could raise the issue this way: "I'm pretty concerned about money right now. Let's sit down and talk using the floor." Such a statement tells your partner that you are raising an important issue and want to discuss it using added structure. This is the most common use of this ground rule. You can be proactive and learn to use the skills before things go downhill on a tough subject.

If things have already escalated, call a Time Out and then use the Speaker-Listener Technique. In the next example, Allison and James used this ground rule to get back on track. Their new skills made a big difference. This evening, they went out to dinner and, before even ordering, got into an argument.

ALLISON: (*matter-of-factly*) This reminds me. Rich and Barb asked us over for dinner next Saturday. I told them I thought we could do it.

JAMES: (*very angrily*) What! How could you tell them we'd go without even asking me? You know I don't want to leave the baby with your mother again.

ALLISON: (*angry, but speaking in a low, serious tone*) Lower your voice. People are staring at us.

JAMES: (*just as loud as before and just as angry*) So what? Let them stare. I'm sick and tired of you making decisions without talking to me first.

ALLISON: Don't talk to me like this.

JAMES: How 'bout I don't talk to you at all?

At that point, James got up, left the restaurant, and went to the car. He paced a bit, fuming and muttering about how difficult Allison could be at times. Then he got in the car, intending to drive away and leave Allison at the restaurant. "Wouldn't that serve her right?" he thought. As he cooled off, he thought better of that idea. He got up, walked back into the restaurant, took his seat across from Allison, picked up a menu and handed it to her, and said, "OK, you have the floor."

Although it might have been better to postpone this conversation, James decided he wanted to talk it out right away, but more productively. Allison went with it, and they had an excellent discussion of the issue. As they passed the menu back and forth, others in the restaurant must have thought they couldn't make up their minds about what to order. Their transition to greater structure took them from what could have been a real meltdown to a victory in an area where there had been defeat in the past. Experiences like this serve to boost your confidence in your ability to work together and keep your relationship strong.

GROUND RULE 3: *When working on an issue, we will separate Problem Discussion from Problem Solution.*

As we stated in the previous chapter, it's critical to be clear at any given time about whether you are discussing or solving a problem. Too often couples rush into finding a solution, only to find that the solution doesn't work because it was premature and not based on a good discussion. This adds to rather than solves the problem and can result in feelings of hopelessness about the problem and even the relationship.

Go back to Chapter Two and review the conversation between Dana and Mark about Zachary and day care. Notice how they had a great discussion but didn't seek a specific solution. They each expressed and heard one another's concerns. They were ready to try problem solving on this issue. Let's pick it up from where they left off.

DANA: I think we're ready for problem solving. What do you think?

MARK: I agree. I feel like we had a good discussion and got a lot on the table. Now working on some solutions would be great.

With these simple comments, they have made the transition from Problem Discussion to Problem Solution and demonstrate that they've learned the value of separating the two. Discussion and solution are different processes with different goals. Problem Discussion is about understanding each other. Problem Solution is about taking action together. Each works better when you give both of them places in your relationship.

GROUND RULE 4: *We can bring up issues at any time, but the Listener can say, "This is not a good time." If the Listener does not want to talk at that time, he or she takes responsibility for setting up a time to talk in the near future (usually within twenty-four to forty-eight hours).*

This ground rule ensures that you won't have an important or difficult talk about an issue unless you *both* agree the time is right. There's no point having a discussion about anything important unless you're both ready to talk about it.

Unfortunately, most couples talk about their most important issues at the worst times: dinnertime, bedtime, when the baby is demanding attention, as soon as you walk in the door after work . . . You get the picture. These are times when your partner may be a captive audience, but you certainly don't have his or her full attention. In fact, these are often the most stressful times in life, so they are not good times to talk things out.

This ground rule assumes two things: (1) you each are responsible for knowing when you are capable of discussing something and giving your full attention to your partner, and (2) you can each respect the other when he or she says, "I can't deal with this right now." There simply is no point trying to have a discussion unless you are both ready to hear each other.

Perhaps you're thinking, "Isn't this just a prescription for avoidance?" That's where the second part of the ground rule comes in. The partner who is not up for the discussion takes responsibility for making it happen in the near future. This is critical. Your partner will have a much easier time putting off the conversation if he or she is confident you will really follow through, usually within twenty-four to forty-eight hours. This may not always be practical, but it works as a good general rule.

And what about late at night? This is a tricky time for many parenting couples because most of us are so busy that bedtime can seem like the only time to talk. Most often it's a bad time to try to have important discussions because you will be fatigued. You will minimize unproductive discussion and maximize sleep if you both can agree to put off discussion of the issue until the next day. If you follow this ground rule, you will learn to trust that discussions, rather than being avoided, can be temporarily postponed until they can be effective.

Here's an example. Martina and Alex have a thirteen-month-old son. As is typical of many couples with young children, they have little time for sleeping, much less discussions. They are often alone only at bedtime, after the baby is finally asleep.

ALEX: I can't believe how Matt wants to hear the same story ten times in a row. I thought he'd never get to sleep.

MARTINA: It's the same with naps. You'd think he would be bored to death with those stories.

ALEX: I would. Speaking of boring things, we need to talk about those life insurance decisions. I know that agent will call back any day.

MARTINA: I know it's important, but I just can't focus right now. I think I could focus on about ten minutes of reading, and that's about it.

ALEX: Pretty wiped? Me, too. Well, what would be a good time to talk about this?

MARTINA: No guarantee I will be alive, but I think I might have the energy around lunchtime tomorrow. Could you come home? Maybe we'll get lucky and catch Matt on his nap.

ALEX: Sounds good. Let's read a little and crash.

It is now Martina's responsibility to raise the topic tomorrow and to make this discussion happen. This should be fairly easy because their agreement is specific. They may be too tired and busy for there ever to be a perfect time to talk this out, but there are times that are better than others.

To add a variation of this ground rule, you may want to come to an agreement that certain times are never good for bringing up important things. For example, many couples agree never to bring up anything significant within thirty minutes of bedtime. These couples decided they're just too tired at bedtime, and it's important to be relaxing and winding down. Other couples also include transition times: when they are preparing to leave home or arriving back home, on dates, at mealtimes, and so forth. However, the next ground rule is very helpful if you want to protect these special times from conflict.

GROUND RULE 5: *We will have weekly couple meetings.*

Most couples don't set aside a regular time for dealing with issues and problems. As a result, the issues and problems take control of the couple by popping up at times when they can't be dealt with effectively. The primary advantage of having a regular weekly couple meeting is that both of you know there is a specific time and place to deal with issues and problems—to conduct the business of the relationship. Setting aside specific time for its upkeep indicates you are making your marriage a high priority. You may be thinking, "How will we ever find time to do this? With the baby we already don't have enough time for everything." Actually, taking the time for regular couple meetings saves time. Couples tend to come to meetings having thought through issues and with the goal of working through issues and problems in a constructive and productive manner.

When there is a designated time to deal with issues and problems, they are much less likely to pop up in the middle of your fun or intimate times. And if they do, they can be put in their place by your postponing discussion until the next couple meeting. It's so much easier to delay bringing issues up until another time when you know there will *be* another time. Pursuers can relax because they'll have their chance to raise their issue. Withdrawers are encouraged to bring up concerns they have, because there's a meeting just for this purpose.

You will likely be surprised by how much you can accomplish in thirty minutes or so of concentrated attention on an issue. During couple meetings, you can talk about specific issues or problems, talk about your relationship, or practice communication skills, which includes using all the skills and techniques you have learned in the first part of this book. Many couples use some of the time to review and plan the week ahead, determining who will do what and planning for couple time: time for fun, friendship, and intimacy.

When you first start holding couple meetings, you might find you need to hold them more than once a week or that they may need to be longer. This is common when there's a backlog of issues and problems to deal with. As you learn to communicate more effectively and take better care of your couple relationship, your couple meetings will probably become shorter.

You may be thinking this is a pretty good idea, but to put this idea into action, you must be consistent in taking the time to make the meetings happen. You may want to skip meetings at times, but we encourage you not to give in to this urge. If you do, you lose the safety and security of predictable couple meeting time and open the door to the return of destructive patterns of communication.

If you get to a meeting and have little to deal with, fine. Have a short meeting, but be sure to have a meeting. You might use the time to plan a reward for yourselves for dealing effectively with issues and making your relationship strong. When a specific problem is the focus, work through it using the Problem-Solving Process you learned in the previous chapter. Keep the appointment and use the time to keep your relationship strong.

GROUND RULE 6: *We will make time for the great things: fun, friendship, intimacy, and spirituality. We will agree to protect these times from conflict and the need to deal with issues.*

Just as it's important to have time set aside to deal with issues in your relationship, it's critical that you set aside time for enjoying the best parts of your marriage and protect these times from conflict. You can't be focusing on issues all the time and have a really great marriage. You need some nurturing and safe times for relaxing—having fun, talking as friends, making love—when conflict and problems are off-limits. This is such an important point for parents that we'll discuss it in the chapters on friendship, fun, and intimacy later in the book.

For now, we'll emphasize two points embodied in this ground rule. First, set aside specific time for these great things. Second, if you're already spending time together in these ways, don't use it to bring up issues you have to work on. And if an issue does come up, table it for a later time, such as your couple meeting.

The example of Alexandra and Byron that we presented earlier in this chapter makes this point well. They were having a relaxing and romantic weekend, which wasn't the time to focus on one of their key issues. Using Time Out and the Speaker-Listener Technique helped them get refocused on the reason they had gotten away. But it's better still if you agree in the first place to keep such issues off-limits during such positive times.

If you agree to use these ground rules, you are agreeing to control the difficult issues in your relationship rather than allowing them to control you, a real danger with the time demands and fatigue of parenting. Instead of having arguments whenever things come up, usually at the worst times, you are agreeing to deal with the issues when you both are able to do it well, when you are both under control.

EXERCISE

Your exercise for this chapter is very straightforward: discuss these ground rules and try them out. You and your partner may want to modify one or more of the ground rules or come up with additional ground rules to make them work better for you. That's fine. Tailor them to your unique couple relationship and your particular situation as new parents. The key is to take a hard look at these rules and give them a chance to work in your relationship. Discuss the ground rules as listed here. Agree to try them out for at least two weeks. Then discuss them again to decide whether you need to modify or add to them. Periodically review the ground rules to reevaluate the need for modifications or additions. And reward yourselves for using the ground rules!

Ground Rules for Handling Issues

1. When conflict begins to escalate, we will call a Time Out and either try talking again, using the Speaker-Listener Technique, or agree to talk about the issue later at a specified time, using the Speaker-Listener Technique.

2. When we're having trouble communicating, we will use the Speaker-Listener Technique.

3. When working on an issue, we will separate Problem Discussion from Problem Solution.

4. We can bring up issues at any time, but the Listener can say, "This is not a good time." If the Listener does not want to talk at that time, he or she takes responsibility for setting up a time to talk in the near future. (You both need to decide how "the near future" is defined.)

5. We will have weekly couple meetings. (Schedule the time now for your weekly couple meeting. There is no time like the present.)

6. We will make time for the great things: fun, friendship, intimacy, and spirituality. We will agree to protect these times from conflict and the need to deal with issues.

Part II

Going Deeper
Dealing with Core Issues

I n this part of the book, we'll turn our attention to core issues that become more obvious and problematic as you become parents. We'll look at deeper issues—often awakened or magnified by parenthood—that drive conflicts, as well as expectations that affect nearly everything in your relationship. We'll explore the origins of core values and beliefs and why they become more important when a baby joins the family. The material on commitment and forgiveness speaks to some of the most powerful themes in marriage. In this part of the book we want to increase your awareness of issues you need to work through together in order to have a great marriage as a parenting couple.

5

The Difference Between
Issues and Events

So far, we've focused on how you can manage conflict and disagreements in your marriage. Now we want to offer help in dealing with everyday happenings and long-term arguments. All couples experience frustrating events, and all couples have difficult issues, but these events and issues tend to be magnified by parenthood. In this chapter, we'll help you understand how issues and events are connected and how important it is to deal with them separately. Then we'll discuss the deeper, often hidden issues that affect relationships, especially as you try to balance meeting the needs of your child and those of your partner.

ISSUES VERSUS EVENTS

As we pointed out in Chapter Three, the major issues most married couples say cause problems are money, sex, communication, children, and housework. Other things couples commonly fight about are in-laws, recreation, alcohol and drugs, religion, and careers. Although these issues are important, we find that couples argue most frequently about the small, day-to-day happenings of life. We call these *events*. We want to help you separate events from issues and then to separate issues that are more apparent—such as money, communication, sex—from the deeper, often hidden, issues that affect your relationship. An example will help you see what we mean.

Ellen and Greg have big money issues, especially since the baby came. One day, Ellen came home from work and put the checkbook on the kitchen counter as she went to change the baby's diaper. When Greg looked at the checkbook and saw a $150 entry to a department store, he was furious. When Ellen walked back into the kitchen with the baby, she was looking for a hug or a "How was your day?" Instead, the conversation went like this:

GREG: What did you spend $150 on?
ELLEN: (*very defensive*) None of your business.
GREG: Of course it's my business; we just decided on a budget and you're already blowing it.

Suddenly they were in a huge argument about money. But it happened in the context of an event—Greg discovering Ellen had spent $150. It was actually for a gift to celebrate Greg's promotion, but that never came up.

Arguments like this about events are common. Issues and events work like the geysers in Yellowstone National Park. Underneath the park are caverns of hot water under pressure. The issues in your relationship are like these pressure points. The unresolved issues are like cauldrons of pressure. The issues that give you more trouble contain the greatest amount of heat. The pressure keeps building when you aren't talking about issues in constructive ways. Then events trigger the messy eruption.

Many couples with young children deal with important issues only in the context of triggering events. Let that sink in for a moment. For Ellen and Greg, so much negative energy is stored up around the issue of money that it's easily triggered. They never sit down and talk about money in a constructive way, as a separate issue. Instead they argue when bills come, checks bounce, and so forth. They never get anywhere on the big issues because they spend their energy dealing with the crises of events. What about you? Do you set aside time to deal with issues ahead of time, or do you wait until events trigger them?

Another couple, Marcus and Keisha, had avoided talking about the intrusion of relatives in their relationship. One evening they were taking a walk with the baby—the first time they'd been able to talk all week. As they strolled along talking, Marcus got a call on their cell phone from his mother. When the call ended, Keisha confronted Marcus.

KEISHA: Why do you always let her interfere with our relationship? This is the first time we've been able to talk all week.

MARCUS: (*really steaming*) There you go again, blasting me when we finally have some time together.

KEISHA: (*sounding indignant*) Well, I didn't know we were bringing your mother along!

MARCUS: (*dripping with sarcasm*) Ha, ha. Real funny, Keisha.

Their evening was destroyed. They never even finished their walk. They spent the night arguing about his mother calling and whether or not she interfered in their lives.

Events tend to occur at the most inopportune times—when you're ready to leave for work, coming home from work, going to bed, out to relax, busy with the baby, having friends over, and so forth. These are usually the worst times to deal with issues.

HOW TO DEAL
WITH TRIGGERING EVENTS

We're suggesting that you overcome the urge to argue about the issue right at the moment an event triggers it. The key to dealing with this urge is saying to yourself, "I don't have to deal with this right now. This isn't a good time. We can talk later." There are times when simply dropping the matter for the moment is the best strategy.

In the argument we just described, Keisha could have said, "That phone call from your mother really set off an issue for me. I'd like to talk about it later." This way, she would have acknowledged the event but left the issue for a time when they could deal with it more effectively. Likewise, Marcus could have said, "Listen, let's take a Time Out. I can see you're upset, but let's wait for a better time to talk about this issue. How about tonight after we get the baby to bed?" If they had been practicing the skills we've presented so far, this could have saved their evening by containing the event so that it didn't trigger the explosive unresolved issues about his mother and their time together. That's what we mean by separating issues from events. It means not being at the mercy of events but instead controlling them to some degree so that they don't drag you into unproductive arguments about issues.

Marcus and Keisha also could have tried to talk about the issue for a few minutes, agreeing to have a more thorough discussion later. Marcus might have said, "Let's talk about what just happened for a few minutes and then try to move on and have a nice evening together." You can use the Speaker-Listener Technique if you want to be sure you both feel heard, then let the subject go until later.

There never seems to be enough time when a baby joins the family, so there's pressure to deal with issues as they're triggered by events. It seems there's not time now and there won't be time later either, so couples dive right in. Then they wind up in a marital minefield, with issues being the explosives and events being the detonators. You never know when you're going to step on another mine. You feel tense around each other instead of open and relaxed. Though what you want most is simply to enjoy each other as best friends, you end up feeling uptight around each other instead. The effect on your marriage can be devastating.

Practicing the things we've been teaching makes it more likely you'll handle events better as you take the time to deal with important issues. This way, you maintain a level of control as to where, when, and how you will deal with issues.

HIDDEN ISSUES

Most of the time people can recognize the issues being triggered by events because they have almost the same content. With Ellen and Greg, his looking at the checkbook was the event, and the issue was money. That's not hard to figure out. But you'll also find yourselves getting caught up in fights around events that don't seem to be attached to any particular issue. Or you'll find you aren't getting anywhere when talking about particular problems, as though you are spinning your wheels.

These are signs that you aren't getting at the real issues. The real issue isn't money, careers, housework, leaving the toilet seat up, or putting the diaper on backwards. The real issues are deeper and more elusive. We call these *hidden issues*, and they often drive the really destructive arguments.

When we say these issues are hidden, we mean they usually aren't being talked about openly or constructively. They are the key issues that often get lost in the flow of the argument. For instance, you may be aware of feeling uncared for, but when certain events occur, that's not what you talk about. Keisha may have been aware that she felt Marcus didn't think she was as important as his mother, but that's not what they talked about. They couldn't see the forest (the hidden issue) for the trees (the event).

So events are everyday happenings, such as dirty dishes or a bounced check. Issues are those larger topics, like money, sex, and in-laws, with which all couples must deal. Hidden issues are the deeper, fundamental issues that lie underneath the arguments about issues and events. We see at least six hidden issues in our work with parenting couples: power, caring, recognition, commitment, integrity, and acceptance. There are probably others, but these six capture a lot of what goes on in relationships.

Hidden Issues of Control and Power

With control issues the question is, Who will have the status and power? For instance, who decides who will earn the money and who will take care of the baby? Are your needs and desires just as important as your partner's, or is there an inequality? Is your input important, or are major decisions made without you? Who's in charge? If you deal with these kinds of issues a lot, you may be dealing with a hidden issue of control.

This issue is easily triggered as you become parents because there are so many decisions to make and issues to address. It may seem like the baby is the one who is really in control of your life, which can make you even more sensitive to control issues with your partner. You may often find yourself feeling that your partner is trying to control you or that you need to be in control. A power struggle can arise over just about anything.

Whatever the topic or disagreement, control issues are least likely to damage your relationship when there's a good sense of being a team and when each partner's needs and desires are considered in decisions. Some people are hypersensitive about being controlled by others because they've experienced a very controlling authority figure in the past, usually a parent. Such experiences can result in a lack of trust and in negative interpretations that their partner is trying to control them.

It's no accident that money is rated the number one problem area for couples. So many decisions revolve around money. If you have significant power or control issues in your marriage, it's likely you struggle a lot with money as well as any number of other things. Money in and of itself isn't the deeper issue, but it's an issue that provides many events for triggering the deeper issues of control and power.

Whenever you must make a decision together, especially if it's an important one, the control issue can be triggered. When you disagree, one or the other of you gets your way, or you'll compromise.

But it's hard to compromise or let your partner win an argument if it will make you feel controlled or powerless. It's best to keep such issues from being a problem in the first place. Working together as a team is the best antidote to the hidden issue of control.

Hidden Issues of Needing and Caring

A second area for hidden issues involves caring. Here the main theme is the extent to which you feel loved and cared for by your partner. The caring issue is involved when you feel your emotional needs aren't being met. It is likely that one or both of you will at times feel replaced by the baby in your partner's affections.

Tom and Laura repeatedly fought over the cleanliness and neatness of the house after Tom returned to work when their baby was ten days old. But the status of the house wasn't the real issue. Since the baby entered the family, Tom felt Laura no longer loved him— a hidden issue of caring. So he was always harping at her about dirty dishes and things being a mess. He was very aware of feeling uncared for, but in their arguments about the house he didn't talk about it.

For her part, Laura was thinking, "Who made him the cleanliness police? Doesn't he have a clue about what taking care of a baby involves?" Laura had a hidden recognition issue, which we'll explore further in a moment. Our mutual hidden issues often underlie our arguments. *You can't have a big argument about something small or relatively insignificant unless there's a hidden issue involved.*

Hidden Issues of Recognition

The third type of hidden issue involves recognition. Does your partner appreciate your activities and accomplishments? Whereas caring issues involve concerns about being cared for or loved, recognition issues are more about feeling valued by your partner for who you are and what you do. They are easily activated by the changes in roles and responsibilities that occur with becoming parents.

Continuing the previous example, Laura didn't think Tom gave her any credit for taking care of the baby. She thought he believed she just played with the baby all day. He seemed to have no idea how challenging it was to try to meet the seemingly endless demands of a totally dependent infant. As a recovering cleanliness fanatic, Laura was proud to be putting care of the baby ahead of household chores. The couple finally made time to talk.

TOM (SPEAKER): It seems like the baby has replaced me in your life. We used to talk and cuddle. You used to be interested in what I was doing and thinking. Now it seems everything is just baby, baby, baby.

LAURA (LISTENER): *(summarizing in her own words)* So you feel left out and like everything centers around the baby.

TOM (SPEAKER): *(validating her)* Yeah. I just need to know there's still a place in your life and heart for me.

LAURA (LISTENER): You need to know I still love you and want you.

TOM (SPEAKER): Exactly. *(hands Laura the floor)*

LAURA (SPEAKER): Well, I do love you, more than ever. Now I love you not only as my husband but as the father of our child. *(reaches over and gives him a big hug)* When you make comments about the house being dirty or messy, I feel really hurt. I never imagined how much work one little baby could be.

TOM (LISTENER): So you feel hurt when I comment about the house. And the baby is more work than you thought he would be.

LAURA (SPEAKER): *(nodding)* Yes. I thought I'd have plenty of time to take care of the baby and keep up the house. I feel like I'm just in survival mode.

TOM (LISTENER): This isn't how you expected it to be, and you're hangin' on by a thread.

LAURA (SPEAKER): I'm trying so hard to be a good mother and a good wife and still take care of the house. I don't feel like I'm doing a good job at anything. Most days I can't even seem to get dressed.

TOM (LISTENER): *(reaches out and takes her hand)* You're trying hard, and it doesn't seem you're doing anything well. *(Laura nods, with tears welling up in her eyes, and hands him the floor.)* Honey, I'm so proud of you. You're a wonderful mom. I think I have a much better appreciation now of how time consuming it is to take care of the baby. I'll try to do a better job of understanding, and I'll pick up more of the household chores.

As you can see from the end of their conversation, talking about their deeper concerns paved the way for greater connection rather than alienation. But it's difficult to talk about such issues if you can't talk safely! That's the key: to be able to talk about these kinds of deeper issues rather than let them operate as hidden issues in arguments. Tom and Laura's discussion is another example of how difficult it can be to solve the problem about the event (the condition of the house) unless you are communicating well enough to get the hidden issues out in the open.

A hidden issue of recognition indicates that you want your partner to recognize and appreciate what you contribute to the relationship and family. How long has it been since you told your partner how much you appreciate what he or she does?

Hidden Issues of Commitment

The focus of this fourth hidden issue is the long-term security of the relationship expressed by the question, Are you going to stay with me? One couple, Alice and Chuck, had huge arguments about where he was and how he was spending his time. For Alice, the hidden issue was commitment. She started feeling really vulnerable during pregnancy, and these feelings grew stronger after the baby was born. She wanted to know where Chuck was at all times—who he was with and what he was doing. She had two friends whose marriages had fallen apart not long after they became parents, and she was increasingly fearful this might happen to her and Chuck.

Chuck had no plans to leave. In fact, he was working more hours and picking up odd jobs to earn enough money so that Alice could stay home with the baby. But because Alice had never talked about her fear, Chuck wasn't given the opportunity to alleviate her anxiety by affirming his commitment. This issue kept fueling explosive conflict through events connected to it.

When your commitment to each other is secure, it creates a feeling of real safety in your relationship. This safety comes from the honest belief that you will be there for one another, through good times and bad, for the rest of your lives.

Sometimes the issue of commitment is triggered by one partner's success. In healthy relationships, partners tend to take pride in each other's accomplishments. In distressed relationships, people tend to be threatened by their partner's success. One partner's success may be seen as providing more opportunity for that person to leave the relationship. Success can also trigger hidden recognition issues because the other partner may feel a lack of recognition and appreciation in comparison.

Many people who have gone through divorce—their own or their parents'—or other forms of abandonment as children, struggle with fears about commitment. Do you worry about your partner's long-term commitment to you and the marriage? Have you talked about this openly, or is this issue expressed through events in your relationship? In Chapter Eight we'll focus more in depth on how commitment issues affect relationships.

Hidden Issues of Integrity

The fifth type of hidden issue deals with integrity. Have you ever noticed how upset you get when your partner questions your feelings or motives? These events can spark fury.

With Bryant and Lesley, arguments frequently included hurtful statements about each other's intentions. They had a serious problem with negative interpretations of each other. Here's a typical example.

LESLEY: You forgot to pick up more diapers.

BRYANT: *(feeling a bit indignant)* You didn't ask me to pick any up. You asked me if I was going by the store, and I told you I wasn't.

LESLEY: *(really angry at what she sees as his lack of caring about what she needs)* You said you'd pick some up, but you just don't give a damn about me or the baby.

BRYANT: *(feeling thoroughly insulted)* I do care, and I resent your telling me I don't.

Her caring issue is out in the open here, although they aren't exactly having a constructive talk about it. But his issue has more to do with integrity. He feels insulted by Lesley calling him an uncaring, inconsiderate husband who never thinks about her needs or the baby's. He really does care, so he feels judged. Each winds up feeling invalidated.

As we pointed out earlier in this book, it's not wise to argue about what each other really thinks, feels, or intends. Don't tell your partner what's going on inside, unless it's about *your* insides! To do otherwise is guaranteed to trigger the issue of integrity. And almost anyone will defend his or her integrity when it's questioned.

Acceptance: The Bottom Line

One issue seems to underlie all the others listed here: the desire for acceptance—which is often experienced as fear of rejection. At the deepest level, people are motivated to find acceptance and avoid rejection in their relationships. This reflects the deep need we all have to be both respected and connected.

You can see this issue come up in many ways. Some people are afraid that if they make their real desires known, their partner will reject them. A lowered sense of self-worth intensifies such concerns. Sometimes partners will ask for what they want indirectly by saying something like, "Wouldn't you like to make love tonight?" rather than doing so directly by saying, "I'd like to make love with you tonight." Their real desires aren't stated clearly because of fear of rejection.

Let's look more closely at a couple with issues of acceptance. Elena and D.J. are the parents of a six-month-old daughter. They haven't had much of a sexual relationship since the baby was born. This has become more and more of an issue for Elena.

ELENA: I feel like no matter what I do you never want to touch me or be with me. Do you think I'm fat?

D.J.: (*thinking, "Here we go again"*) Don't be ridiculous. You've worked hard to get your figure back since the baby.

ELENA: When I initiate something and you don't want to do anything, I feel like you're rejecting me. How do we say, "This isn't a good time"?

D.J.: (*wanting to short-circuit the repeated argument*) All my focus has been on the baby, and when she's asleep, I'm not making enough effort toward you.

Issues around intimacy often spring from an underlying hidden issue of acceptance. If you don't feel accepted, it's difficult to open yourself to true intimacy. And if your partner doesn't want to be intimate, it's easy to assume, as Elena does, that your partner is rejecting you rather than declining intimacy at that time. The hidden issue of acceptance is often triggered as you become parents. Maintaining open and constructive communication can do a lot to reveal and deal with hidden issues at such times when partners tend to feel vulnerable. (We'll discuss ways to protect and enhance your intimate relationship in Chapter Twelve.)

Recognizing the Signs of Hidden Issues

You can't handle hidden issues unless you can identify them. There are four key signs that hidden issues are affecting your relationship.

Wheel Spinning

One sign of hidden issues is finding yourselves spinning your wheels as you talk about the same problem over and over again. When an argument starts with you thinking, "Here we go again," you should suspect hidden issues. You never really get anywhere on the problem because you aren't talking about what really matters—the hidden issue. Tom and Laura could talk forever about the state of the house but would never solve the problem. Until they got to the hidden issues, problem solving would be premature and ineffective. As it turned out, once they had a good discussion, there was no longer a problem to solve.

Trivial Triggers

A second clue to hidden issues is that minor things get blown way out of proportion. You can't have a big argument about something trivial unless there's a hidden issue. Something bigger is at stake.

Avoidance

A third sign of hidden issues is that one or both of you are avoiding certain topics or levels of intimacy. If walls have gone up between you, it often means important, unexpressed issues are affecting the relationship. Perhaps it seems too risky to talk directly about feeling unloved or insecure. The trouble is, however, that these concerns have a way of coming up anyway.

Couples avoid many topics, reflecting hidden issues in relationships. For example, we have talked with many couples from different cultural or religious backgrounds who avoid talking about these differences. This usually reflects concerns about acceptance. The deeper question is, Will you accept me fully if we really explore our differences? Avoiding such topics not only allows hidden issues to remain hidden but also puts the relationship at greater risk because these important differences can have great impact on a marriage.

Other common taboo subjects in marriage include issues of sex, weight, and money—all of which tend to demand discussion as you become parents. There are many sensitive topics that people avoid dealing with in their relationships out of fear of rejection. What issues do you avoid talking about?

Many couples also avoid certain kinds and levels of intimacy, which may be a symptom of hidden issues. Men often complain that their partners aren't as affectionate as they used to be. Women often say the reason is that they don't feel valued and cared for in the marriage. As a result, they pull back from intimacy, especially sexual closeness. Men notice this and press even more for physical affection to regain their connection. The women pull back further, feeling their partners are only interested in sex. Unpleasant events begin to occur routinely in the bedroom.

Scorekeeping

A fourth sign of hidden issues in your relationship is that one or both of you start keeping score. Scorekeeping is hopelessly biased in your favor because you are with yourself constantly and not always with your partner. Therefore you see all you do for the relationship but not all your partner is doing. Even when you are both contributing equally to the relationship, scorekeeping will lead you to believe you are doing more. If you're keeping score, you're headed for trouble. It could mean you're not feeling recognized for what you contribute to the relationship. It could mean you are less committed. It could mean you're feeling controlled, so you're keeping track of the number of times your partner has taken advantage of you. Whatever the issue, it can be a sign that important things are not being talked about.

Handling Hidden Issues

What can you do when you realize hidden issues are affecting your relationship? You can recognize when one may be operating and start talking about it constructively. This will be easier if you are cultivating an atmosphere of teamwork using the techniques we've presented thus far. We strongly recommend using the Speaker-

Listener Technique when you are trying to explore such sensitive areas.

Another important strategy is to deal with the issue in terms of Problem Discussion, not Problem Solution. Beware of the tendency to jump to premature solutions. In our opinion, the deeper the issue, the less likely problem solving will be the answer. What you need first and foremost is to hear each other and understand each other's feelings and concerns. Such validating discussions have the greatest impact on hidden issues because they work directly against the fear of rejection. There is no more powerful form of acceptance than really listening to the thoughts and feelings of your partner in an understanding and respectful way.

You might also realize one talk usually won't resolve a hidden issue. Hidden issues are like onions with many layers. As you feel safe enough to discuss one issue, or layer of the onion, you are likely to find another issue, or layer, lying beneath it. It may take many discussions to get to the real core issue, and it takes working through many layers of hidden issues. It's worth the time and effort to do so because of the incredible sense of closeness and connection that typically results from this process.

Our goal in this chapter has been to give you a way to explore and understand some of the most frustrating aspects about intimate relationships. You can prevent a lot of damage by learning to handle events and issues with the time and skill they require. Using the model presented here along with the skills and techniques presented in Part One of this book will help you do just that.

For too many new parents, the hidden issues never come out. They fester and produce fear, sadness, and resentment that can erode and destroy the marriage. It doesn't have to be that way. When you learn to discuss deeper issues openly and with emphasis on validating each other, what had been generating the greatest conflicts can actually draw you closer together.

In the next chapter, we turn to the subject of expectations, the source of myriad hidden issues. The next chapter will help you understand what you expect of one another and where these expectations come from.

EXERCISES

Think through the following exercises individually, and jot down notes about your thoughts. Then talk together about your thoughts.

Signs of Hidden Issues

Think through the list of signs that hidden issues may be affecting your couple relationship. Do you notice one or more of these in your relationship? What do you notice?

Wheel spinning

Trivial triggers

Avoidance

Scorekeeping

Identifying Hidden Issues

Next, we'd like you to consider which hidden issues might be triggered most often in your couple relationship. Note if there are certain events that have triggered or keep triggering the issues. On a piece of paper, write down the events that trigger each of the following issues:

Power and control

Caring

Recognition

Commitment

Integrity

Acceptance

Working Through Hidden Issues

Plan some time together to talk about your observations and thoughts. Most couples have certain hidden issues that come up repeatedly. Identifying these can help draw you closer together as you each learn to handle these issues with care. These are likely to be sensitive issues. You'll want to discuss them using the safety and structure of the Speaker-Listener Technique. Your emphasis needs to be on understanding your partner's point of view as fully and clearly as possible, not on resolving some immediate, concrete concern.

6

Unmet Expectations and What to Do About Them

In Chapter Five, we explained how hidden issues can fuel conflict and create distance between partners. Now we're ready to build on those ideas by focusing on expectations: what they are, where they come from, and whether or not they are reasonable or achievable. As you become parents you will become far more aware of your expectations of your partner and your relationship, and they are much more likely to become sources of dissatisfaction and conflict. At the end of this chapter is a very important exercise that will help you explore and share your expectations for your relationship. In fact, this entire chapter is designed to prepare you for that exercise. It's that important.

Exploring your expectations will also help you understand how issues—hidden or not—get triggered in your relationship. Becoming parents and parenting together will raise many issues for both of you. Along with the skills we've taught so far, exploring your expectations will give you the best shot at preventing the kinds of frustrating conflicts we discussed in Chapter Five.

HOW EXPECTATIONS
AFFECT RELATIONSHIPS

We have expectations for every aspect of a relationship. In Part One of this book, we discussed how expectations can become powerful filters that can distort your understanding of what happens in your relationship because people tend to see what they expect to see. In Part One, we focused on how perception can be distorted because of filters.

In this chapter, we focus on your expectations of how things are supposed to be in your relationship. For example, you have specific expectations for such minor things as who will change the baby's diapers or get up with the baby at night—the stuff of events. You have expectations about common issues, such as money, housework, in-laws, and sex. You also have expectations for the deeper, often hidden, issues—how power will be shared (or not shared), how caring will be demonstrated, or what commitment is in your relationship. Expectations affect everything!

To a large degree, we are disappointed or satisfied in life depending on how well what is happening matches what we expected— what we think *should* happen. It is the fit between expectations and reality that is key. Therefore, expectations play a crucial role in determining our level of satisfaction in marriage and parenting together.

Consider Zoey and Max. They've been married for about two years, and things have gone pretty well. Since the baby came, however, Zoey has been upset about Max continuing to go out once or twice a week with his guy friends to play ball, go to sporting events, or to a movie. Like many couples, they have a lot of expectations and issues to resolve about what's OK and what's not. Sometimes the event of his going out triggers huge arguments between them, like this one.

ZOEY: (*feeling agitated*) I don't see why you have to go out again tonight. You've been out a lot lately.

MAX: (*obviously irritated, rolling his eyes*) How many times do we have to argue about this? I go out once a week and that's it. I don't see any problem with that.

ZOEY: Well I do. Your guy friends are all single. You're not only married, you have a child.

MAX: So?

ZOEY: So they're out looking for women.

MAX: (*angered, feeling attacked and accused of being unfaithful*) We don't go out hunting for women. We just enjoy each other. I don't like that you don't trust me.

ZOEY: I just don't think a married man with a baby needs to be out so often with his single friends.

MAX: (*turning away and walking out*) You sound jealous. I have to leave now. I'll be back by ten.

This argument is about expectations. Zoey didn't expect that Max would continue going out with his friends so often once they became parents. She thinks this is something single guys do, not married men, especially those with a child. Max doesn't think there's anything wrong with going out with his friends. It's very important to him. He has cut back since he got married, and he can't understand why it bothers Zoey so much.

In this example, neither expectation is outrageous. What's much more important is that their expectations don't match, and this is fueling conflict. You can imagine that hidden issues of caring and control are also at work. Zoey could be wondering if Max really cares to be with her or is assuming responsibility as a parent, considering that he still wants to go out regularly with his male friends. Max could be feeling that Zoey is trying to control him. They each think the other's expectations are unfair and unrealistic.

EXPECTATIONS AND HIDDEN ISSUES

When events trigger hidden issues, they usually do so because some expectation wasn't met. What underlie *power* issues are expectations about how decisions and control will be shared—or not shared. What underlie *caring* issues are expectations about how one is to be loved. What underlie *recognition* issues are expectations about how your partner should respond to who you are and what you do. What underlie *commitment* issues are expectations about how long the relationship should continue and, most important, about safety from abandonment. What underlie *integrity* issues are expectations about being trusted and respected. Under it all, there are the core expectations about being *accepted*, which we all have. A *hidden issue can't get triggered in the first place unless an expectation has been violated*.

WHERE EXPECTATIONS COME FROM

Expectations build up over a lifetime of experiences. Most expectations are based in the past but still operate in the present. The three primary sources of our expectations are our family of origin, our previous relationships, and the culture in which we live.

Family of Origin

Your family experiences as you grow up lay down patterns, both good and bad, that become models for how you think things should or will be. You learned your expectations from what your parents said and what you observed. No one comes to marriage or parenting as a blank slate.

For example, if you observed your parents avoiding conflict, you may have developed the expectation that couples should seek peace at any price. So if there's disagreement and conflict, it may seem the world is going to end. Or if you observed your parents being very affectionate, you may have come to expect the same in your marriage. If your parents divorced, you may have some negative expectation in the back of your mind that marriages don't last.

Your being a child of their parenting significantly influenced how you observed your parents as parents. You couldn't really be an objective observer because you were directly involved. Your feelings and experiences of being parented influence the expectations of parenting you learned from your own parents.

Because each family is unique, there is often a mismatch between expectations. Deena and Tyrell provide a good example. Tyrell's parents were very traditional. His father was the breadwinner and head of the household. His mother was homemaker and primary parent. Tyrell was used to his father being the primary decision maker in the family. Deena's family was quite different. Her parents shared work and family responsibilities fairly equally. She watched them problem-solve and make decisions on a more equal basis and was just as likely to turn to her father for parental support as her mother.

As you might imagine, Deena and Tyrell have faced some challenges determining who does what in their marriage, especially since they became parents. Deena is beginning to think she married a control freak who doesn't really want to be a father, and Tyrell isn't sure his wife is the woman he thought she was. After repeated arguments they decided to try discussing this sensitive issue using the Speaker-Listener Technique. This is just part of their discussion, but you can see how they were able to get some issues on the table.

DEENA (SPEAKER): The key for me is, I thought we'd be sharing things more—earning money, parenting, decision making, chores—because that's what I grew up being used to. But it seems you want to be the big boss and expect me to take care of everything at home.

TYRELL (LISTENER): You thought we'd be sharing everything because that's what you grew up to expect, and we're not. And you feel like I'm the boss and you have to do everything at home.

DEENA (SPEAKER): Exactly. I never thought a lot about the expectation, but I can sure see I've had it, and it's affecting us.

TYRELL (LISTENER): So you're saying that you've had this expectation but really haven't been aware of it. Yet you can see it's affecting us negatively.

DEENA (SPEAKER): Yes. That's just what I mean. (*floor switch*)

TYRELL (SPEAKER): I can understand better now why you've seemed so peeved with me. But I've just been trying to be a good husband and that means taking care of you and the baby by earning money, making decisions, and letting you run the house.

DEENA (LISTENER): So what looked to me like you being controlling was really you just wanting to be a good husband.

TYRELL (SPEAKER): Yes. That's it. Because of my own background, I thought that's how it's done. I guess my parents were pretty traditional, but it worked, and I guess I expected to follow their example.

DEENA (LISTENER): You've just been following the example your parents set in your family.

TYRELL (SPEAKER): I don't want to control you or control our lives. I thought we'd work together as a team. I guess what I learned in my own family is getting in the way.

DEENA (LISTENER): You want to work as a team, but what you learned in your family is getting in the way.

TYRELL (SPEAKER): Right. I think we need to set aside time to talk about this more and really lay out our expectations of each other and how we want our marriage and our family to be. We're not our parents.

Deena and Tyrell weren't even aware of how their expectations from their families of origin were influencing their behavior as partners and parents. Once they began to understand and talk openly about their expectations—where they came from and the effects of their pasts on their relationship—they felt they were being heard and respected. They were then able to negotiate how they wanted their relationship and family to be.

If we had space, we could give thousands more examples. The point is that you each have powerful expectations that come from your families of origin. Understanding this can be an important first step toward dealing effectively with those expectations and reducing the conflict arising from them.

Previous Relationships

You've also developed expectations from previous relationships you've had. You have expectations about how to kiss, what's romantic, how to communicate about problems, how recreational time should be spent, who should make the first move to make up after a fight, and so on.

Suppose, for example, that in a previous relationship, when you began to open up about painful childhood events you got dumped. Logically, you may have developed the expectation that if you want to be accepted, you can't share those aspects of yourself. On a deeper level, you may expect that people can't be trusted with knowing the deepest parts of who you are. If so, you'll pull back and withhold a level of intimacy in your present relationship.

Studies show that people who have come to expect that others can't be trusted have more difficulties in relationships. If you look at such people's past experiences, their expectations will usually make sense. Yet their mistrust can lead to trouble if it is so intense that they can't even allow someone they really love to get close. If this is your situation, it is all the more reason to learn how to make it safer for verbal intimacy in your relationship.

Many expectations are about such minor things that it's hard to imagine they could become so important—but they can. Their importance depends on what meanings and issues are attached to the expectations. For example, Phil's past girlfriend had drilled into him that she didn't want him opening doors for her. He thought, "OK, no big deal." Now, with his wife Gina, he was finding quite the opposite. She liked men to hold doors and would get upset with him if he forgot. He had to work hard to unlearn the expectation he'd finally learned so well.

Such events as door opening happen pretty often in life. For Phil and Gina they triggered conflict because she would interpret his trouble remembering as a sign that he didn't care about her. This is another example of negative interpretation causing more damage than the actual event. Believing his devotion was being challenged, Phil would get angry at Gina. This just confirmed what she already believed—he didn't care.

Cultural Influences and Backgrounds

A variety of cultural factors can influence your expectations: books, television, movies, and so forth. What expectations would you develop about marriage or parenting, for example, from watching thousands of hours of TV in the United States? For most of us, this is not a hypothetical question. We receive powerful messages about what is expected or normal from shows like *The Simpsons*, *Home Improvement*, *Friends*, *The Cosby Show*, and *Roseanne*. Some of these expectations from television are reasonable. Most are not. What expectations do people learn from the soaps or from talk shows with such topics as "Women who have affairs and the men who love them"?

It doesn't take growing up in different countries to lead to cultural differences. Coming from different parts of the same country or even different parts of the same city can result in learning different rules, values, and expectations for all kinds of things. These expectations cover such areas as child-rearing practices and discipline, sexuality, money management, and roles in marriage. It's very important to understand these differences and how they affect your relationship rather than to assume you share the same viewpoint. You probably don't, and in some ways this is likely to surprise you.

WHAT TO DO ABOUT EXPECTATIONS

Expectations can lead either to massive disappointment and frustration or to deeper connection between you and your partner. There are three keys to handling expectations well: be aware of what you expect, be reasonable in what you expect, and be clear about what you expect.

⊘ Be Aware of What You Expect

Whether you are aware of them or not, unmet expectations can lead to great disappointment and frustration in your relationship. And when they continue to be unmet, they can shift from disappointed expectations to angry demands.

People bring to their relationships a host of expectations about marriage and parenting that are never made clear. These expectations are found in the fine print of our unwritten contracts for our marriages. The problem is, people don't know what's in their partner's version of the contract when they get married. They don't get to read the fine print. Many of our fine-print expectations are virtually unconscious—making them very difficult to be aware of. We don't mean to say that all expectations are deeply unconscious, but many do become such a part of us that they function automatically.

One important clue that unmet expectations are functioning is disappointment. It's a good habit to stop a minute when you're disappointed, sad, or angry and ask yourself what you expected. Doing this can help you become aware of important expectations that otherwise may be unconsciously affecting your relationship and your family.

Brian would become very sad when he'd ask his wife, Ashley, to go fishing with him and she'd say, "That's OK. I really should stay with the baby. Go ahead without me and have a great time." Ashley would rather stay home with the baby and do a little gardening. Brian worked very hard during the week as a repairman, and fishing was the greatest relaxation for him. Ashley didn't care for fishing but really wanted Brian to feel OK about having a nice time without her.

Brian's sadness led him to realize that he expected they would share this very important interest of his and eventually share it with their child as well. What did Ashley's lack of interest mean? Ashley loved Brian dearly, but the expectation or hope that she'd become interested in his hobby stirred sadness about deeper issues of wanting to feel cared for. Once he was aware of his expectation and the reasons for his sadness, he was able to express what fishing with her meant to him. Ashley had no idea. Although she didn't love fishing, she was glad to go more often once she knew it meant so much to him. Once you have become aware of an expectation, the next step is to consider whether your expectation is reasonable.

Be Reasonable in What You Expect

As we noted earlier, many important expectations just aren't reasonable or realistic. Some unreasonable expectations are very specific. For example, is it reasonable to expect that your partner will never disagree with you about parenting decisions? Of course not. Yet you'd be surprised how many people expect this. Is it reasonable to expect that once you're married your partner will give up all contact with old friends? Some people expect this, but that's not realistic either.

When partners' expectations are unreasonable, their relationships are more likely to be distressed. Acting on unreasonable expectations is likely to lead to conflict.

For example, Megan and Dan have been married for three years and have a six-month-old daughter. Dan is a plumber, and Megan continues to do bookkeeping for a small business from home while she cares for the baby. Dan's job often demands long hours and working on weekends. Romance has become a huge issue for them. While they were dating, Dan would regularly bring Megan flowers. He sent her love notes every day and often brought her little love gifts. They would spend days off exploring museums together or taking long bike rides through the country.

Megan expected all this to continue after they were married and became parents. When it didn't, she thought Dan had stopped loving her and that perhaps their marriage had been a mistake. The situation came to a head in a major fight. Although you can certainly continue to be romantic after you're married and become parents, Megan's expectations were just not reasonable. Unless the couple can negotiate some way through this problem, it may threaten Megan and Dan's future together.

Sometimes couples who learn and use the skills and techniques we are presenting in this book develop an unreasonable expectation that they will not have to keep at it, that conflicts will be a thing of the past because they've worked productively on issues for a time. We do hope couples who consistently use these techniques will have fewer and less intense negative events. But events will always occur, and sometimes couples fall back into their old patterns. There's a difference between being perfect and handling issues well.

One of the most destructive and unreasonable expectations you can have is that your partner will meet all your needs and heal all your wounds from life. This expectation will always lead to disappointment and dissatisfaction, yet it's a common expectation in relationships.

Be Clear About What You Expect

A specific expectation may be perfectly reasonable but never clearly expressed. Your partner can't do anything about something he or she doesn't know about. So it's crucial to tell your partner about your important expectations. We all tend to assume that our partner's model of the ideal marriage is the same as ours.

We assume our partner knows what we want, so we don't bother to clearly state what we need. Many partners believe that if they need to ask, something is wrong. Even worse, many think that if they ask their partner and their partner responds, then the outcome isn't meaningful. They say, "If I have to ask for a hug, it really doesn't mean much," or "If I have to ask you to change the baby's diaper, you aren't really helping." Actually, when you ask and your partner responds, that's evidence of your partner's love and commitment.

Unless you make your expectations clear, you'll have trouble working as a team. You can't work from any kind of shared perspective if you don't share your perspective. You need to be aware of your expectations, willing to evaluate them, and willing to share them with your partner. Otherwise, expectations have the power to trigger some of the hottest issues and the hidden issues in your relationship. If you don't deal with expectations openly, you also miss an opportunity to define a mutual vision of how you want your marriage to be.

The main exercise for this chapter is as important as any in this book. It takes time to do it well. It also takes considerable follow-up. We hope you can find the time and motivation to do the work. If you do, you will improve your understanding of mutual expectations. Combining that knowledge with the skills you are learning can have a major impact on the strength of your relationship—both now and into the future.

As you move into parenthood you're likely to be surprised by how many additional expectations you become aware of. Pregnancy, birth, and parenting are fertile ground for issues, hidden issues, and their underlying expectations. Be watchful for and sensitive to their presence and their effects.

In the next chapter, you'll learn more about core values and beliefs and how they become more important to your relationship as you become parents.

EXERCISES

The following exercise is designed to help you explore your expectations. Spend time thinking carefully about each area and write down your thoughts so you can share them later with your partner. You may have expectations in many other areas. Feel free to add them to the list. Consider everything that seems significant to you. Most couples find this type of exercise very helpful to their relationship. Take as much time as you need to complete these exercises carefully and completely. The effort will be extremely beneficial to your relationship.

Getting to Know Your Expectations

The goal of this exercise is to help you become aware of your expectations of your couple relationship: how you want or expect it to be, rather than how it is now. Jot down what you expect about each area, whether or not you think the expectation is realistic or legitimate. The expectation is what matters because it will affect your couple relationship whether it's reasonable or off the wall. Jot down what you really think, not what you think you "should" think or what you think is the "correct" response. Also jot down what you observed or learned about each of these areas in your family as you were growing up. This is where many of your beliefs and expectations come from.

What are your expectations about each of the following?

1. The time perspective of your relationship. Do you think in terms of "till death do us part"? Are you thinking long-term?

2. Sexual faithfulness. Is it acceptable to be intimate with someone other than your partner? Should your partner have friends of the opposite sex?

3. Love. Do you expect to love each other forever? Do you expect this to change over time? What does being loving and caring mean to you? How do you expect love to be expressed?

4. Your intimate relationship. What are the practices, frequency, and taboos of your sensual and sexual relationship with your partner? Who should initiate lovemaking? Should your intimate relationship change as you become parents?

5. Romance. What is romantic for you? What is your particular language of love? How do you expect your partner to be romantic? Should the romance continue throughout your marriage?

6. Children. Did you want this child? Do you want more children? What are your expectations about raising your child? How will your baby be fed? Will your baby be allowed to suck its thumb? Use a pacifier? How about discipline? Education? Extracurricular activities?

7. Children from previous marriages. If you or your partner have children from a previous marriage, where do you want them to live? How do you expect you and your partner should share in raising these children? Discipline? Involvement in their lives and activities?

8. Work, careers, and provision of income. Whose responsibility is it to provide the financial support of the family? Whose career or job is more important? Yours? Your partner's? How will each of your careers or jobs be affected by your becoming parents? Will either you or your partner reduce your out-of-home work time to take care of the baby? What are your expectations of how you will use parental leave when the baby comes? What about work after your nest is empty? Retirement?

9. The degree of each partner's emotional dependency on each other. Do you want to feel taken care of? In what ways? How much do you expect to rely on each other to get through tough times? What about depending on family and friends for support? In what areas would you expect to be more emotionally independent?

10. Basic approach to life. As a team? As two independent individuals?

11. Loyalty. What does that mean to you?

12. Communication about problems in the relationship. Do you want to talk these out? If so, how? What about the expression of strong emotions, such as anger? What about using outside help to deal with your problems?

13. Power and control. Who do you expect should have more power in what kinds of decisions? Who should control the money? Who should discipline the kids? What happens when you and your partner disagree in a key area? Who should make the final decision? Who seems to have the most power in your relationship now? How do you feel about that?

14. Household tasks. Who should do what? How does the current division of household labor look in relation to what you ideally expect? How do you expect it will change when the baby comes?

15. Religious beliefs and observances. Where, when, and what rituals do you expect to follow? How should holidays be celebrated? How will this change when the baby comes?

16. Time together. How much time do you want to spend together? With the baby? Alone? With friends or family, at work, and so forth? Should all activities be shared, or can you each have your own interests?

17. Sharing feelings. What do you expect about sharing all your thoughts and feelings? Are there thoughts or feelings that shouldn't be shared?

18. Friendship with your partner. What is a friend? How do you envision friendship with your partner? Should your partner be your best friend?

19. The little things in life. Should toothpaste be squeezed from the top or the bottom? Should the toilet paper go over the top or around the bottom? Should the toilet seat be left up or down? Who should send greeting cards? Really think about the little things that have irritated you or have been going really well. What do you want or expect in each area?

20. Forgiveness. How important is forgiveness in your relationship? What should happen when there is a need for forgiveness?

21. Now, with your mind primed from all of the work you've done, consider again the hidden issues we described in Chapter Five. Do you see any ways now that some of these deeper issues of yours might influence your expectations? What do you expect, want, or fear in the areas of power, caring, recognition, commitment, integrity, and acceptance?

22. List any other expectations you have about how things should be. Some other areas might include money (saving and spending), free time, recreation, TV, use of alcohol and drugs, your interactions in public, and relatives.

Reasonable Expectations

Now go back and rate each expectation on a scale of 1 to 10 for how *reasonable* you think the expectation really is—with 10 meaning completely reasonable ("I really think it's OK to expect this in my couple relationship") and 1 meaning completely unreasonable ("I can honestly say that although I expect or want this, it's just not a reasonable expectation"). For example, suppose you grew up in a family where problems were not discussed, and you are aware that you honestly expect or prefer to avoid such discussions. You might now rate that expectation as not very reasonable.

Next, place a big check mark by each expectation on your list that you feel you've never clearly discussed with your partner.

Sharing Expectations

After you and your partner have finished the expectations exercises so far, schedule times together to discuss each of the areas either of you thinks is important. Don't try to do this all at once! You'll need to plan a number of discussions, each covering only one or two expectations. Because you'll probably be dealing with sensitive issues, you might want to use the structure and safety of the Speaker-Listener Technique. The goal of these discussions is to come to a full and clear understanding of each partner's expectations and beliefs.

As you deal with each issue, discuss the degree to which you both feel the expectations are reasonable and discuss what you want to agree to do about these expectations. Think about your overall, long-term vision for your couple relationship. What expectations do you share about your future together?

From the standpoint of giving you a lot to think about and discuss, this chapter is probably one of the hardest in this book. In addition to carefully going through the exercises, you might want to read the chapter over another time or two. Really think through what your key expectations are and how they affect your relationship. You'll probably want to return to this chapter and these exercises after you've worked through the entire book. Thinking through the rest of the book may influence your expectations, particularly as they relate to becoming parents.

7

The Importance of
Core Values and Beliefs

Core beliefs and practices affect couples over the life span, but probably never so deeply as when couples become parents. As a childfree couple, you may be able to lead somewhat independent lives. But as you become parents, differing values and beliefs that never caused conflicts before can blow up because they affect important things, such as parenting decisions and the values you want to model for your children.

Although beliefs and practices can enhance a relationship when they are shared, differences here can greatly intensify conflict. Core values and beliefs about life, its meaning, and how one should live most often have their origins in spiritual or religious beliefs. Although not everyone is religious or spiritually inclined, there are key points of relevance here for all couples. For many people, the spiritual or religious realm embodies core belief systems. All people have some type of core belief system, and we'll use that as the focus for much of what we have to say here.

We don't want to preach about what you should believe. Rather, we want to suggest that what you do believe—and, more important, practice—affects your growing family. Rather than being an area of risk for you, this is an area about which we want you to be able to talk openly and make decisions as to how you can best share life together. We do freely advocate certain key values that are widely accepted as leading to better marriages and families.

If you aren't usually interested in religious or spiritual issues, you may be skeptical about the relevance of what we have to say. Or if you're very committed to a particular faith, you might see this chapter as "watered down" or too secular. Either way, we invite you to explore the kinds of impacts these dimensions can have on relationships as your family grows. We want you and your partner to have meaningful discussions that will produce understanding, reduce conflict, and promote intimacy.

We'll start with a focus on religion because most of the relevant research has been conducted in that context. That's because religious behavior is pretty easy to measure, in contrast to the idea of spirituality; agreement about spiritual meanings and practices is not as easy to come by.

RESEARCH ON RELIGIOUS INVOLVEMENT

Studies of religious practice and belief in marriage abound, and there are implications from these studies that can benefit all couples. That's because many religions codify core beliefs, values, and practices that promote stability and health in relationships. If we consider some of what those findings may be about, we can highlight key implications for all couples—religious or not.

Who Gets Married?

Religious people are more likely to get married in the first place. Lower rates of marriage among the nonreligious are attributed to two factors. First, religious involvement brings people together. Second, people who are less religious are, in general, less conforming— they tend not to see themselves fitting into traditional structures in society. Therefore, they may be less interested in such institutions as marriage.

Religion and Marital Quality

Numerous studies suggest religious belief and practice may have a favorable impact on marriage. For example, couples who are more religious tend to be more satisfied in their marriages. They are also less likely to divorce. In one of our studies, married subjects who rated themselves as more religious showed somewhat higher levels of satisfaction, lower levels of conflict about common issues, and higher levels of commitment.

Those who were more religious, especially those who were conservative, were more likely to say divorce is wrong. They were also likely to believe that if they had problems, there would be significant social pressure to stay together and make it work. And they were more likely to report being satisfied in sacrificing for one another and having a stronger team identity. These findings make sense given the values emphasized in traditional religious groups.

Another study found that more religious women reported greater sexual contentment in terms of frequency of orgasm and openness of communication with their husbands about sex. This was in comparison to moderately religious and nonreligious women. These same women also reported higher overall marital satisfaction.

Some of the most recent research in this field suggests that couples derive the greatest benefits from religious life when they are involved in it together. To sum up, something about the factors associated with religious involvement gives couples an edge in keeping marriages strong. Before we examine this in greater detail, let's look at research on something relevant to more and more couples—interfaith marriages.

Interfaith Marriages

People are increasingly likely to marry out of their faith, for all sorts of reasons. Research consistently shows that such couples are much more likely to divorce. When people of different backgrounds marry and have little allegiance to those backgrounds, we would assume that the risks for divorce are lower. Many interfaith marriages start out just fine, with couples thinking that they can beat the odds and that "love conquers all." Although love can conquer a lot—especially if it's translated into loving and respectful behavior—the more there is to conquer, the greater the risk of failure.

Things can heat up around these differences for a couple of key reasons. First, people tend to get more religious or spiritually inclined as they age—perhaps because death gets closer. Second, as couples become parents, they face a host of decisions about how the child is to be raised regarding religious and spiritual beliefs. This is the time when your past religious upbringing can become critical, even if you don't see yourself as "a believer." Here are some of the decisions and questions that come up:

Do you have a boy circumcised by religious ceremony, by a physician, or not at all?

Does the baby get baptized? Dedicated? Does baptism happen later, at the age of accountability and personal belief, or when the child is an infant?

What do you do about religious holidays? Christmas, Rosh Hashana, Passover, Easter, Ramadan, Earth Day, and so forth?

What about religious schooling? Parochial or public school? Sunday school? Hebrew school?

What about bar mitzvahs, confirmations, dedications, and so on?

For example, Josh and Mercedes married after falling in love in college. The problem was, he was Jewish and she was Catholic. His parents were alarmed that he'd date a gentile. Hers were concerned, but they figured Josh was a passing fancy. He wasn't.

Mercedes's parents began to get pretty worried. "How could she not marry a Catholic boy?" Mercedes and Josh felt pressure from both families to cool it. But they really did love each other, so what did religion matter? Children? No problem. "We'll let them choose for themselves what to believe." Parents? No problem. "They'll learn to accept our marriage." Religious practice? No problem. Neither was particularly involved or observant at this point in life, so their thought was, "You do your thing; I'll do mine."

Things went along fairly well for Josh and Mercedes until the fourth year of marriage, when she got pregnant. For Mercedes, the idea of having a child was wonderful but marred by concerns: "What kind of world am I bringing this baby into?" These natural anxieties led her to a serious reevaluation of her faith. There was no other context that seemed as relevant for grappling with such questions. For Josh, his vision of himself as a father returned him to interest in his faith. "What if I have a son? I can't have a physician do the circumcision."

Mercedes talked with a priest and began attending mass again. Josh wondered whom to call to get a circumcision done if he had a son. In returning to church, Mercedes got to thinking about baptism. The priest said, "Infants must be baptized." She now believed this was critical.

As it turned out, they had a son, Benjamin. They had decided to have him baptized and circumcised in religious ceremonies. The trouble was that in order to do the baptism, the priest wanted Mercedes to commit to raising Benjamin as a Catholic. To make things more complicated, the couple couldn't find a mohel who would circumcise their son, because he was born to a gentile woman who hadn't converted to Judaism. They ended up doing neither.

Mercedes and Josh made compromises that worked for a couple of years. Both parents read Bible stories to Benjamin, and he certainly enjoyed celebrating both Hanukkah and Christmas. But it got tougher and tougher. By the time Benjamin turned four, each parent felt more and more pulled to see Benjamin educated in his or her own tradition. Conflicts became more frequent and more intense. They agreed that it would be pretty confusing to expose Benjamin to different teachings, but neither was willing to give up on Benjamin learning their faith.

Josh and Mercedes became increasingly alienated as they experienced the frustration of not being able to come to an agreement that made any sense. Negative feelings intensified to the point that their conflicts about Benjamin were erupting in all aspects of their relationship. One by one, key areas of intimacy suffered under the weight of the conflict about Benjamin. In frustration and isolation, they separated and moved toward the idea of divorce.

When they began to consider separation, they realized things had gone too far. Their marriage and their child were too important to throw away. It took a great deal of effort, and help from a counselor, but Josh and Mercedes learned to manage conflict more effectively and developed a plan to deal with their different beliefs. They still face challenges around these issues but are better able to handle them constructively.

Couples can make interfaith marriages work. Doing so just takes more work than other couples might have to do. But even that depends a lot on how committed each partner is to a belief system. When one or both partners in an interfaith marriage are not strongly committed—and when they don't become more committed later as a result of changes in life—such differences in background will be much less likely to produce friction and conflict.

To summarize, couples who are more religiously inclined and are from same-faith backgrounds appear to have an edge in maintaining satisfying marriages and avoiding divorce. We would now like to offer an analysis of why this might be, in hopes of stimulating you to consider how to strengthen your own relationship.

Although we'll focus our understanding on pretty down-to-earth explanations, we recognize that some of you may also consider more spiritual explanations for such effects. We focus on two key factors:

(1) the value of social support for your relationship and (2) the effect of having a shared worldview. Let's look at these in detail.

SOCIAL SUPPORT

No matter what else they might do, religious and spiritual beliefs bring groups of similarly minded people together. There's a benefit for most people in being part of a social group—religious or not—as long as they have a clear sense that they belong or "fit" into the group. Studies have consistently shown that people who are more isolated are at greater risk for emotional problems like depression and suicide, health problems, and poverty. Many studies demonstrate how much more vulnerable you are if you have significant stress but no social support system to help you. It's just not healthy for most humans to be isolated.

For many, religious involvement brings ready-made social support. Activities from spiritual (worship, prayer, reading, study, discussion groups) to social (coffee hour, ice cream socials, picnics, group outings, dinners, softball leagues) provide easy points of connection in a community that shares things in common. What are your social supports at this time? Who cares about the two of you and that you are becoming parents? *Our key point is that it's important for all couples to have a strong support system for their relationships.* Are you socially connected to a group that supports and somehow helps your developing marriage and growing family? If not, do you want to be? Who will be around to help you through the challenges of parenting? These are important questions for you and your partner to address directly. You'll have the opportunity to explore your support needs and your social network in greater depth in Chapter Fifteen.

SHARED WORLDVIEW

A shared belief system—including mutual understanding about the meanings of life, death, and marriage—makes it easier for the two of you to develop a vision of your future together. In turn, having a relationship vision supports the long-term view of commitment.

In most religions, there's a common understanding and language system for thinking and talking about core beliefs. So another explanation for the benefit of religious involvement is that couples who are more religious have a belief system that facilitates developing and maintaining the shared worldview.

Again, although you may not be religious, we think it's important for *all* couples to consider the impact of their worldviews on their marriage and the importance they place on parenting. Do you share core values and beliefs? How are the two of you handling similarities and differences in views? Think about these questions as we look at three specific areas in which your worldview can affect your marriage—core relationship values, moral judgments, and expectations.

Core Relationship Values

Let's focus on four key values that many belief systems and religious faiths emphasize—values with obvious positive implications for all relationships, including marriage: commitment, respect, intimacy, and forgiveness. When you and your partner have similar core beliefs, it's likely that you will have a similar understanding about these values and how you can give life to them in your marriage. Regardless of couples' core beliefs, we see the need for all couples to have some way to reinforce such values.

Many belief systems emphasize *commitment,* in terms of both dedication and constraint. Although there are great differences among belief systems about the morality of divorce, there is wide agreement across beliefs about the value of commitment. Long-term relationships need a sustained sense of commitment. The importance of commitment is reflected in our devoting the entire next chapter to the topic.

Respect is a core value emphasized in most religious or spiritual groups. Although various religions include beliefs others may reject, most systems nevertheless emphasize respect for the value and worth of others. Respect is a core need of all people. As a couple, you need to share a value system that has a strong emphasis on respect for each other.

Even if you have significant disagreements and differences, you can show respect for one another in how you communicate. We've taught you how to do this through validation. You show interest in and respect for your partner even when you see things differently. You can't have a good relationship without basic respect.

Intimacy is prized in most religious and spiritual systems. Although the concept may be understood differently, it's usually emphasized and encouraged, especially in marriage. One way to think about everything we're saying in this book is that couples need to have clear ways to maintain and enhance intimacy. Furthermore, poorly handled conflict can damage all that is intimate. All couples seeking long-term, satisfying marriages need to value intimacy, as well as to preserve and protect it. In Chapter Twelve, we will examine intimacy and how it is affected by becoming parents.

Forgiveness is a core theme for the health of relationships. Long-term healthy relationships need an element of forgiveness. Otherwise, partners can allow emotional debts to build in ways that destroy the potential for intimacy and teamwork. Forgiveness is so important that we will spend an entire chapter dealing with this topic. Marriages need forgiveness to stay healthy over the long term.

We hope you can see how the four core values discussed here are reflected in the skills and techniques we've been teaching you throughout this book. Religious belief systems have been emphasizing these values for thousands of years in ethics, codes of conduct, and standards for dealing with others. Our understanding of marital success and failure leads us to emphasize these same values. They are relevant to every couple but become more prominent as you become parents. As you practice the skills and techniques we advocate, you are acting on values such as these.

Expectations

Another way your worldview can significantly affect your marriage is in shaping your expectations in such areas as marital roles, child rearing and discipline, intimacy, and dealing with in-laws. The potential for differences in expectations to spark conflict is so great that we spent the previous chapter encouraging you to make such expectations clear—no matter where they come from. When two people share a perspective on key relationship expectations, they are going to have an easier time negotiating life together. Shared expectations lead to shared rituals and routines that guide couples more smoothly through the transitions and trials they must confront daily.

In religious systems, such viewpoints tend to be very clear and codified in beliefs and rituals, which may make it easier to have a shared worldview in terms of everyday expectations. This could explain, in part, why couples who are more religious and those with similar belief backgrounds have a somewhat easier time in marriage and parenting together. Sharing a structured belief system simplifies dealing with many expectations in that they don't have to be worked out or negotiated. Couples who aren't religiously involved can derive this same benefit if they share some philosophical viewpoint that makes it easier to maintain a shared viewpoint on expectations.

In summary, you and your partner may hold different perspectives, even if you were raised similarly. When you think about religious and spiritual differences, a lot is at stake. The same is true for any core belief system, such as a philosophy of life. Everyone has beliefs, and it's unlikely that a couple exists in which both partners line up perfectly on all dimensions. The point is that you need to grapple with the effects of your beliefs on your relationship and parenting. The exercises for this chapter are designed to help you do just that—grapple. We want you to explore your beliefs on religious or spiritual dimensions and talk them over together.

Exploring and sharing clearly what you believe and expect about some of these key questions can be an enriching if not eye-opening experience in your relationship. Talking about these issues with respect can be a very intimate experience. Try it and see what we mean.

In the next chapter, we will focus on the concept of commitment. This is a topic of great importance for relationships—one about which people tend to have quite a few expectations, especially as they move into parenting together.

EXERCISES

The following exercises will help you explore the core values and beliefs in your life, first taking a more general view and then examining them in relation to becoming parents.

Core Values and Beliefs

The following questions are designed to get you thinking about a broad range of issues related to your values and beliefs. There may be other important questions we've left out, so feel free to answer questions we don't ask as well as those we do. Jot down an answer to each question as it applies to you. This activity will help you think more clearly about the issues and will also help you when it comes time to talk with your partner about them. *As you think about and answer each question, it can be especially valuable to note what you were taught as a child versus what you believe or expect now as an adult.*

Questions for Reflection

1. What is your core belief system or worldview? What do you believe in?

2. How did you come to believe in this viewpoint?

3. What is the meaning or purpose of life in your core belief system?

4. What was your belief growing up? How was this core belief practiced in your family of origin? In religious practice? In some other way?

5. Do you make a distinction between spirituality and religion? What is your view on these matters?

6. What is the meaning of marriage in your belief system?

7. What vows will you say, or what vows did you say? How do they tie into or reflect your belief system?

8. What is your belief about divorce? How does this fit with your belief system?

9. How do you practice or expect to practice your beliefs in your relationship? Through religious involvement, spiritual practices, other behaviors? How do you want to practice your beliefs?

10. What do you think the day-to-day impact of your belief system should be on your relationship?

11. Are there specific views on sexuality in your belief system? What are they? How do they affect you and your partner?

12. How will your children be raised with respect to your belief system?

    Does the baby get baptized? Dedicated? Does baptism happen later at an age of accountability and personal belief, or when the child is an infant?

    Do you have a boy circumcised by religious ceremony, by a physician, or not at all? What is the basis for your circumcision decision?

    What about your child's education? Religious or public schooling? Sunday school? Hebrew school?

What about bar mitzvahs, confirmations, dedications, and so on?

What involvement do you expect from clergy and your religious or spiritual community in preparing for parenthood and raising your child?

13. Do you give, or expect to give, financial support to a religious institution or other effort related to your belief system? How much? How will this be determined? Do you and your partner agree on this?

14. Do you see potential areas of conflict regarding your belief systems? What are they?

15. What do you believe about forgiveness in general? How does forgiveness apply in a relationship such as the one you have with your partner?

16. In your belief system, what is your responsibility to other human beings?

17. How do you observe or expect to observe religious holidays? Which holidays will you observe? Christmas, Rosh Hashana, Passover, Easter, Ramadan, Earth Day?

18. What does your belief system include with respect to other people?

19. Are there other questions about values and beliefs you can think of and answer?

After you and your partner have finished this exercise individually, schedule time to discuss these expectations together. These are not easy issues, so plan on a number of discussions. What new issues are raised for you through these discussions? Use the Speaker-Listener Technique if you'd like some additional structure for dealing with these sometimes difficult issues. If any new expectations come up, talk about the degree to which you both feel they are reasonable or unreasonable and discuss what you want to agree to do about them.

Values and Beliefs Will

As we become parents, most of us gain a new appreciation of our own mortality. Some of us then prepare a will, which typically specifies who gets what when we die. For this exercise, we'd like you to take a slightly different approach to writing a will. If you and your partner were both to die, what values and beliefs would you want to be sure are instilled in or passed on to your child? Take time to think about this individually, and make notes. You may want to go back to the questions for reflection in the preceding exercise to guide your thinking. When you have each done some serious thinking, schedule a couple meeting to share what you've come up with. You may want to start your discussion using the Speaker-Listener Technique. You may also want to use brainstorming. You'll probably need to continue the discussion over several sessions and again periodically after your baby is born and as your child grows.

8

Commitment

The Glue That Holds Relationships Together

M ost married couples consider commitment the glue that holds their relationship together. The kind and depth of your commitment has a lot to do with your chances of staying together and being happy. What better time to think about your commitment than when you are adding a new family member. Commitment is the foundation of your relationship and the foundation of your child's security.

THE COMPLEXITY OF COMMITMENT

In this chapter, we'll explore the meaning of commitment and focus on ways to apply the major implications of commitment to maintaining a healthy and long-lasting marriage. First we'll discuss two couples in some detail. Each reflects a different type of commitment. Notice what's similar and what's different as you consider these marriages.

Charlie and Meg Greeley: Ball and Chain

Charlie and Meg married nine years ago and have a two-year-old son, Michael, and three-year-old daughter, Melissa. Although Meg and Charlie were eager to become parents, reality has not lived up to their expectations. Things got tough for them after Melissa arrived and haven't gotten better. In order for Meg to have more time with the kids, she cut back to working part-time. Charlie changed jobs and increased his work hours to make up for her lost income. The stresses of work and parenting have left Charlie and Meg feeling tired and distant.

Meg has often considered divorce and increasingly finds herself thinking about leaving her husband. Like many men, Charlie feels unhappy in the marriage but hasn't considered divorce much. He hopes for more in the relationship but thinks that trying to get closer just doesn't work. Charlie has become anxious Meg might leave him, yet he believes energy invested in the marriage is wasted. "Maybe things will get better when the kids leave home," he thinks.

Meg and Charlie work around others they find attractive. Brad is a single, good-looking man at Meg's work who has made it clear he's interested in her. She's been seriously contemplating an affair and finds herself thinking about it more and more.

Meg believes she puts more into the marriage than Charlie does, and with little in return for her time and effort. She thinks Charlie is married more to his job than to her, while Charlie believes it's his working so hard that allows her more time with the children. She resents that he doesn't seem to appreciate all she's done for him in providing support, making a home, and taking care of the kids.

As Meg thinks about divorce, she grapples with difficult questions. She wonders how the kids would respond to divorce. Would it hurt them? Would Charlie fight for custody? Would it be hard to get a divorce? How could she afford a lawyer? She wonders how she would support herself and the kids on her income. Who would get the house? Could either of them afford to keep the house alone? If she were to marry again, would another man accept her children?

As Meg considers these questions, she decides that the costs of getting a divorce are greater than she wants to bear, at least for now. She's not happy in the marriage, but she weighs this against the pain and stress divorce could bring. A dark cloud of despair hangs over her, and she feels trapped. Although staying isn't great, she decides that at least for now it's better than leaving.

Bruce and Amy Johnson: Full Commitment

Amy and Bruce were married seven years ago, and their first child is on the way. Although they've had stressful times, they have few regrets about marrying each other. Becoming parents turned out to be much more difficult than either imagined. They had difficulty getting and staying pregnant, and this pregnancy has been rocky, with Amy in and out of premature labor. Despite the challenges, Amy and Bruce feel each other's support as they face life together.

Not only do they approach life as a team, but they also regularly do things that reaffirm their dedication. They talk about what they want to do in the future—even the distant future. They change their schedules to accommodate each other's needs. Each has resisted the temptation to dwell on "what ifs" when they're frustrated in the marriage. Most important, they keep a clear emphasis on *we* as they go through life.

Everyone has regrets at times in marriage, but for Amy and Bruce these times are few. They genuinely respect and like each other, do things for each other, and talk openly about what they want in marriage and life. Because of religious convictions, each resists thinking about divorce, even in the rough times. Each is willing to support the other in attaining what he or she desires in life. Simply put, they feel like a team.

The Greeleys and Johnsons have very different marriages. The Greeleys are pretty miserable, and the Johnsons are enjoying life. Both marriages are likely to continue for the time being—reflecting some kind of commitment. But it's not just the level of happiness that differentiates these two marriages. The Johnsons have a much different, fuller kind of commitment. To understand the difference, we need to understand commitment better.

WHAT IS COMMITMENT?

What do you think of when you think of commitment? There are two common ways to think about commitment. The commitment of dedication, or *personal dedication*, refers to the desire to maintain or improve the quality of the relationship for the mutual benefit of both partners. Personal dedication is characterized by the desire—and associated behaviors—not only to continue in the relationship but also to improve it, sacrifice for it, invest in it, link personal goals to it, and seek the partner's welfare, not just one's own.

In contrast, *constraint commitment* refers to forces that keep individuals in relationships whether or not they are dedicated. Constraint commitment may arise from either external or internal pressures. Constraints help keep couples together by making ending the relationship more costly—economically, socially, personally, or psychologically. If dedication is low, constraints can keep people in relationships they might otherwise want to leave.

Meg and Charlie Greeley have a commitment characterized by constraint. Meg in particular is feeling a great deal of constraint and little dedication. She feels compelled to stay in a dissatisfying marriage for a host of reasons: kids, money, family pressure, and so on. Charlie also has high constraint commitment and little dedication, though he's less dissatisfied with their day-to-day life.

Like Meg and Charlie, Amy and Bruce Johnson have a good deal of constraint commitment, but they also have a strong sense of dedication to each other. Any thriving marriage will produce a significant amount of constraint over time. In fact, happier, more dedicated couples are just as likely to have considerable constraints as less satisfied, less dedicated couples at similar points in life. Happier couples just don't think a lot about constraints, and when they do, they often draw comfort from them.

Let's look more closely at the composition of the glue that holds relationships together. We could spend more time looking at constraints, but we won't. Although constraints are very important to marital stability, they aren't nearly as important to the ongoing quality of your marriage as dedication. Dedication involves elements about which you can make daily choices—choices that will strongly influence your future together.

The Commitment of Personal Dedication

What we want to do here is present the most common features of dedication in strong relationships. *Desiring the long term* refers to wanting the relationship to continue into the future: wanting and expecting your relationship to last; wanting to grow old together. Desiring the long term is a core part of dedication that plays a critical role in the day-to-day quality of marriage, especially through the ups and downs of parenting together.

The priority of the relationship refers to the importance you give your relationship relative to everything else. When people are more dedicated to their partners, they are more likely to make decisions for the relationship when it competes with other things for time and attention. When dedication is weaker, the relationship is more likely to take a back seat to things like work, kids, and hobbies.

Unfortunately, as people get busier, too many partners end up doing what Scott Stanley, in his book *The Heart of Commitment* (Nelson, 1998), calls "No-ing" each other rather than "knowing" each other: "No, I don't have time to talk tonight." "No, I'm too tired to even think about making love." "No, I can't take Friday off to be at the baby's doctor's appointment, I have that project due." "No, I promised Dad I'd come over Saturday and help him with the yard." To protect your relationship at this crucial time of transition, you've got to become good at saying no to other things in your life that aren't as important in the long run as your happiness together.

The Greeleys have allowed their marriage to become a low priority, and they are suffering for this. Their marriage isn't bad so much as neglected. It's possible to turn this situation around. Amy and Bruce Johnson are truly important to each other. There are times when Bruce feels Amy is overly involved with the pregnancy, but he doesn't seriously doubt he matters to her. Likewise, Amy sometimes thinks Bruce is too involved with work, but she recognizes his dedication to her and the baby on the way.

We-ness refers to the degree to which one views the relationship as a team rather than as two separate individuals focusing primarily on what's best for themselves. In we-ness, "we" transcends "I" in your thinking about your relationship. It's crucial to have a sense of an identity together if the relationship is to be satisfying and to grow. If you do not have this sense of being a team, conflict is more likely, as you will see problems as "me against you" instead of as "us against the problem."

We aren't suggesting that you merge your identity with your partner's or that you lose your sense of self. In fact, as we'll mention later, it can be challenging for you as parents to hang onto a clear sense of who you are. Rather, we're suggesting it's healthy to have a clear sense of two individuals coming together to form a team. Dedicated couples enjoy this sense of being a team. Instead of selfishly grappling to get their own way, they feel that the team's goals are at least as important as their individual goals. What a difference this makes in how you view life together.

Satisfaction with sacrifice is the degree to which people feel a sense of satisfaction in doing things largely or solely for their partners' benefit. The point isn't to be a martyr but to find joy in an honest choice to give of yourself for your partner. Research indicates that people who are doing the best in their marriages are those who feel good about giving to one another—and they're also those who report they would give up the most for their marriage and partner. Relationships are generally stronger when both partners are willing to make sacrifices. If you aren't both willing to sacrifice, you will probably have a relationship that at least one of you is in mostly for what you can get, with little focus on what you can give. That's not a recipe for happiness or growth.

Meg and Charlie have stopped giving to each other. Charlie doesn't think he'll get anything back if he gives more, and Meg feels she's already giving more than her share. Neither feels like sacrificing anything at this point.

Alternative monitoring refers to how much you keep an eye out for potential alternative partners. The more you are attracted to other potential partners, the less your personal dedication to your current partner. Do you find yourself frequently or seriously thinking about being with people other than your spouse? We emphasize "seriously" because almost everyone is attracted to other people from time to time.

Dedication is in jeopardy if this attraction has become strong, especially if you have a particular person in mind. Highly dedicated people mentally devalue attractive potential partners. This is something about which you have a choice. Bruce has been tempted a couple of times by people at work, especially a woman named Libby. Although aware of the attraction, Bruce considered it a threat to his marriage and made himself focus on Libby's negatives rather than her positives. Though tempted to look, he focused on why the grass *wasn't* greener on the other side of the fence. To keep your marriage strong, keep your focus on tending to your own lawn rather than yearning for the grass on the other side of the fence.

HOW DOES COMMITMENT DEVELOP? HOW DOES DEDICATION DIE?

Dedication is believed to develop mostly out of the initial attraction and satisfaction in relationships. Think back over your relationship. Because you liked being together, you became more dedicated to staying together. As your dedication to one another grew, you probably noticed you became more relaxed about the relationship. In most relationships, there's an awkward period during which the desire to be together is great but the commitment is unclear. This ambiguity produces anxiety about whether or not you'll stay together. As your mutual dedication became clearer, the relationship seemed safer to invest in.

Because of your dedication, you made decisions that increased constraint. For example, as dedication grows, a couple will decide to go from a dating relationship to becoming engaged. As dedication grows further, they decide to become married, buy furniture, buy a house, have children, and so on. Each of these steps, taken as a reflection of dedication, adds to the constraint. Essentially, today's dedication becomes tomorrow's constraint. It's normal for the level of constraint to grow in marriage.

When it comes to having children, research suggests that it is the couples who feel most committed and sure of their marriages who are most likely to want to parent together. Becoming parents is a particularly significant milestone, both in terms of the meaning of the relationship and the changes that will come about. It's a very important time to display your dedication to one another.

Greater dedication will usually lead to greater satisfaction, and dedication grows out of satisfaction. When truly dedicated, people are more likely to behave in ways that protect their marriage and please their partner. So the effect on satisfaction is positive. It's comforting to see that your mate really cares about you and protects your relationship from all the other options available.

If most couples have high levels of dedication early on, when engaged or early in marriage, what happens to kill dedication for some couples over time? For one thing, if the partners don't handle conflict well, their satisfaction with the marriage will steadily decline. And because satisfaction fuels dedication, dedication begins to erode along with satisfaction. With dedication in jeopardy, giving to one another erodes further, and satisfaction takes a dive. There is a downward spiral.

Dedication erodes when people feel that their efforts no longer make a difference. This is another way poorly handled conflict kills a marriage. You begin to believe no amount of dedication matters, and it becomes difficult to keep trying. When you reach this stage, you are well on the road to a high-constraint, low-dedication, low-satisfaction marriage, if not divorce. This is *not* where you want to be.

The secret to satisfying commitment is to maintain not just constraint but dedication at high levels. Although constraint commitment can add a positive, stabilizing dimension to your marriage, it can't give you a great relationship. Dedication is the side of commitment that is associated with great relationships. Dedicated couples report not only more satisfaction with their relationships but also greater levels of self-disclosure and less conflict about the problems they have.

Are you just existing in your relationship, or are you making it all you hoped it would be? Now that you have a better understanding of commitment, let's focus on how to apply some of this information to maintaining a healthy and long-lasting marriage.

THE IMPORTANCE OF A LONG-TERM VIEW

At the heart of it, when people are committed, they have a long-term outlook on the relationship. This is crucial for one simple reason: *no relationship is consistently satisfying.* What gets couples through tougher times is the long-term view commitment brings. They have an expectation that the relationship will make it through thick and thin.

We're not saying everybody should devote Herculean effort to save their marriage no matter how abusive or destructive. For the great number of couples who genuinely love each other and want to make their marriages work, however, a long-term perspective is essential for encouraging each partner to take risks, disclose about self, and trust the other to be there when it really counts. In the absence of a long-term view, people tend to focus on the immediate payoff. This is only natural. If the long term is uncertain, we concentrate on what we're getting right now.

What we have called the hidden issue of commitment (Chapter Five) is easily triggered when the future of the relationship is uncertain. When commitment is unclear, in place of a feeling of *acceptance*—a core issue for everyone—there is pressure to perform. The message is, "You'd better produce, or I'll look for someone who can." Most of us resent feeling we could be abandoned by someone from whom we expect to find security and acceptance. Not surprisingly, people usually won't invest in a relationship with an uncertain future or reward. The Greeleys are held together mostly by constraint. There isn't the sense of a future together that comes from both dedication and constraint.

In contrast, other couples don't have the perfect marriage—who does?—but they have a strong expectation of a future rooted in balanced commitment. They talk about plans for life *together*. They've maintained their commitment, especially their dedication. They do things for one another, show respect, and protect their marriage in terms of priorities and alternatives.

For these couples, the long-term view allows each partner to give the other some "slack," leading to greater *acceptance* of imperfections and failings over time. Where the Greeleys experience anxiety or resentment around the core issue of acceptance, the Johnsons feel the warmth of a secure commitment—each conveying to the other the powerful message "I'll be here for you." That's the essence of commitment. It's not only believing you'll be there for one another in the future but also that you can count on one another through the ups and downs of life.

Trashing the Long-Term View

Sometimes commitment becomes a weapon in a fight. Although Meg and Charlie Greeley aren't going to divorce any time soon, the topic sometimes comes up in bad arguments. Consider the following conversation and its effects on trust, power, and commitment.

CHARLIE: Why does this house always look like a pigsty?

MEG: Because we have two little kids and two big dogs.

CHARLIE: I end up having to clean up all the time, and I'm tired of it.

MEG: Oh, and I don't clean up? When you're here, you disappear into your shop. I'm the one cleaning up constantly—not you.

CHARLIE: Yeah, yeah, I disappear all the time. You just don't give a damn about this marriage. I don't even know why we stay together.

MEG: Me neither. Maybe you should move out.

CHARLIE: Not a bad idea. I'll think about it.

At the end of the fight each was trying to convince the other they weren't committed. You can't get much more short-term than to suggest divorce. If you're trying to keep your marriage on track, don't bring up the topic of divorce, period. Likewise, don't threaten to have affairs. Such statements trash the long-term view. They erode trust and reinforce the perception that it's risky to invest.

Although expecting a child and parenting are wonderful times for couples, they are also very stressful. This is a time in your life when you want to go out of your way to demonstrate your commitment to one another. Pregnant and nursing women report feeling less secure in their marriages because they feel vulnerable and dependent on their partners. There could hardly be a more important time in life to demonstrate commitment to one another to dispel the anxieties that normally arise. Now we turn to another set of implications of commitment in a discussion of selfishness and self-centeredness.

SELFISHNESS

Our culture encourages devotion to self. Notions of sacrifice, teamwork, placing a high priority on our partner, and the dedicated relationship have not enjoyed much positive press lately. In fact, our society seems to glorify self and vilify whatever gets in the way. We all pay for these attitudes.

In contrast, we suggest that dedication is fundamental to healthy relationships and that selfishness is fundamentally destructive. Self-ishness may sell in our culture, but it doesn't bring lifelong happy marriages.

Dedication is more about being team-centered or other-centered than about being self-centered. To be team-centered is to be sensitive to your partner, to take your partner's perspective, to seek to build your partner up, and to protect your partner in *healthy* ways, *because you are a team*. It means making your partner's health and happiness a priority; doing what you know is good for your relationship—like listening to your partner—even when you don't particularly want to; and protecting your commitment from alternative attractions.

These acts of giving to one another, like acts that demonstrate commitment, are particularly crucial when you are making a major transition, such as becoming parents. Your life is in an upheaval of sorts now, and it's going to take time to adjust to the newest member of the family. If this child is your first, the change in who you are as a couple is profound. It's a key time to protect your identity as a couple.

Selfish attitudes and behavior can and will kill a relationship. Such attitudes aren't compatible with dedication. Dedication reflects we-ness and, at times, sacrifice. You just can't have a great marriage when each partner is primarily focused on what's best for self. In a culture that reinforces self, it's hard to ask, "What can I do to make this better?" It's a lot easier to ask, "What can my partner do to make me happier?"

We are *not* advocating martyrdom. A "martyr" does things for you not out of concern for what's best for you but because the mar-tyr wants to put you in debt. This is not dedication. Such behavior is usually insecurity and selfishness masquerading as "doing good."

The key is to think about not only *what* you do for your partner but also *why* you do it. Do you do things with the attitude, "You'd better appreciate what I'm doing"? Do you often feel your partner *owes* you? There's nothing wrong with doing positive things and wanting to be appreciated. There is something wrong with believing you are owed, as if your positive behavior were building up a debt for your partner. The kind of deeply intimate, caring, and lasting marriages most people seek are built and maintained on dedication to one another expressed in the kinds of constructive behavior we advocate throughout this book. Too many people are self-centered so much of the time that they will never truly experience the kind of relationship they deeply desire.

When you boil it down, commitment is about knowing you will be there for each other in the future and that you can count on one another in the present. There's no better time of life than now, as you become parents, to do all you can to affirm your commitment to one another.

EXERCISES

There are several exercises to help you get the most out of this chapter as you become parents. You'll have the opportunity to examine your constraint and dedication commitment, consider your priorities, and explore the power of commitment in your relationship.

Assessing Constraint Commitment

Jot down your answer to each item using the following scale to indicate how true the statement seems to you: mark 1 if you strongly disagree, 4 if you neither agree nor disagree, and 7 if you strongly agree.

1. The steps I would need to take to end this relationship would require a great deal of time and effort.

2. A marriage is a sacred bond between two people that should not be broken.

3. I would have trouble finding a suitable partner if this relationship ended.

4. I stay in this relationship partly because I wouldn't want the children to grow up without both parents in the home.

5. My friends or family really want this relationship to work.

6. I would lose valuable possessions if I left my partner.

7. I stay in this relationship partly because my partner would be emotionally devastated if I left.

8. I couldn't make it financially if we broke up or divorced.

9. My lifestyle would be worse in many ways if I left my partner.

10. I feel trapped in this relationship.

11. It is important to finish what you have started, no matter what.

12. I stay in this marriage partly for the sake of the kids.

Your answers to these few questions can tell you a lot. What constraints are you aware of? How powerful are these constraints? What kind of constraints did you rate higher?

Most important, do you feel trapped or stuck? Just about everyone does from time to time, which is normal. Having a good deal of constraint but not feeling trapped is normal in a healthy couple relationship. The best relationships are those in which both partners are dedicated to each other *and* feel comfortable with the stability implied by constraint.

Assessing Personal Dedication

These next items will help you gauge your level of dedication. Use the same rating scale you used to examine constraint commitment: 1 = strongly disagree, 4 = neither agree nor disagree, and 7 = strongly agree.

1. My relationship with my partner is more important to me than almost anything else in my life.

2. I want this relationship to stay strong no matter what rough times we may encounter.

3. It makes me feel good to sacrifice for my partner.

4. I like to think of myself and my partner more in terms of "us" and "we" than of "me" and "him" or "her."

5. I am not seriously attracted to anyone other than my partner.

6. My relationship with my partner is clearly part of my future life plans.

7. When push comes to shove, my relationship with my partner comes first.

8. I tend to think about how things affect us as a couple more than about how things affect me as an individual.

9. I don't often find myself thinking about what it would be like to be in a relationship with someone else.

10. I want to grow old with my partner.

We can give you an idea of what your score means on these dedication items. To calculate your score, simply add up your ratings for each item. In our research—working with a sample of people who were mostly happy and dedicated in their relationships, including those dating for a few months as well as those married for over thirty years—the average person scored about 58 on this scale. If you scored 58 or above, we'd bet you're pretty highly dedicated. However, your dedication may be quite low if you scored below 45. Whatever your score, think about what it may mean for the future of your marriage.

Considering Priorities

An important way to look at dedication is to consider your priorities. How do you actually live your life? What does this say about your commitment?

Divide a piece of paper into three columns. In the first column, list what you consider *your* top five priorities in life, with number one being the most important. Possible priority areas might include work and career, your partner, the baby, religion, house and home, sports, future goals, education, possessions, hobbies, pets, friends, relatives, coworkers, television, car. Feel free to list whatever is important to you. Be as specific as you can. Now, in the second column, list what *you* think *your partner* would say are *your* top five priorities. For example, if you think your partner would say work is your top priority, list that as number one. In the third column, list what *you* believe are *your partner's* top five priorities.

When both of you have completed your lists, compare them. Don't be defensive. Consider how the answers each of you have given affect your marriage. If you see a need to make your relationship a higher priority, talk together about specific steps you can take to make this happen. You might find it helpful to use the Problem-Solving Process you learned in Chapter Three. Part Three of this book will suggest additional ways to make your relationship a higher priority.

Exploring the Power of Commitment

Think about your answers to the following questions, then meet and talk with your partner about your reflections. What is your point of view, and what are you doing in this relationship?

1. What is your outlook on this relationship? Do you have a long-term view? Why or why not? If you have a long-term view, are you comforted by it, or do you feel trapped or stuck?

2. To what extent do you engage in scorekeeping? Do you notice the positive efforts your partner makes for you and the relationship? Can you try to notice the positive efforts more? Do you think some things are unfair and feel the need to confront your partner about them? Will you do that constructively?

3. Does your basic orientation in your marriage reflect more self-ishness or team-centered sensitivity? What kinds of things do you do that express selfishness? What things do you do that demonstrate a desire to meet your partner's needs?

4. Has the dedication between the two of you eroded to danger-ously low levels? What do you want to do about this?

5. If your relationship is going well, what do you think is the most important factor keeping it that way?

Now schedule some time to talk. These talks should be handled carefully. We suggest you use the Speaker-Listener Technique to share some of your most important impressions. Take this more as an opportunity to come together than as an excuse to get defensive and angry.

9

Forgiveness and the Preservation
or Restoration of Intimacy

We all tend to look to marriage as a refuge, but, because we are human, there is a risk of getting hurt from time to time. Your chances of being hurt deeply by your partner increase as you become parents. Put-downs, avoidance, negative interpretations, abusive comments, forgetting something important, making decisions without regard to your input—all these can hurt, and all happen more easily when the baby is crying, you're tired, and each minute seems precious.

Unless you have very unrealistic expectations, you realize both of you will commit "sins of omission and commission" over the course of your marriage. Minor infractions are normal and should be expected. It's far more valuable to learn how to move on at these times than to expect them not to happen at all. Major "sins" may happen as well. When that's the case, you will need to make more of an effort to put the events in the past. The more significant the issues or events causing harm, the more likely it is that you will need some of the specific steps we'll recommend later in this chapter.

THE NEED FOR FORGIVENESS

Let's look at two different parenting couples for whom forgiveness is an issue. Although both examples demonstrate the need for forgiveness, the infractions are very different—one is relatively minor, the other is major—and they have very different implications.

Oops, I Forgot: The Steadmans

Tyler and Kira Steadman have been married four years and have an eight-month-old daughter, Adriana. They have experienced the typical challenges of new parenthood but in general have handled them with skill and respect. Like many new moms, Kira was reluctant to leave Adriana to have some time for herself. Although she and Tyler had had a few dates, while Tyler's mom took care of the baby, it was challenging to get away in between Adriana's breast-feedings. What Kira really longed for was some time with her friends without the baby. Through discussion and problem solving, she and Tyler were able to negotiate for Kira to go to lunch and a movie with her girlfriends. This was no minor accomplishment.

On the big day, Kira spent the morning playing with Adriana, doing household chores, and eagerly anticipating her outing. Tyler was playing golf with his friends and promised to be home by 11:00 A.M. so that Kira could finish getting ready and meet her friends at the restaurant by noon. When 11:00 A.M. came and went and Tyler wasn't home, Kira became concerned. There was no way to reach Tyler at the golf course, because he and his friends could be at any of three different courses. By 12:15, Kira was livid; she called her friends at the restaurant to tell them she wouldn't be able to make it. After she hung up the phone, she sat down and cried. When Tyler waltzed in the door at four in the afternoon, the exchange went something like this:

KIRA: (*very distressed*) Where on earth have you been?

TYLER: (*noticing how upset Kira is and her swollen, red eyes*) Oh, no! This was supposed to be your big outing with your friends. I totally forgot.

KIRA: Where were you? You were supposed to be here by eleven. We had this all planned out. How could you do this to me?

TYLER: It completely slipped my mind. We ended up having to go to all three courses before we could get a reasonable tee time. I was so distracted by the late start, I forgot I was supposed to be home early.

KIRA: Not only did you blow my big day, you totally embarrassed me. I had raved about how wonderful and caring you were to make sure I finally got some time for myself. I set you up as a glowing example to my friends. Some example you turned out to be!

TYLER: Honey, please, please forgive me.

Should she? Of course. What does it mean for her to forgive in this context? Now consider a very different example—one in which the same questions have much more complicated answers.

The Grass That Looked Greener: The Carters

Anthony and Jayne Carter have been married for ten years. After seven years of marriage and lots of quality time as a couple, Anthony and Jayne decided to start a family. Unfortunately, this was not as easy as they had anticipated.

After two miscarriages, Jayne became pregnant again. The pregnancy was difficult, with Jayne in and out of the hospital for premature labor. For the last four months of pregnancy, life was totally disrupted as every effort was made to maintain the pregnancy and have a healthy baby. Jayne gave birth to a healthy boy, Jeremy, but her labor was long and complicated, and she ended up having a cesarean birth followed by complications. Needless to say, Jayne and Anthony's journey into parenthood was less than smooth and took its toll on their couple relationship.

By the time Jeremy was four months old, Jayne noticed that Anthony was gone more and more. She might have noticed a change in their intimate relationship, but that had fallen by the wayside during the difficult pregnancy. Anthony worked long hours during the day and often into the evening, or he returned to the office after dinner. His job demanded a lot, but did he really have to be gone that much? Without much time or talking together, it was hard to know what was going on. When Jayne tried to raise the issue, Anthony would either avoid the conversation or withdraw as soon as possible.

Jayne began to feel she didn't know Anthony anymore and suspected he was having an affair. She'd been attracted to other men, so why couldn't it happen to him? She'd call his office when he was supposed to be working late, and he was rarely there. When she asked about this, he'd say he must have been down the hall in the copy room or talking with a colleague. That didn't wash with Jayne.

Eventually Jayne got sick and tired of being suspicious. One evening she told Anthony she was going to see a friend and left. They had arranged for a baby-sitter so that he could go back to work. Borrowing her friend's car, Jayne followed him as he left the neighborhood. She followed him to an apartment complex, noting the door he entered. She sat and sat for three hours. She got up to look at the name on the mailbox—Roxanne something-or-other.

She felt a growing knot in her stomach that was matched by the lump in her throat. Now what? She decided to knock on the door. After ten minutes, a woman came to the door wearing a bathrobe.

ROXANNE: (*seeming quite tense*) Can I help you?

JAYNE: (*outwardly calm but falling apart inside*) Yes. Please tell Anthony I'm here and would like to speak to him.

ROXANNE: (*gaining composure*) Anthony? Who's Anthony? You must have the wrong apartment.

JAYNE: (*sarcastically*) Maybe I could take a look.

ROXANNE: I don't think so. Look, you have the wrong address. Good-bye!

JAYNE: (*yelling out as the door closes*) Tell Anthony I'll be at home—if he remembers where that is.

Anthony cruised in an hour later. He denied everything for three days. Jayne was quite sure of herself and wasn't about to back down. She told Anthony to get out. "An affair is bad enough, but if you can't even admit it, there's nothing left for us to talk about."

Anthony began drinking and disappeared for days at a time. Jayne felt even more alone and betrayed. Although she still loved Anthony, her rage and resentment grew. I thought I could trust him. I can't believe he would leave me for someone else! And leave his son as well!

As his denial crumbled, Anthony's sense of shame was so great that he was afraid to deal with Jayne. He would just stay away from home. Yet he was really bothered that Jayne was being so tough. In a way, he found new respect for her. No begging or pleading for Jayne, just toughness. He liked Roxanne but didn't want to spend his life with her. It became clear that he wanted to be with Jayne and Jeremy.

Of course Jayne didn't feel tough at all. She was in agony. There was no chance that she would stay with Anthony unless he dealt with her honestly. She wasn't sure whether she wanted to stay in the marriage or end it.

Jayne came home one night to find Anthony sitting at the kitchen table with a look of pain on his face.

ANTHONY: (*desperately*) Please forgive me. I'm not sure what happened. I'll get help.

JAYNE: (*cool outside, raging inside*) I'm not sure what happened either, but I think you know a lot more than I do.

ANTHONY: (*looking up*) I guess I do. What do you want to know?

JAYNE: (*icily*) I'd like to know what's been going on, without all the lies.

ANTHONY: (*tears welling up*) I've been having an affair. I met Roxanne at work. We got close, and things sort of got out of control.

JAYNE: I guess they did. How long?

ANTHONY: What?

JAYNE: (*voice raised, anger coming out*) How long have you been sleeping with her?

ANTHONY: Five months. Since the office party. Look, I couldn't handle things here at home. There's been so much distance between us with all the problems before and since the baby.

JAYNE: (*enraged*) So what! What if *I* couldn't handle it? I didn't go looking for someone else. I don't want you here right now . . . just go. (*turning away, heading into the next room*)

ANTHONY: If that's what you want, I'll go.

JAYNE: (*as she walks away*) Right now, that's just what I want. Leave me alone. Just let me know where you'll be for Jeremy's sake.

ANTHONY: (*despondent*) I'll go to my parents'. That's where I've been lately.

JAYNE: (*sarcastically*) Oh, thanks for telling me.

ANTHONY: I'll leave. Please forgive me, Jayne, please.

JAYNE: I don't know if I can. (*goes upstairs as Anthony slips out the back door*)

At this point, Jayne had some big decisions to make. Should she forgive Anthony? Could she forgive Anthony? She had already decided she might never trust him again. He clearly wanted to come back, but how would she ever know he wouldn't do this again the next time they had problems?

What do you think? Should she forgive? What does it mean to forgive Anthony in this situation?

WHAT IS FORGIVENESS?

Forgiveness is a decision to give up your perceived or actual right to get even with, or hold in debt, someone who has wronged you. Forgive is a verb. It's active. It's something you must decide to do! When one of you fails to forgive, you can't function as a team because one of you is kept "one down" by being indebted to the other.

In this sense, refusing to forgive is the ultimate in scorekeeping, with the message being "You are way behind on my scorecard, and

I don't know if you can catch up." In that context, resentment builds, conflict increases, and, ultimately, hopelessness sets in.

As we've seen, infractions can be small or large, their accompanying sense of debt being small or large as well. Tyler has a much smaller debt to Kira than Anthony has to Jayne. At any rate, statements such as those that follow express the opposite of forgiveness:

"I'm going to make you pay for what you did."

"You're never going to live this down."

"You owe me. I'm going to get even with you."

"I'll hold this against you for the rest of your life."

"I'll get you for this."

As harsh as these statements may sound, the sentiments they express are quite relevant for marriage. When you fail to forgive, you act out these kinds of statements—or state them openly. We'll focus on some of the most important issues about forgiveness. They usually have more to do with what forgiveness isn't than what it is.

What Forgiveness Isn't

You hear the phrase "forgive and forget" so often that the two ideas get equated when they in fact have nothing to do with one another. This is one of the greatest myths about forgiveness. Can you remember a painful wrong someone has caused in your life, for which you feel you have forgiven that person? We bet you can.

Just because you have forgiven—and given up a desire to harm another in return—doesn't mean you have forgotten the event ever happened. Fortunately, when people say "forgive and forget," they usually mean that you need to put the infraction in the past. If putting it in the past simply means you've given up holding it over your partner's head, that's fine.

One misconception related to forgiveness is the belief that if a person still feels pain about what happened, he or she hasn't really forgiven. You can still feel pain about being hurt in some way yet have fully forgiven the one who harmed you.

Jayne Carter may come to a point of completely forgiving Anthony, as we have defined forgiveness here. She may work through her rage and desire to hurt him back. However, even in the best of circumstances, what happened will probably leave her with a permanent wound.

In the Steadmans' case, the way in which Tyler hurt Kira is far less severe, with fewer lasting consequences. As it turned out, Kira did forgive him. She didn't dwell on it. However, when reminded of it, she remembers. That doesn't mean she's holding it over Tyler or trying to get even. She has forgiven; she just has a painful memory along the road of their marriage.

You may be wondering, "But, in forgiving, aren't I saying that the one who did wrong isn't responsible for what he or she did?" This is the second big misunderstanding about forgiveness. When you forgive, you're saying nothing about the responsibility of the one who did wrong. People who have done wrong are responsible for their actions, period. Forgiving them does not absolve them of their responsibility for their actions.

In this light, it's important to distinguish between punishment and consequences. You can be forgiven from the standpoint that your partner is not looking to hurt or punish you, but you can still accept and act on the consequences of your behavior.

Let's summarize so far. If you've been wronged by your partner, it's up to you to forgive or not. Your partner can't do this for you. It's your choice. If you've wronged your partner in some way, it's your job to take responsibility for your actions and, if necessary, take steps to see that it doesn't happen again. This assumes that the infraction is clear and that you are both humble and mature enough to take responsibility. If you want your relationship to move forward, you need to have a plan for forgiving. Even if you don't want to forgive—perhaps because of your own sense of justice—you may still need to do so for the good of your marriage.

The Steadmans followed this model in the ideal sense. Tyler took complete responsibility for being late—apologizing and asking Kira to forgive him. She forgave him, having no intention of holding it against him. Their relationship was actually strengthened by the way they handled this event. Kira gained respect for Tyler in his total acceptance of responsibility. Tyler gained respect for Kira in her loving and clear desire to forgive and move on.

Before we move on to specific steps you can take to keep forgiveness going, we want to discuss a crucial distinction—between forgiveness and restoration in a relationship. What do you do if one partner can't or won't take responsibility? How can you move forward?

What If You've Been Wronged, But Your Partner Won't Take Responsibility?

Forgiveness and restoration usually go hand in hand in a relationship, as they did with Tyler and Kira. The two of them quickly restored intimacy and openness in their relationship—neither erected barriers. Each handled his or her own responsibility without complication. When partners do this, restoration will naturally follow. What we mean by restoration is that your relationship is repaired for intimacy and connection.

But what do you do if you've been wronged in some way and your partner takes no responsibility? Do you allow the relationship to continue as it was? For one thing, you must be open to examining the possibility that your partner really didn't intend to do anything wrong, even though you were hurt by what happened. There can be a sincere difference in the interpretation of what happened and why.

Kyle and Dana Rush experienced such an event. They had been married three years, with things generally going well, and were expecting their first child. Although they weren't handling conflict well, their dedication remained strong. They were in the process of turning the spare room into a nursery. Kyle had been eager for Dana to finish the sorting and cleaning so that he could paint and set up the crib. One Saturday while Kyle played ball with the guys, Dana's nesting instinct took hold and she diligently sorted and scoured. When Kyle came home, he was thrilled that the mess was gone and that he could start his work.

The next day, when he was prepping the room for painting, he wondered where his box of memorabilia had gone. He had saved all his trophies, awards, and news clippings from his years as a success-ful student athlete. Kyle looked forward to sharing this part of him-self and his history with his child. The problem was that Dana, in her cleaning frenzy, had accidentally thrown the battered box away, and it had already been picked up by the garbage collector.

When Kyle realized the box was gone, he was furious. He ac-cused Dana of being "stupid and insensitive." He felt she didn't care and that throwing his stuff out was just another sign of her failure to accept him an athlete.

What happened was unfortunate. Kyle had every right to be upset. Those memorabilia were irreplaceable treasures to him. But it really was a mistake. The event triggered an acceptance issue for Kyle; yet he was being unfair in accusing Dana of intentionally hurt-ing him. This was a very negative interpretation. In fact, she was trying to do something for his benefit.

When you have been harmed in this way, it's OK to expect an apology—not because your partner *intended* to hurt you but because a mistake did hurt you. Dana can apologize to Kyle. But he has a long wait ahead if he needs to hear her say, "You're right; I threw out your things because I don't accept the successful athlete part of you. I'll work on it." Not likely.

Whether or not you both agree on the nature of the infraction, you can still move ahead and forgive. To do so can be difficult, but if you don't, you and the relationship will suffer. In fact, there's good reason to believe that when you hang on to resentment and bitter-ness, you put yourself at risk for psychological and physical prob-lems, such as depression, ulcers, high blood pressure, and rage.

Suppose it is clear that your partner did something very serious and wrong and isn't going to take any responsibility. That's a far tougher case. Sometimes people forgive the one who wronged them but don't reconcile the relationship because of the severity of what happened—or if the wrongdoer denies responsibility. Anthony did something incredibly wrong, and Jayne would be foolish to reconcile unless he takes responsibility *and* changes. He must be responsible for his own behavior if the marriage is to have any chance of moving forward. Sure, they are *both* responsible for letting their relationship slip. They had grown distant, and neither is more to blame than the other for that. However, it was his decision to have the affair. He's responsible for that action, not her.

When Anthony showed up in the kitchen, asking for forgiveness, the worst thing Jayne could have done would have been to pretend everything had returned to normal. It hadn't. You can't sweep things like this under the rug. Jayne could have decided then to forgive him—but that's a separate decision from whether or not she should allow a full restoration of the relationship. Here is what we mean.

When Anthony came back to the house that night, Jayne didn't know what level of responsibility he was taking for the affair. "What if he really blames me for it? What if he thinks it's my fault for being so involved with the baby and not being more affectionate?" If she thought he felt justified or wasn't serious about changing, why should she allow restoration of the relationship? It really would be a risk to take him back. Still, she can forgive. Either way, it will take time.

Here is what actually happened. For a few days, they had some nasty talks on the phone. With so much tension, it was easy to escalate. Yet Anthony persistently stated his desire to rebuild the marriage.

Jayne asked Anthony to the house for a talk one night after the baby went to sleep. She poured out her pain and anger. He listened. She focused on how his behavior had affected her, not on his motives and weaknesses. He took responsibility to the point of a sincere apology. He didn't blame her for the affair. Now she thought there was a chance they could get through this. Their talk concluded this way:

ANTHONY: I've had a lot of time to think. I made a very bad choice that hurt you deeply. It was wrong of me to have a relationship with Roxanne.

JAYNE: I appreciate the apology. I needed to hear it. I love you, but I can't just pick up where we left off.

ANTHONY: What do you want me to do?

JAYNE: I don't know. I've got so many questions. I just know I needed to hear you say you'd done something very wrong.

ANTHONY: Jayne, I did do something wrong. I know it. It's also clear to me . . . clearer than it's been in a few years . . . that I want this marriage to work. I want you, not someone else.

JAYNE: I'd like to make it work, but I'm not sure I can learn to trust you again.

ANTHONY: I know I hurt you deeply. I wish I could undo it.

JAYNE: I suppose I can forgive you, but I also need to believe it won't happen again.

ANTHONY: Jayne, I'd like to come back home.

JAYNE: OK, but I need to know we'll get help to get through this.

ANTHONY: Like a therapist.

JAYNE: Yes, like a therapist. I'm not sure what to do next, and I don't want to screw this up. If you'll agree to that, I can handle you coming home.

ANTHONY: That makes sense.

JAYNE: Don't expect me to go on like nothing's happened. I'm incredibly angry with you right now.

ANTHONY: I know, and I won't pressure you to act like nothing happened.

JAYNE: OK.

As you can see, Jayne really opened up, and Anthony validated her pain and anger. He didn't get defensive. If he had, she was prepared to work on forgiveness but end the marriage. She gained hope from this talk.

Jayne knew she could forgive but realized it would take time. She's also no fool. She knew they needed help. There was a lot to work through if they were going to restore their relationship.

Anthony did the best he could under the circumstances. Next day, he called around to find the best therapist. He wanted a professional who knew what they needed to do to move forward. This showed Jayne he was serious about repairing their marriage—giving her some evidence of long-unseen dedication.

The relationship could not be restored until they made the effort. It took time, but they did the work. Jayne will never forget, but the ache becomes more bearable each day. They were able to move through forgiveness and on to restoration of their relationship.

What About Regaining Trust?

Whatever the incident, suppose forgiveness proceeds smoothly and you both want restoration. How do you regain trust? It's not easy. There are four key points to keep in mind:

1. *Trust builds slowly over time*. Trust builds as you gain confidence in someone being there for you. Jayne can only regain her trust in Anthony slowly. The best thing that can happen is for time to pass without a serious breach of trust. That takes commitment and new ways of living together. They can't afford to let the same kind of distance build up again. If Anthony has another affair, it will.

2. *Trust has the greatest chance of being rebuilt when each partner takes appropriate responsibility*. The most important thing Anthony can do to regain Jayne's trust is to take full responsibility for his actions. If Jayne sees Anthony doing all he can to bring about change, her trust will grow. Through his effort, she gains confidence that things can get better—not perfect, but better. It's easier to trust when you can clearly see your partner's dedication to you.

Jayne can also help rebuild Anthony's trust. For one thing, he'll need to see she doesn't plan to hold the affair over his head forever. If she reminds him about it, especially during arguments, he won't be able to trust that she really wants him to draw closer and move ahead.

3. *If you've lost trust, recognize you can do more today to further damage it than to regain it.* It takes a long time to regain trust, but only a moment to crush it. If Anthony comes home tonight and is still trying, Jayne will gain a little more trust. But if he comes home two hours late with no explanation, Jayne's trust will evaporate. Mistakes are going to happen, but the commitment to change must remain clear. The commitment says you have the motivation and are making the time to rebuild trust.

STEPS YOU CAN TAKE TO BRING ABOUT FORGIVENESS AND RESTORATION

So far, we've focused on the meaning of forgiveness and what it takes to bring it about. Now we want to give you a more specific and structured approach for ensuring forgiveness. We don't mean to imply that forgiveness is easy, but we want you to be able to move forward with some specific steps to get you through the toughest times.

The steps outlined here are much like the process we suggested for problem solving. These steps can work well to guide you in forgiveness when you are dealing with a specific event or recurring issue.

We'll use the example of Dana and Kyle to highlight key points of each step. These steps will summarize many of the points made in this chapter as well as provide a road map for handling forgiveness.

Step 1: Schedule a Couple Meeting to Discuss the Specific Issue Related to Forgiveness

If an issue is important enough to focus on in this way, do it right. Set aside time without distractions. Prepare yourselves to deal with each other openly, honestly, and with respect. As we said in Chapter Four regarding ground rules, setting aside specific time for dealing with issues makes it more likely you will actually follow through and do it well.

After the initial rush of anger, Dana and Kyle agreed to work through the memorabilia incident. They set aside time on an evening when they were both rested and calm.

Step 2: Set the Agenda to Work on the Issue in Question

Identify the problem or harmful event. You must both agree that you are ready to discuss it in this format at this time. If not, wait for a better time.

When Dana and Kyle met, the agenda was pretty clear: how to forgive and move on from what happened with his box of memorabilia. They agreed this was the focus of their meeting, and they agreed they were ready to handle it.

Step 3: Fully Explore the Pain and Concerns Related to This Issue for Both of You

The goal in this step is to have an open, validating discussion about what happened that harmed one or both of you. You shouldn't try this unless you are willing to hear and show respect for your partner's viewpoint. The foundation for forgiveness is best laid through one or more good discussions.

Validating discussions go a long way toward dealing with the painful issues in ways that bring you closer together. This would be a great place to use the Speaker-Listener Technique. If there's ever a time to have a safe and clear talk, this is it.

Using the Speaker-Listener Technique, Dana and Kyle talked for about thirty minutes. She really heard his anguish about losing the things that meant so much. He listened to how badly she felt for him—for his loss. He also validated her statement that she hadn't intended to throw out his things. They felt closer than they had in quite awhile.

Step 4: The Offender Asks for Forgiveness

If you have offended your partner in some way, a request for forgiveness is not only appropriate but healing. An apology is a powerful addition to a request for forgiveness because it validates your partner's pain. Saying "I'm sorry. I was wrong. Please forgive me" is one of the most healing statements possible.

Apologizing and asking for forgiveness are a big part of taking responsibility for how you have hurt your partner. This doesn't mean you sit around and beat yourself up for what you did. You have to forgive yourself, too!

But what if you don't think you've done anything wrong? You can still ask your partner to forgive you. Remember, forgiveness is a separate issue from why the infraction occurred. Even if you don't agree you did anything wrong, your partner can choose to forgive. That's harder, but it can be done.

Listen carefully to your partner's pain and concern. Even if you feel you've done no wrong, you may find something in what your partner said that can lead to a change on your part for the better of the relationship.

Step 5: The Offended Agrees to Forgive

Ideally, the offended person clearly, openly acknowledges the desire to forgive. This may be unnecessary for minor infractions, but for anything significant this step is important. A clear statement makes the willingness to forgive more real, more memorable, and it increases accountability between you for healing.

There are several implications of this step. In forgiving, you are attempting to put the event in the past. You are agreeing you will not bring it up in the middle of future conflicts.

You both recognize that this commitment to forgive does not mean the offended will feel no pain or effects from what happened. But you are moving on. You're working to repair the damage and restore the relationship.

For many people, it also makes sense to make a personal commitment to forgive yourself when you have done something wrong. Punishing yourself endlessly for past behavior will do neither you nor your mate any good. Instead, put that energy into moving forward and making positive changes in your life and your relationship.

Step 6: If Applicable, the Offender Makes a Commitment to Change Patterns or Attitudes That Give Offense

Again, this step depends on your agreement that there is a specific problem with how one of you behaved. It also assumes that what happened is part of a pattern, not just a one-time event. For the Steadmans and the Rushes, this step is not very relevant. For the Carters, it's critical.

If you have hurt your partner, it also helps to make amends. When you make amends, you make a peace offering—not because you "owe" your partner but because you want to demonstrate your desire to get back on track. It's a gesture of goodwill. One way to make amends is to do unexpected positive acts, which shows your desire to keep building your relationship.

In Dana and Kyle's case, Dana arranged an intimate dinner at his favorite restaurant. She went out of her way to show he was special to her. He had already forgiven, but this gesture took them farther on the path of healing. Besides, it was fun. Their friendship was strengthened.

Step 7: Expect It to Take Time

These steps are potent for getting you on track as a couple. They can move the process along, but you may each be working on your side of the equation for some time to come. You are likely to hurt each other as you parent together. It's not whether or not this happens that counts most but rather how you deal with those hurts. Even when painful events come between you, you *can* heal your relationship. It is your choice to do so. These steps will help you get started.

EXERCISE

There are two parts to this exercise, one to do individually and one to do together.

Individual Work

First, spend some time thinking about areas where you harbor resentment and reluctance to forgive in your relationship. Write them down. How old are these feelings? Are there patterns of behavior that continue to offend you? Do you hold things against your partner? Do you bring up past events in arguments? Are you willing to push yourself to forgive?

Second, spend some time thinking about times you may have hurt your partner. Have you taken responsibility? Did you apologize? Have you taken steps to change any patterns that give offense? Just as you may be holding onto some grudges, you may be standing in the way of reconciliation if you have never taken responsibility for your part.

Working Together

As is the case with everything else we've presented, when it comes to forgiveness, practice is important to put positive patterns in place. Therefore, we recommend you meet together at least a couple of times and work through some issues following the steps presented in this chapter. Start with less significant events or issues to get the feel of things and build confidence and teamwork.

If you have identified more significant hurts that the two of you have not dealt with, take the time to sit down and tackle them. It's risky, but if you do it well, the resulting growth in your relationship and capacity for intimacy will be worth it.

Part III

Relationship Enhancement
Maintaining the Great Things

People get married to have a lifelong companion and partner. Like flowers without sunlight and water, many marriages wither and die from lack of attention to the best parts of the relationship: friendship, fun, and intimacy. Often these relationship riches are allowed to slip away as couples become parents. We want to help you keep this from happening. We will discuss each of these great aspects of relationships and teach you techniques to keep them alive and well in your relationship.

10

Preserving and Protecting Friendship

What people seem to want most in a mate is a best friend for life. For too many couples, this is a hope rather than a reality. Many couples start out as friends but don't remain so because they don't nurture and protect their friendship. Friendship often suffers when a baby enters the family. Fatigue, stress, and the new and multiple demands on your time tend to push friendship down the priority list. It's crucial to work to maintain your friendship as you deal with all the changes and challenges of parenthood. We want to help you strengthen and preserve your friendship now and for many years to come.

WHAT IS A FRIEND?

Typically people say a friend is someone who supports you, is there for you to talk with, is a companion in life; someone you relax with, play with, open up to, and count on. We talk and do fun things with friends. In this chapter, we'll focus on the talking side of friendship, and in the next chapter we'll focus on the role of fun in building and maintaining your friendship and your relationship. Falling short of the expectation of being friends can lead to strong feelings of disappointment and sadness.

BARRIERS TO FRIENDSHIP

To get an idea of what can happen to friendship over time, let's look at some common barriers.

There's No Time

We all lead busy lives, but life becomes exponentially busier and more complicated when a baby enters the family. On top of the demands of financial support of the family and basic household duties, you will have someone who requires care twenty-four hours a day, seven days a week. Friendship, the very core of your relationship, often takes a back seat to these competing demands.

Lisa and Christopher are a dual-career couple with a three-month-old daughter, Lindsey. Although they were happy with their marriage and life together, they felt they were losing something.

CHRISTOPHER: We used to sit around for hours talking about things like politics or the meaning of life. Now we hardly have time to sleep and eat. We're lucky to talk about the essentials that get us through the day.

LISA: You're right. It used to be so much fun just being together, listening to what we each thought about things.

CHRISTOPHER: Those talks really brought us together. Why don't we still have them?

LISA: We don't take time like we used to. Now, we've got Lindsey, the house—not to mention work.

CHRISTOPHER: It seems like we're letting something important slip away.

All too often, couples fail to take the time to talk as friends. This time to relax and talk gets crowded out by other demands; in other words, that time is no longer high on couples' list of priorities. When couples are dating, they somehow find time to be together, no matter how busy they are. Life may be a little less crazy at that stage, but finding time to be together is nevertheless a higher priority. Not making the time isn't the only reason friendship weakens over time, however.

We've Lost That Friendship Feeling

Many people say they were friends with their partners to begin with but aren't any more. Now they're *married* or *married with children*, as though these are states incompatible with being friends. Most couples seem to become business partners, without the pleasures of being friends.

The strongest marriages have maintained a solid foundation of friendship over the years. Jen and Pierre have been happily married for forty years. When we asked, "What's your secret?" their answer was, "Commitment and friendship." They have always made the time to talk as friends. They've maintained a deep respect for one another as friends who freely share thoughts and feelings about all sorts of things in an atmosphere of deep acceptance. That's kept their bond alive and strong.

Don't buy into the expectation that if you're married and parenting together you can't remain friends. You can!

We Don't Talk Like Friends Anymore

Think for a moment about a friendship you enjoy with someone other than your partner. How often do you have to talk with that person about problems between the two of you? Not often, we would bet. Friends aren't people with whom we argue a lot. In fact, one of the nicest things about friendships is that you usually don't have to work out issues. Instead you're able to focus on mutual interests in a way that's fun for both of you.

Friends talk about sports, spiritual matters, politics, philosophy of life, fun things they've done or will do, hopes, dreams, and thoughts about what each is going through at this point in life. In contrast, what do parenting couples talk most about? Who does what at home, problems with money and budgets, problems with the baby, problems with getting the car fixed, concerns about who has time to complete some project around the house, concerns about in-laws, problems with the neighbor's dog, concerns about each other's health. The list goes on and on.

Evan and Kate had made the mistake most parents do. They were on their first "date" in seven months, since Avery was born. When dessert was served, Evan said, "You know, we got a baby-sitter so we could have some time just for us. All we've talked about since we left the house is Avery. Let's make the baby off-limits until we go back home." *You need time to connect as husband and wife, not just as parents.* You have to make the effort to separate friendship time from time to talk as parents. You can marvel at the wonders of being parents as part of friendship talk, but you need to put the business of parenting in its place—with the other business of your relationship.

If couples aren't careful, most of their talks end up being about problems and concerns—not points of view and points of interest. Problems and concerns are part of married life and parenting, and must be dealt with. But too many couples let these issues crowd out the other, more relaxed talks they once shared and enjoyed. And because problems and concerns can easily become events that trigger issues, there's much more potential for conflict in talking with your partner than with a friend. That brings us to the next barrier.

We Have Conflicts That Erode Our Friendship

One of the main reasons couples have trouble staying friends is that friendship gets disrupted when issues come up in the relationship. For example, when you're angry with your partner about something, you're not going to feel much like being friends. Or worse, when you do have the time to be friends, conflicts come up and take you out of that relaxed mode of being together. We believe this is the chief reason some couples talk less and less like friends over the years— they aren't keeping their issues from damaging their friendship.

One couple, Cindy and Kevin, were having real trouble preserving friendship in their relationship. They had been married for eight years and had a one-year-old daughter. They bred dogs together but hadn't been away to a dog show since before Cindy got pregnant. They finally left the baby with Kevin's parents and went to a dog show for the weekend. This was the first chance to be away alone in over two years.

They were sitting in the hot tub of the hotel, really enjoying talking together about the show and the dogs they breed when a conflict came up that ended their enjoyable time together.

CINDY: (*very relaxed*) This is such a nice setting for the dog show.

KEVIN: (*equally relaxed, holding Cindy's hand*) Yeah. This is great. I can't believe we're really alone together.

CINDY: It seems too good to be true. You know, since we have some time, we really should talk about whether or not I have to go back to work next month like we planned.

KEVIN: (*tensing up*) We had that all planned out. You know how much we depend on your income. We've had to use almost all our savings for you to be home with the baby this long.

CINDY: (*sensing his tension, and now her own*) Well, what if I've changed my mind?

KEVIN: (*growing angry*) You can't do that. We can't make it on my income alone. You have to go back to work.

CINDY: (*angry and getting out of the tub*) Who put you in charge of the world?

Notice what happened here. There they were, relaxed, spending time alone together, being friends. But their talk turned into a conflict about an issue—their hot issue of money. What had been a great talk as friends turned into a nasty fight as partners.

When couples aren't doing a good job of keeping issues from erupting into their more relaxed times together, it becomes difficult to keep such positive times going in the relationship. The worst thing that can happen is your letting time to talk as friends become something to avoid. As we said earlier in this book, partners develop the perception that talking—including talking as friends—leads to fighting. This is one of the main reasons some couples lose touch with friendship over time. But as we'll see, you *can* prevent that from happening.

I Already Know My Partner Very Well

It's easy for people to assume that their partner doesn't change much over time. Couples begin to assume that it won't be interesting to talk as friends. They think they already know what their partner thinks about everything. But this isn't possible. Everyone grows and changes over time. We experience new events, new ideas replace old, and we are touched by the many things that happen to us and around us. You and your partner are taking on the new identity of parent and will need to get to know each other in that role. You can't know what new thoughts, ideas, and responses your partner is having unless you're able to talk as friends.

PROTECTING FRIENDSHIP IN YOUR MARRIAGE

Now that we've covered some of the common barriers to keeping friendship alive and well, we want to share some tips to help you protect this vital part of your relationship. These recommendations can work for building, rebuilding, or maintaining friendship in marriage. They work because they capture what couples do to nurture friendship in the first place.

Make the Time

Although it's great to be friends no matter what you're doing, we think you can benefit by setting time apart specifically for talking as friends. To set the time, you must *make* the time. And making time is not easy when you are parents. It's too easy to be occupied with problems, concerns, and just making it through the day.

We mentioned how Jen and Pierre had preserved and deepened their friendship over the forty years they had been married. One of the things they did to keep friendship alive was take time to be alone together. They would take long walks together and talk as they walked. They'd go out to dinner. They'd take weekend vacations from time to time, without the kids. They always made the time, and it's been paying off for forty years.

If couples truly believe friendship is important, they need to plan time to be together as friends. To plan this time you must make the friendship aspect of your intimacy a top priority. Doing so is one of the most beneficial investments you can make in your relationship. You need to put some boundaries around all the other things you do in life so as to carve out time for friendship. The investment of time to nurture your friendship with your partner is well worth it. You will feel better as a person, be a better parent, and do better in your work if your marriage is doing well. But that's not all you need to do to protect friendship.

Protect Your Friendship Time from Conflict and Issues

In Part One of this book, we focused on skills and techniques for handling conflicts well, such as using the Speaker-Listener Technique, good problem-solving skills, and ground rules. In Part Two, we added to this theme by presenting information about core issues. These strategies are powerful tools for dealing with conflict. You didn't get married in order to handle conflict, but you do need to handle conflict well if you want to protect your friendship and intimacy. To do so entails setting time aside to deal with issues as issues, taking Time Out when conflicts are intruding on times you set aside for friendship, and forgiving one another for problems in the past so you nurture the trust that friendship thrives on.

Never use things shared in moments of intimacy as weapons in a fight. Nothing adds fuel to the fire like betraying a trust in this way. Doing so is incredibly destructive and creates huge barriers to future intimacy. If you're getting so angry that you are even *tempted* to do this, you probably aren't handling issues well enough in your relationship. You may need to work harder—together—on all the skills we emphasized in the first two parts of this book. It takes a lot of practice to get to the point where you can handle conflicts with skill and respect.

You might be surprised by how powerful it can be for the two of you to agree that some times are "friend times" and therefore off-limits for conflicts and issues, including parenting issues. For example, you could decide that whenever you take a walk it's automatically friend time. Or you could go out to dinner and specifically agree that "This is friend time tonight, OK?" That way, you're working together to define the times you are "off duty" from the business of your marriage. Even better, you can decide that unless you have both agreed to deal with an issue at a particular time, you will be in friendship mode.

Begin Again to Talk as Friends

Listen like a friend listens. Good friends listen without being defensive. You don't have to worry so much that their feelings will be hurt or that they'll be offended. That's because a friend cares about what you think and feel, and relationship issues are rarely at stake. Our friend and colleague Bill Coffin once noted, "A friend is someone who's glad to see you and doesn't have any immediate plans for your improvement." When you're talking as friends, you are not trying to change one another. You can both relax and just enjoy the conversation. Even when we share serious issues or problems, we don't want a friend to tell us what to do; we just want him or her to listen. It feels good to know someone cares. Friends often provide that kind of support, and you can do this for each other in your relationship.

Don't focus on solving problems, unless it's a problem one of you has that has little to do with the other. Also, don't give unwanted advice. Most of the time, with a friend, you don't have to solve a problem. When you feel pressed to do so, it's easy to cut off discussions that can bring you closer together. That's why it's so important not to talk about relationship issues when you're together as friends—there's too much temptation to solve something and give advice. Focus on each other when in friend mode, not on issues between you.

Try It

We recommend you set aside time to talk as friends. Let's summarize the ways to make this happen:

- Ban problem issues and relationship conflicts from these times.

- Find time when you can get away from the pressures and demands of life—including the baby. Don't answer the phone. You might consider going out to dinner and leaving the baby with a sitter.

- Focus on topics of personal or mutual interest.

- Listen to each other in ways that deepen the sharing between you.

Although you might think these points sound contrived, they are necessary to preserve and protect your friendship. As we said at the beginning of this chapter, friendship is a core expectation people have for marriage. If you make and protect time for friendship, your relationship will blossom and continue to grow throughout your marriage. If you don't make time for friendship, it will slip away.

Like so many other things you've learned in this book, friendship is a skill. To keep your friendship strong, you may have to work at it a bit, but we can't think of anything more important to the long-term health of your relationship than to stay friends.

∽

In this chapter we've outlined some of the things that make friendship work, especially in how you communicate. In the next chapter we focus on fun. This is another area of intimacy and friendship in relationships that couples often take for granted and allow to slip away.

EXERCISES

The purpose of these exercises is to help the two of you reconnect as friends and develop a plan to build time for friendship into your weekly routine.

Reconnecting as Friends

Plan a quiet, uninterrupted time to talk as friends. It's best if you can be "off duty" as parents—when the baby is asleep or with someone else. Take turns picking topics of interest to each of you. Ban discussion of relationship conflict issues, problem solutions, the baby, and parenting. You might want to consider some of the following topics.

- Some aspect of your family of origin that you've been thinking about.

- Personal goals, dreams, or aspirations.

- A recent book or movie. Pretend you are professional critics, if you like.

- Current events, such as local or national news, sports, or politics.

Another approach to reconnecting as friends is to take turns pretending to be your favorite TV interviewers; interview your partner about his or her life story, including what it's like to be a new parent. This can be a lot of fun, and it's really in the spirit of listening as friends. The best interviewers on TV are very good at listening and drawing their guests out of themselves. Try to draw one another out in your sharing together as friends.

Building Time for Friendship

Friendship time won't just happen. You and your partner will need to develop a plan to build time for friendship. Particularly after the baby comes, planning will probably mean blocking in friendship time on the family calendar. If friendship time is important enough, you can make it happen. It is essential to the health and life of your couple relationship. Use the Problem-Solving Process to develop a plan to build friendship time into your weekly routine. Start with planning how you will make it happen *this week*.

Preserving and Protecting Fun Together

The focus of this chapter is on how to continually revitalize your relationship by increasing your fun together. Like friendship, fun is one of the great ways to stay close together but is all too easily neglected and allowed to fall by the wayside as you become parents.

THE IMPORTANCE OF PRESERVING FUN

Research has shown that the amount of fun couples have together is strongly related to their overall marital happiness. Good relationships stay great when you're preserving both the quantity and quality of your enjoyable times together. First we'll look at some barriers to fun in marriage. Then we'll teach you how to keep fun alive in your relationship, even when you are parents.

BARRIERS TO FUN

Most couples start out having lots of fun together during the dating phase of their relationship. These times play an important part in developing a positive and intimate bond between you. But, for too many couples, fun fizzles out as time goes on. Let's look at some of the reasons this happens.

We're Too Busy

Early in relationships, people tend to put a high priority on going to the movies, window shopping, walking hand in hand, going bowling, and so forth. But couples often stop making time for fun. That's the way it was for Miguel and Lucia. They used to spend many Saturdays at the beach swimming, talking, and lying in the sun. They took long walks along the sand and talked about their future together. When they got married, they continued to go to the beach, but less frequently. A few years later they had their first child; their baby was a delight for them, but they began to spend much less time going out and having fun like they used to. Over time they noticed life wasn't as enjoyable as it used to be. They were happy together, and their five-year-old marriage was solid, but something was missing.

It may seem obvious when you stop to think about it, but sometimes it's easy to overlook the obvious: *life is more enjoyable when you regularly make time to do fun things together.* Having fun together "recharges your batteries." If you don't make these times happen, the busyness of life will take them from you.

Ian and Erin are a good example of partners who have preserved time for fun in their marriage. When they married they vowed they would always maintain the friendship and fun in their relationship. When they decided to become parents they agreed they were partners first and would do whatever it took to maintain their relationship. Their baby is now seven months old, and they only messed up the week the baby was born.

They have at least one "adults only" date every week. Over the course of their marriage they've tried lots of things and vary what they do for fun together—dinner, a movie, swimming, dance lessons, walking in the park, watching the sun set, and so forth. Since the baby came, they also have at least one family fun time each week. These have ranged from taking the baby to the park to cross-country skiing with the baby in a backpack. They are determined not only to continue to have fun but also to teach their child the importance of fun in a healthy life. Fun is a priority in their marriage.

We're Parents Now, So We're Not Supposed to Have Fun

One of the expectations people sometimes hold about becoming parents is that it's serious business and should be undertaken in a mature way. It's now time to be an adult and leave childish playfulness behind. Hogwash! You should be an involved parent and a responsible member of society, but you also need to let your hair down and have fun together. Being a parent is a *great* reason to fully express your playful and fun-loving side. Children are superb at teaching parents how to play and have fun, if you're open to learning.

At the end of life, when people are asked what they wish they had done differently, few say, "I wish I had worked more hours" (or sold more widgets or completed more projects). People usually say they wish they had spent more time enjoying their spouse and children. Don't postpone enjoying life to the fullest. Make sure fun and play are essential parts of your relationship *now*.

We Have Conflicts That Ruin Our Fun Time

Mishandled conflict is a real killer of fun time together. As we've emphasized so often, handling problems poorly can just about ruin all the enjoyable aspects of a relationship.

Robin and Geoff were a couple who made time for fun. But all too often they would be out to have fun, and some event would trigger an issue that would destroy the playfulness of the moment. They were introduced to infant massage after the baby came, and later thought they'd like to explore adding massage to their adult relationship. They arranged for a baby-sitter so that they could go to a couples' massage class. They thought, "This will push us to have fun in a new way." Great idea!

The instructor was making a point about paying attention to your partner's reactions. Geoff whispered to Robin, "That's a great point." Robin whispered back, "I've been trying to tell you that for years." Geoff was instantly offended. He felt attacked, and pulled away from Robin, folding his hands across his chest in disgust.

This event triggered some hot issues for Geoff and Robin. For years, Robin had felt Geoff didn't listen well to what she said (a hidden issue of caring). She was hurt that he hadn't cared enough to remember her making the same point the instructor was making. Geoff had been feeling that Robin was critical of nearly everything he did, especially his parenting. Now he felt she was attacking him when he was trying to improve their relationship by taking this class together. He felt rejected, wondering, "Can't she even lay off when we're out to have fun?" On this evening, they didn't recover well. Geoff suggested they leave the class early and go home. They did— in silence.

There will be occasions for all couples when conflict erupts during fun times. But when it happens too often, fun times aren't much fun anymore. The whole idea is to share a relaxing time together that creates an enjoyable experience. Poorly handled conflict will blow this all away. Remember Ground Rule 6: "We will agree to protect these [fun] times from conflict and the need to deal with issues."

GUIDELINES FOR KEEPING FUN IN MARRIAGE

Now that we've discussed some barriers that can keep fun from being a regular part of your relationship, we want to present some ideas for keeping fun alive and well as you become parents.

You may be thinking you know how to have fun and don't need help in this area. If so, that's great. You can still use these tips to help you stay on track.

Make the Time

It's hard to have fun together as a parenting couple without setting aside time for it to happen. We suggest you make this a high priority for your relationship. To make the time, you may actually have to pull out your calendars and schedule fun time together. This may not sound spontaneous or romantic, but for most parenting couples, there's so much else going on that it takes deliberate action to make the fun times happen. Early in your relationship, you probably had no trouble making time for fun. But once real life sets in and the baby comes, it's common to find that your fun time has fallen by the wayside. People say it's quality time that's important. *But you need a quantity of time together to have that quality time.*

As parents, you will need to find someone you trust to care for the baby so you can have time alone together. Nothing helps you relax more than being out to have fun and knowing your little one is safe with someone you trust. Don't limit yourselves to having someone come in to take care of the baby. Couples often long for time alone together at home. This is probably why many couples work out arrangements with other parents to trade off child care so they can have time alone together at home. You may feel guilty for wanting or needing time alone to play together as a couple. *Remember that the best way to be a great parent is to be sure to take care of you and your couple relationship.* Self- and couple care recharge your "parenting batteries."

When you are making time for fun, try to arrange for time without the possibility of distraction. For example, if your job requires you to wear a pager or carry a cell phone, do you really have to have it with you when you've carved out time to play with your partner? It's not very relaxing to know you could be beeped or phoned at any moment. Some parents are able to be more relaxed if they know the baby-sitter can reach them if necessary. If this is the case, you might want to carry a pager or cell phone with the strict order not to be contacted unless it's absolutely necessary. Once you learn your baby is not only safe but also probably having fun with another care provider, you will be able to relax more and have even more fun.

When their baby was eight months old, Morgan and Jason realized they hadn't been on a date since before the baby was born. They decided this wasn't acceptable and set out to restore the fun and friendship time in their relationship. The next weekend, they had Morgan's mom come over to take care of the baby, and they went on a real date, which reminded them of what they had been missing. They rededicated themselves to making couple time a priority. On the following Friday, despite Morgan's mom being available to take care of the baby, they were both too tired to go out. Of the next six weekends, they managed to have dates on only two. They decided part of the problem was that it was too easy to cancel their plans, and doing so was detrimental to their relationship.

They promised themselves at least one evening out together each week. They registered for Friday night ballroom dancing lessons. It wasn't that either had a burning desire to learn ballroom dancing; they were both interested, but because they had to pay up front for the classes, they felt it would increase their likelihood of getting out the door. They only made it to about half the classes, but they always had a date together on Friday night. Once they had child care arranged and a place to go, actually getting out became easier. They no longer have to trick themselves into making time for fun. They realize how essential it is to keeping their relationship strong and growing.

If you establish a pattern of taking time for fun together, you are likely to see positive effects on your adult couple relationship and your relationship with your baby. It's worth it!

Protect Fun from Conflict

As we discussed in the previous chapter, mishandled conflict is a real killer of fun times together. We'll make the same point again in the next chapter on your intimate relationship. Poorly handled conflict can ruin the most enjoyable aspects of your relationship. You can be in control of when and how you'll deal with issues, and you can protect your wonderful times together from negative patterns that are so destructive.

If you work at making time for fun together, you may be tempted to deal with issues during these times. For example, you're going on a date and one of you thinks, "As long as we have this time together, why don't we talk about how we can get the baby to sleep through the night?" Bad idea! If at all possible, don't mix dealing with issues, including parenting issues, with fun time. You will be best able to follow this advice if you are both clear when it is "fun time." That way, you both understand the ground rule you've agreed to follow and can guard your fun time together.

So here's the key: work on issues in the time set aside for doing just that. If issues get triggered during fun time, set them aside. Come back to them and handle them well, but not in time reserved for fun. The sense that conflict could erupt at any moment isn't compatible with relaxed playfulness.

Brainstorm About Fun Activities

OK, you've set aside time for fun, and you've agreed to put conflicts aside to protect that time. Now what? Some of you have gotten rusty at coming up with fun things to do together. You can regain this ability. You just have to work at it a bit.

There are many activities couples do for fun. What do you do? Are you in a rut? Sit down together and think about the most enjoyable, interesting, and fun things you've ever done, or things you would like to do together. Make a list to which you both contribute, putting down all ideas no matter how foolish or outrageous they may seem. Part of the fun is in brainstorming about fun—throwing out the wackiest ideas you can. Avoid getting into ruts.

To help you get started, we'll share some of the great ideas we've heard from couples. Sometimes it only takes hearing what works for others to get your mind spinning in some creative directions.

You can reminisce about the past—going backwards into the future. Such memories are important to talk about to help you remember the fun times you had as well as encourage you to have more fun times in the future. You can go out to dinner and share fantasies. For example, what would it be like to give up life as you know it and sail around the world for a year or two? Or, what would you do if you won the lottery?

You can exercise or try some massage together. Many couples enjoy going to the movies. You could also just rent a movie and cuddle up on the couch with some popcorn. You could bake cookies together, ride bikes, go for a hike, or go to the beach and collect seashells. Fun doesn't have to be something elaborate or expensive.

Over the years, we've noticed that when couples brainstorm about fun things to do, sex usually isn't mentioned until other things come up. Couples tend to forget that sexual intimacy is one of the most fun things they can do together. Several variations to suit your personal preferences should be included on your list. How about setting aside an evening without the baby just to make love?

Get Going

One thing that can really help you get more fun going is to have a list of fun things already made. You can both contribute items to the list. Or, as was suggested in *A Couple's Guide to Communication* (Research Press, 1976) several years ago, make a fun deck by taking a stack of index cards and writing an idea on each card. Or you can make a fun jar by writing your ideas on pieces of paper and putting them in a jar to draw from. Try listing twenty-five to thirty ideas to start with. Make sure you include a variety of ideas with different price tags (be sure to include *free* things), time requirements, and so forth.

Once you have your list, deck, or jar, set aside particular times to choose activities—and do them. Don't let anything stop you! Each of you pick three things. Trade cards. Then each choose one fun thing your partner picked and take responsibility for making it happen. That way you're each picking something you know your partner will like, and, because you get to make the selection, you know you'll like it too. Don't worry about which one your partner wants you to pick. If you don't get to do it today, you'll have another chance tomorrow!

You may want to make two decks or jars: one for fun things to do together and another for fun things to do as a family. Although it is *essential* that you have separate *couple* fun time, you can increase your overall fun and cover the times when you can't get a sitter by including ideas for family fun time.

You can choose to intensify the effort at times. For example, you could each pick three things from your list, deck, or jar, and over the next weekend do all six. Try breaking the fun barrier!

If you follow the key points in this chapter, you will be qualified for a degree in relationship fun. You can do it! Early in relationships, having fun comes easily. Even when you are parents, it's not all that hard if you make the time, protect that time, and work as a team to make fun happen. In addition to the potentially huge benefits to your couple relationship, think of the wonderful example you'll be setting for your child.

EXERCISES

These exercises will guide you through the steps discussed in this chapter for having fun together.

Creating a Fun Deck or Fun Jar

Sit down with your partner and think about the most enjoyable, interesting, and playful things you've ever done or would like to do together. This is a brainstorming session, so let all your creative juices flow! Have fun coming up with ideas. As you come up with ideas, jot them down either on three-by-five cards to make a fun deck or on small pieces of paper to make a fun jar. Follow the instructions we just covered in the "Get Going" section.

Having Fun Together

Develop a plan to build time for fun into your weekly routine. Go for it! After the baby comes, try to include couple fun times *and* family fun times—but don't lose that playful time as a couple.

12

Hello Baby, Goodbye Sex?
Protecting and Enhancing Your Sex Life

Almost everything we've discussed in this book has the potential to affect your intimate relationship. Problems in other aspects of your relationship often get played out in the bedroom. Fatigue, stress, and the seemingly endless demands of a baby can increase conflict in your relationship. As with friendship and fun time, intimacy can be pushed down the priority list and all but forgotten. When you actually have the opportunity to lie down alone together, it can be almost impossible to stay awake to do anything! You've no doubt heard lots of horror stories. Many couples expect their sex life to vanish with the appearance of the first diaper, if not before. Unfortunately, as with other expectations, this can become a self-fulfilling prophecy.

It's a myth, though, that becoming parents means kissing your sex life goodbye. We don't mean to imply it will be easy to maintain your intimate relationship as parents. It's not easy to have a great sex life even without kids. But we'd like to accentuate the positive and teach you ways to enhance your intimate relationship as you become parents. The physical and mental changes of expectant and new parenthood force you to relate in new and different ways both sensually and sexually, which can add new dimensions to your intimacy.

As strange as it may sound, pregnancy can be an aphrodisiac. You don't have to worry about getting pregnant, which can be a real turn-on. The full breasts and curves of the pregnant body can excite men and help women feel sexy. Often the physiological changes of pregnancy increase a woman's sexual responsiveness, which can excite her partner as well.

On the down side, many women feel very self-conscious about their body when pregnant. After the birth of the baby, breasts that are leaking milk may not be the most inviting playground. And a screaming baby or anxiety about how you're going to pay the bills can kill just about anyone's sexual arousal. In this chapter, we'll examine the effects of pregnancy and parenthood on your intimate relationship, including how to enhance your sensual and sexual relationship before and after the baby comes.

INTIMACY DURING PREGNANCY

It's important to realize that your intimate relationship isn't a blank slate when you become pregnant or a baby joins the family. Couples usually have a history of intimacy together. Most couples enjoy the physical closeness of the marital relationship and initially spend lots of time cuddling and caressing each other and making love. Over time, however, the pressures and demands of life tend to erode the physical relationship. Couples often become efficient at having intercourse and end up "making do" rather than "making love" in the fullest sense. Your intimate relationship as you become parents is built on and influenced by the foundation of your existing relationship. Keep this in mind as you read on.

There are no real "rules" about intimacy during pregnancy. This is a great time for relaxing, enjoying the woman's changing body, talking a lot, touching each other, and experimenting with new ways, both sensual and sexual, of being intimate and expressing affection. The old ways of relating intimately are unlikely to continue to work. You can look at this as a crisis or seize the opportunity.

Let's consider an example. Once they became pregnant with their first child, Randy and Quyen were forced to change their intimate relationship. Like many women, for the first few months of pregnancy, Quyen experienced almost constant nausea, severe fatigue, and extreme breast tenderness. She had little interest in intercourse but wanted to continue to feel close to Randy. Randy's desire for intimacy was unchanged.

On the advice of some friends who had recently become parents, Quyen and Randy combed the library and bookstores for books on improving intimate relationships. They got all kinds of ideas on how to enhance their sensual relationship. They learned some massage techniques and tried massaging each other's hands, feet, and heads. They experimented with different scented oils and found some that actually reduced Quyen's nausea. Because they were forced to do things differently, they realized they had been in a rut in their intimate relationship and used this opportunity to expand their intimacy repertoire by incorporating these new techniques.

Rediscovering Sensuality

There are both sensual and sexual components of intimacy, and it's important to understand and maintain both parts. Sensuality includes the pleasurable touching, caressing, stroking, massaging, and holding close that provide sensations we've learned to associate with feeling cared for and loved—acts that provide physical pleasure in nonsexual ways. Sensuality isn't always associated with making love.

Unfortunately, over time many couples tend to bypass the sensual and move almost exclusively to goal-oriented sexual behavior. This leads to problems, because touching is a basic part of your overall intimacy. Quyen and Randy were reminded of the importance of sensuality and learned some new ways to regain this part of their intimacy.

Communicating Desires

Quyen's changing body and discomforts of pregnancy also led to their learning to communicate more effectively about their intimate relationship. She and Randy could no longer go by what each wanted or liked in the past.

We recommend you discuss your expectations about your intimate relationship now that you are pregnant, in the safety of a couple meeting and using the Speaker-Listener Technique. Go back to the expectations exercise in Chapter Six. Now that you are pregnant, what are your expectations about sexual practices, frequency, and taboos in your sensual and sexual relationship? Who should initiate lovemaking? These types of discussions are very sensitive. Be sure to be gentle, caring, and validating.

Once you've discussed your expectations, likes, dislikes, needs, and concerns in a couple meeting, communicate clearly and specifically about what feels pleasurable to you while actually touching and making love. Your partner can't know unless you say something. In addition to words, guide your partner's hands to show where and how and how firmly to touch. Because things will continue to change throughout pregnancy and parenting, you will need to keep this line of communication open and revisit these issues regularly.

In midpregnancy, Quyen felt great, and she and Randy enjoyed an active and mutually satisfying intimate relationship. In fact, like many women, Quyen found herself more sexually responsive. This extra responsiveness is due to the increased blood flow through the pelvis and sexual organs during and after pregnancy. Some women experience their first orgasm during pregnancy. Quyen's orgasms were more frequent and more intense.

Fears About Hurting the Baby

As the baby grew and Randy could feel it kicking through Quyen's abdomen, Randy became concerned that penile thrusting during intercourse might hurt the baby. Though he was turned on by Quyen's changing body, he thought it must be wrong to be sexually excited by a pregnant woman and to have sex with a "mother."

He was embarrassed but got up the nerve to discuss this with their midwife, who assured him these were normal concerns. She explained that because the uterus tips forward during pregnancy, he didn't need to worry about "bumping the baby" during intercourse. The midwife also assured him that certain positions, such as man on top, would become too uncomfortable for Quyen before they would possibly harm the baby. His relief upon hearing this information led to renewed lovemaking with his voluptuously pregnant wife.

These kinds of questions can easily begin to drive a wedge between you if you let them. If you have such concerns, be sure to discuss them with your partner.

Changes in Body Image

Many women develop a negative body image during pregnancy, seeing themselves as fat and ugly rather than pregnant. They cannot comprehend how their partner could honestly find them attractive or sexually appealing. When Randy started showing less interest in her sexually, Quyen believed her growing body repulsed him.

Actually, research indicates most men find their mate's changing body beautiful, and marvel at her ability to grow a baby. But because most women don't know this they usually withdraw and hide their body from their partner, which may actually increase his guilt about being aroused by his pregnant spouse. This is not a road to intimacy. These feelings need to be brought into the open. As with other discussions of the sensitive topic of your intimate relationship, it might be a good idea to use the Speaker-Listener Technique.

Changes in Sex Drive

A woman's sex drive can vary significantly during pregnancy. We recommend that you not assume you know what these variations will be, or your expectations may become a self-fulfilling prophecy. As was true for Quyen, in early pregnancy many women have less interest in being intimate because of the physical symptoms of fatigue, nausea, and breast tenderness. In midpregnancy, women often experience a renewed or intensified sex drive. Try to remain open to the possibility of changes for both of you and modify your sensual and sexual activities to accommodate these changes. Regardless of her own sex drive during pregnancy, a woman can still pleasure her partner—and vice versa.

Women may also experience emotional changes during pregnancy. Some women use these changes as a reason to be rude to their partner or as an excuse to curtail intimacy. Contrary to some people's beliefs, women are not "crazy" during pregnancy. Sure, changing hormone levels combined with physical discomforts may result in irritability, but pregnant women are sane, can be functional, and should still be expected to act like civilized human beings. You should explore as a couple any reduction in intimacy and develop a plan to maintain a mutually satisfying relationship.

During the last months of pregnancy, Quyen and Randy faced additional challenges to their physical relationship. Quyen's large girth prevented their bodies from fitting together as they had in the past. Rather than letting this throw them, they returned to the books they had used early in pregnancy. These resources guided them to different positions for intercourse, such as female-on-top and side-lying positions, which minimize pressure on the baby-filled abdomen. They were again reminded to get out of their rut! Remember that if intercourse feels uncomfortable or painful, changing positions may help. Intercourse should *never* hurt.

When There Are Complications

Unlike Quyen and Randy, who experienced a normal, uncomplicated pregnancy, Seth and Cami experienced a very challenging pregnancy. Right from the start there were problems. First Cami had spotting of dark red blood. Once that resolved, she had lots of uterine contractions and was treated for premature labor. She and Seth were scared to death. They were sure they would lose the baby. The obstetrician ordered them to stop all sexual relations. Combined with their fear, this order was like a wall between them. Their intimate relationship ended.

Unlike Quyen and Randy, they were unable to discuss the situation and their feelings productively. Tension rose, and everything and anything escalated into major conflict. Although they gave birth to a healthy baby boy, by Micah's first birthday Seth and Cami had still not resumed their intimate relationship, and the very survival of their marriage was in doubt. When things go wrong sexually for a couple, the changes can't be ignored for any length of time without damage to the couple's relationship.

If, like Seth and Cami, you experience problems during pregnancy, and limits are placed on your intimate relationship, ask your obstetrical health care provider to be *very specific* about what these limits are. Sometimes it means you must not put anything in the vagina—no intercourse, no sex toys, no fingers. Other times it means no sexual arousal or orgasms, even through masturbation or nonintercourse sexual stimulation, because female orgasms cause uterine contractions. Understand specifically what you can and cannot do. Whatever the restrictions, there is always the opportunity for some type of sensual, if not sexual, interaction. And even if the woman can't be stimulated, she can still pleasure her partner.

Victor and Tameco faced different challenges to their intimate relationship during pregnancy. After being married for ten years, they decided it was time to start a family. They never imagined the journey to parenthood would be so long and trying. For two years Victor and Tameco tried to get pregnant on their own. Their obstetrician finally referred them to an infertility specialist. They spent the next two years undergoing countless tests and medical procedures and had two miscarriages.

Their lives began to revolve around Tameco's menstrual cycle. They could no longer be spontaneous in their lovemaking—they had to have intercourse in a specific position at specific times on specific days. The most private aspects of their relationship were constantly under medical scrutiny, and their lives centered around whether or not Tameco got her period. Although they were eventually able to achieve and maintain a pregnancy that resulted in a beautiful, healthy son, Tobias, their trials took a toll on their intimate relationship.

Once Tameco became pregnant with Tobias, it took months before they were convinced they weren't going to lose the pregnancy. They basically had to start their intimate relationship all over again. Thankfully they had an obstetrician who understood what they had been through. He provided guidelines on first building a sensual relationship. They began by taking turns pleasuring each other through nonsexual touch. Once they were able to relax and enjoy such contact, they were allowed to slowly resume sexual touch and, eventually, intercourse. Slowly their intimate relationship became private, spontaneous, and mutually satisfying. They were fortunate to have excellent communication skills that they used conscientiously.

If You Are Adopting

If you are becoming parents through adoption, you may have unresolved feelings about not having your own biological child. Infertility or being unable to bear your own child is often an assault on one's identity as a woman or man. But as a person you are more than your ability to procreate. If your goal is to become parents, focus on that goal rather than on the route by which you get there.

Adoption resource centers usually have professionals who understand and can help you work through unresolved feelings and help you understand that just because you wanted so very much to become parents, that doesn't mean you must be perfect parents or enjoy every minute of parenthood. They also provide opportunities for adopting parents to get together. It is helpful to be reminded you are not alone and to be able to share your experiences with others and to learn from them.

Although most pregnancies are normal and uncomplicated, there can be many challenges to your intimate relationship as your family grows. You can allow this precious aspect of your marriage to falter, or you can use the challenges of this important time in your lives as a wonderful opportunity to explore new ways of relating intimately. Let's turn now to sexual intimacy after birth.

INTIMACY AFTER THE BABY COMES

There are any number of things that affect your intimate relationship after the baby comes, such as your experience of the pregnancy, labor, and birth, or your journey to parenthood through adoption; any continuing physical issues or discomforts; and all the changes that come with having a baby in the house.

Resuming Intimacy After Birth

After the birth of a baby, through the vagina or by cesarean section, sexual intimacy can be resumed physically when vaginal bleeding has stopped and any soreness from incisions or tears is gone—usually two to four weeks after birth. Tenderness can be checked by pressing gently with fingers inside the vagina. You may need to delay resuming sexual activity or to provide sexual stimulation some other way if intercourse is uncomfortable. Sexual intercourse should never be painful. If it is or continues to be painful, check with your health care provider and be sure to get help to resolve the problem. Occasionally, infection, scar tissue, or deep muscle tears may be the problem.

Sometimes couples want to resume intercourse quickly, even within days of birth. If you find yourselves in this situation, you aren't deviant. Each couple and situation is unique. Use condoms until vaginal bleeding has stopped in order to prevent infection in the uterus.

Regardless of when you resume intercourse, unless another pregnancy would be acceptable, you need to take action to control conception. Ovulation can resume before a woman has her first menstrual period after birth, and it's a myth that women who are breast-feeding can't get pregnant.

The Impact of Fatigue

Factors most affecting intimacy after birth are fatigue and finding time for lovemaking. Rafe and Gabriella were exhausted. They hadn't slept for more than three hours at a stretch since Brent was born. Gabriella's bottom was still tender, and she felt "all touched out" from carrying the baby around constantly and breast-feeding. Although she wanted to be with Rafe, it seemed their efforts were jinxed.

When they found time for intimacy, no sooner would they start pleasuring each other than the baby would begin to cry. In addition, Gabriella's breasts leaked milk when she became sexually aroused, which she was certain turned Rafe off. Gabriella felt like a fat and dumpy baby-feeding machine. Rafe was jealous of all the attention Brent got, and wondered whether he would ever win his wife back. They both wondered whether they could or would be good parents.

Going with the Flow

No matter how you become parents, having a baby join the family is going to affect your intimate relationship. Your time will no longer be your own—what you do and when you do it will be greatly affected by the baby. You may be used to cuddling and making love when you wake up, but your baby may have other ideas. Your baby will wake up hungry and demanding to be fed. Saying, "Wait a few minutes" just isn't an option. You may be used to snuggling and making love when you go to bed at night. Especially in the early weeks of parenting, it will be almost impossible to lie down without falling asleep.

This doesn't mean your love life is over or needs to be put on the back burner for eighteen years or so. It just means you'll need to work together to develop a creative plan for continuing your intimate relationship. The name of the game is flexibility.

Though Gabriella and Rafe might seem doomed in their quest for intimacy, they made a joint decision to turn things around. They followed the recommendations we'll be presenting later in this book for managing fatigue and taking care of themselves. They figured out the baby's typical sleep-wake pattern and planned intimate couple time when they anticipated Brent would sleep for at least two hours. Not wanting to depend on the baby being predictable, they regularly had the neighbor girl take Brent for long walks around the block in his stroller and savored their uninterrupted private time.

When Gabriella was able to relax during lovemaking, her bottom no longer hurt. They compensated for the vaginal dryness caused by the hormones that support breast-feeding by using saliva or a water-soluble lubricant. Through their dedicated efforts, Gabriella and Rafe have a mutually satisfying sensual and sexual relationship. Being able to communicate effectively and laugh rather than take things too seriously was a lifesaver.

You and your partner can take the time to plan and maintain your intimate relationship only to find that in a few weeks or months things change yet again as the baby grows and starts sleeping through the night or climbing out of the crib, or you or your partner change jobs or return to work. It's helpful to look at your intimate relationship as being constantly in a state of flux. This will help reduce the chances of frustration and anger. Your intimate relationship has evolved and changed up until now, and it will continue to do so. Think of it as a never-ending opportunity to make things better and more satisfying.

Protecting Your Intimate Relationship

Here are some recommendations to keep your intimate relationship on track. You will note their similarity to those for keeping friendship and fun alive and growing.

Make the Time

Your life is getting more complicated rather than less so. Much of your time, especially in the beginning, will be taken up with baby care and basic life maintenance—cooking, cleaning, errands, and so forth. At first it will seem like you have no time at all for yourself or your couple relationship. But as you get to know your baby and become more skilled in caring for him or her, you will become more efficient in your time management. You will have the same twenty-four hours you had before the baby came; you'll just fill them somewhat differently.

As with friendship and fun time, intimacy is vital to the maintenance and continued growth and revitalization of your relationship. If intimacy is important, you can and will find the time. You will probably need to schedule intimacy. This need may fly in the face of your view of lovemaking as spontaneous, but you will be more likely to be intimate if you determine, in general, when good times might be. Each couple and each family is unique.

It will help to identify when your baby is likely to go to bed, wake up, nap, be able to play alone for a while, and so forth. Then plan to make the most of these potentially undisturbed times. We'll be devoting a whole chapter to identifying and using support. It's very appropriate to have someone care for the baby so you and your partner can be intimate.

Protect Intimate Time from Conflict

As with fun and friendship time, you must cherish and protect from conflict your time together for intimacy. As we have said over and over, as you become parents, your potential for conflict increases. Make conflict and issues off-limits during sensual and sexual times together. *Control your issues rather than letting them control you, and don't take them to bed with you!* You've now learned a number of techniques to manage conflict effectively. It will be very important to make the effort to use them. Changes in your intimate relationship are often early warning signs that all is not well between you and your partner.

In this chapter, we've emphasized several keys for keeping your physical relationship vibrant. Now it's up to you. We don't intend this chapter to be a substitute for sex therapy if you have a history of significant sexual difficulties. If you do, we want to encourage you to work together to overcome the problems. Working with an experienced sex therapist can usually accomplish a great deal. Our focus here has been more to help couples who have a satisfying intimate relationship keep things that way—and make it even better.

EXERCISES

As we close this chapter, we offer exercises that can help you enhance your abilities to connect physically. If you're ready for sensual and sexual enhancement, read on.

Sensate-Focus Exercise

Years ago, Masters and Johnson developed an exercise called the Sensate-Focus. It has two purposes: (1) to keep you focused on sensuality and touching in your physical relationship and (2) to help you learn to communicate more openly and naturally about what you like and don't like in your lovemaking. This exercise can be particularly helpful for enhancing your intimate relationship throughout pregnancy and early parenthood or for reestablishing intimacy after dealing with the prescribed and totally goal-directed sexual activity associated with infertility.

This exercise isn't the time for sexual intercourse. That would defeat the purpose, because we want you to focus on sensuality. Don't be goal oriented, other than by having the goal of relaxing and doing this exercise in a way that you each enjoy. If you want to make love following the exercise, that's up to you. But if you have been having concerns about feeling pressured sexually, we recommend you completely separate these practice times from times when you have sex. In fact, you shouldn't have sex unless both of you fully and openly agree to do so. No mind reading or assumptions!

The general idea is that you each take turns giving and receiving pleasure. The first few times, you are either the Giver or the Receiver until you switch roles halfway through the exercise. When you are in the Receiver role, your job is to enjoy the touching and to give your partner feedback on what feels good and what doesn't. Your partner can't know how you feel unless you tell him or her. You can give either verbal or hand-guided feedback. Verbal feedback means telling your partner what actions feel good, how hard to rub, or what areas you like to have touched. Hand-guided feedback consists of gently moving your partner's hand around the part of the body being touched to provide feedback about what really feels good: where to touch, how to touch, and how firmly to touch.

When you are the Giver, your role is to provide pleasure by touching your partner and being responsive to feedback. Ask for feedback as often as necessary. Be aware of changes in how your partner is reacting—what feels good one minute may hurt the next. Focus on what your partner wants, not on what you think would feel good.

Choose roles and give a hand or foot massage for ten to twenty minutes, asking for and giving feedback. We recommend massages of areas like hands, back, legs, or feet the first few times to get the hang of the technique. This also helps you relax if there are some issues about sexuality between you, which is so often the case with expectant and new parents. Then switch roles. Repeat as often as you like, but also remember to practice these roles in other aspects of your sensual and sexual relationship.

We recommend that you repeat the Sensate-Focus exercise over the course of several weeks, at least twice a week. Assuming all is going well in your exercises, begin to move to other areas for touching. Wherever you want to be touched, including the sexual areas, is great.

Over time, you can drop the rigid emphasis on the Giver and Receiver roles, and work on both of you giving and receiving at the same time, while still keeping an emphasis on sensuality and communicating your desires. If you practice this over time, it will become easier for you to communicate openly about touch. It will also be easier for you to work together in your efforts to keep physical intimacy vibrant and alive as you become parents.

Exploring the Sensual

In addition to doing the Sensate-Focus exercise, set aside a specific time for sensual activities together. This applies to all couples, regardless of whether or not they're engaging in sexual activity. Be sure you won't be interrupted—this is the time for baby-sitters, answering machines, and Do Not Disturb signs!

At the start of this exercise, talk about what's sensual for each of you and what you'd like to try doing to keep sensual experiences in your relationship. Here are some ideas:

- Give your partner a massage, using the Sensate-Focus technique.

- Share a fantasy you've had about your partner.

- Cuddle and hug as you talk to your partner about the positive things you love about him or her.

- Plan a sensual or sexual activity for your next encounter.

- Plan a wonderful meal together. Prepare it together and sit close together—share the meal. You might even try feeding each other.

- Wash your partner's hair.

- Spend some time just kissing.

Re-Romanticizing Exercise

Now that we've discussed the importance of maintaining the friendship, fun, and intimacy in your relationship, you have the opportunity to blend all three together in this exercise.

First think about what your partner is already doing that pleases you. Take a piece of paper and finish the following sentence in as many ways as you can. Be specific and positive, and focus on those things your partner does with some regularity.

- I feel loved and cared for when you . . .

Examples:

Make me a cup of tea

Kiss me before you leave the house

Tell me you love me

Bring me flowers

Snuggle up with me and watch television

Tell me important things that happen to you

Now think about the romantic stage of your relationship—before you got into a rut in your intimacy and before pregnancy and the baby. Are there any caring behaviors you used to do for each other that you're no longer doing? Take another piece of paper and finish the following sentence. Include all the important things your partner did that you haven't forgotten.

- I used to feel loved and cared about when you . . .

Examples:

Wrote me love letters

Held my hand when we walked

Called me on the phone to say how much you loved me

Wanted to stay up late talking and making love

Now think about some caring and loving behaviors you've always wanted but never asked your partner for. These may come from your expectations of the perfect mate, private fantasies, wherever. Take another piece of paper and finish the following sentence. Be as specific as you can.

- I would like you to . . .

Examples:

Massage me for thirty minutes without stopping

Take a shower with me

Buy me a gift as a surprise

Sleep naked with me

Plan a surprise date for the two of us

If you find you are having difficulty coming up with ideas, you can get ideas from others. You can talk with friends, relatives, or co-workers. There are a number of books with great ideas on how to be romantic, which may help you get in touch with what you would like and help you be creative.

Review all three lists and indicate how important to you each caring behavior you listed is by writing a number from 1 to 5 next to each one, with 1 meaning very important and 5 meaning not important.

Sit down with your partner and review each other's lists. Place an X next to anything on your partner's list that you *aren't* willing to do at this time. The rest of the things listed should be those you are willing and able to do. Starting tomorrow, try to do at least one of these behaviors each day, starting with those that are easiest for you to do.

When your partner does a caring behavior, be sure to acknowledge it with a comment of appreciation. These caring behaviors are gifts, not obligations. Do them regardless of how you're feeling about your partner and regardless of the number of caring behaviors your partner does for you—no scorekeeping. These behaviors will reinforce or help restore full-scope intimacy as you parent together.

Part IV

Creating a Healthy Lifestyle

Parenting is the most challenging and demanding job you can have. It's a twenty-four-hour-a-day, seven-day-a-week marathon. New parents often find themselves exhausted and stressed out. They struggle with getting the support they need and wrangle over the division of labor. In order to take care of your self and your marriage, you need to be able to manage these realities of parenthood effectively.

When people become parents, they often reevaluate their lifestyle and are open to changing behavior, developing new habits, and learning new skills. You may develop a new appreciation of your own mortality and want to take better care of your self so that you'll be around for your child. You will probably realize what a powerful role model you will be to your child and want to set a good example.

In this final section of the book, you'll learn skills and techniques to take better care of your self so that you can be a healthier person, partner, and parent. We will discuss managing fatigue and stress, creating a support network that will work for you, and negotiating work and family responsibilities.

13

Managing Fatigue

Fatigue is a universal complaint of new parents. You may be used to sleeping six to nine hours at a stretch, but your baby is likely to sleep for only about two hours at a time initially. And babies don't eat three meals a day. They eat every couple of hours around the clock at first, regardless of whether they are breast-fed or formula-fed. Somehow a total of eight hours of sleep in two-hour chunks feels very different from eight hours of uninterrupted sleep. Though charming, babies tend to wreak havoc on the typical adult schedule. In this chapter we'll teach you some techniques to help you and your partner get the sleep you need.

Think about how fatigue affects your own and your partner's behavior and functioning. When you're tired you tend to be less energetic, have less patience and a shorter fuse, and control your moods more poorly; you just don't think or function as well as when you're rested. Fatigue can also have a negative effect on how you see the world and on all you do. When you're tired, your ability to communicate well together and handle conflict is put to the test. This is an important time to use the ground rules we presented in Chapter Four to keep a lid on things. Like so much else in life, times when you need to be at your best you'll often be at your worst—and worst of all with the person you love most. Our goal is to help you maximize your sleep and rest by teaching you the basics of good sleep, especially with a baby in the house.

PROMOTING GOOD
SLEEP HABITS FOR PARENTS

Many people have poor sleep habits and are chronically tired even without the challenge of a new baby. The following recommendations are appropriate for anyone but are particularly important for parents. Getting enough sleep is essential to coping and being a good parent. Even if you believe you have good sleep habits and feel well rested, you'll want to review the following recommendations. Your routine will change with the arrival of the baby, if not before.

Stop for a moment and consider your current sleep pattern: what time you go to bed to sleep, what time you get up, how many hours you typically sleep each night, and whether you feel you are getting an adequate amount of sleep. Keep this information in mind as you read on.

Establish a Regular Sleep Pattern

Going to bed and getting up at regular times reinforces rather than sabotages your internal biological clock. Try not to vary these times significantly, even on days off or weekends. The goal is to have a regular sleep pattern: falling asleep within fifteen to twenty minutes of getting into bed to sleep, and sleeping for a total of six to nine hours.

Ray and Marte were fairly typical in having developed some lousy sleep habits. They had a TV in their bedroom and would stay up watching late-night talk shows or movies. Because both had to get up early for work, they would sleep in until ten on weekends to "catch up." They also tried to cram in all the social life they could before the baby came—out to dinner or dancing, getting together with friends, seeing plays or movies—not to mention the late nights getting the baby's room ready. They were already exhausted when the baby came.

Starting now: sleep smart. You might want to move the TV out of the bedroom. Rather than staying up late, use your VCR to tape late-night shows. If you're not asleep within fifteen to twenty minutes of getting into bed for sleep or if you wake up during the night and can't get right back to sleep, get up and do a quiet activity, such as relaxing reading, until you feel drowsy. Don't just lie awake or stay in bed tossing and turning. This can lead you to associating your bed with having trouble sleeping. (But be sure to be sensitive to your sleeping partner if you get up during the night.)

When the baby arrives, you and your partner will need to decide what you'd like the baby's bedtime to be. Some parents put the baby down early so that they have some adult time in the evening. Others keep the baby up until they go to bed, hoping to get a longer block of sleep at the beginning of the night. Whatever is best for you, start establishing the baby's regular bedtime as soon as the baby comes.

Take Naps or Rests

Napping can be a lifesaver in the early months of parenting. If you are exhausted, sleep or at least lie down and rest when the baby naps. As long as you don't wake feeling groggy and can still fall asleep within twenty minutes at bedtime, you can nap whenever you are tired. In general, though, naps longer than one hour or within three hours of bedtime—including falling asleep in front of the TV—are likely to interfere with nighttime sleep. Sleep experts recommend "power naps" of twenty to thirty minutes midday for anyone to reenergize themselves.

Nan made the mistake many new parents do. She used every minute the baby napped to write birth announcements and thank-you notes, do laundry, clean up the house, and talk to friends and relatives on the phone. Because she was also up every two hours at night breast-feeding, she was soon exhausted. She felt overwhelmed by the demands of the baby and regularly dissolved into tears; she got into some of the biggest fights ever with her husband. She didn't manage her fatigue well.

Lydia, in contrast, slept or at least lay down every time her baby napped. She and Antonio changed the message on the answering machine so that it provided all the essential information about the new baby and explained that if no one answered they were probably napping and to leave a message. She put a Sleeping—Do Not Disturb sign on the door along with a note asking that all deliveries be made to the next-door neighbor. Although getting up with the baby at night left her tired, she was nowhere near the end of her rope.

Exercise Regularly

Regular exercise promotes sleep. Experts recommend at least thirty minutes of aerobic exercise—exercise that increases your heart rate and makes you sweat—at least four times per week. Try not to exercise within three hours of bedtime—except for sex!—because strenuous exercise wakes you up. You don't need to hire a personal trainer or join a health club to get into a regular exercise program. Walking is about the easiest form of exercise. You can do it anytime, anywhere, and about all you need is a good pair of walking shoes. Any form of aerobic exercise is fine, or mix types for variety. *If you are willing to change one behavior in the interest of your health, experts recommend that it be to exercise.*

You may be wondering how on earth you'll find the energy or time to exercise—especially if your baby has already arrived. This is a great opportunity to use the Problem-Solving Process you learned in Chapter Three. Working as a team will increase the likelihood that you'll develop a plan and follow through with regular exercise—whether you'll be exercising together or taking turns with the baby so each of you can exercise individually. Be creative in your brainstorming.

After working through the Problem-Solving Process, Aaron and Faith decided to take daily walks together. They'd put the baby in the stroller or carry pack and off they'd go. If the weather was too crummy—hot, cold, rainy, snowy, or icy—they would drive to the mall and walk inside. They found their walks had the added bonus of being friendship time. They had some great talks while walking.

Jamal and Anfernee found it worked best to exercise separately. Jamal would stop at the gym on his way home from work or go running when he got home. Anfernee went to aerobics class three evenings a week, which also provided special dad and baby time. On the other days she would go for walks with the baby or ride their stationary bicycle.

Both couples had to gut it out for the first couple of weeks but then began to notice that their energy levels increased and that they were sleeping better and weren't chronically tired. They also felt better about themselves in general, were less stressed, and seemed to bicker less. Teamwork was essential. Each partner encouraged the other to stick with their exercise program and worked together to make it happen.

Your baby will also sleep better with regular exercise. And if your baby sleeps better, you sleep better. In the first several months, before your baby can scoot, crawl, or walk, your baby's exercise is being talked to and played with. Try not to play vigorously with the baby in the hour or so before bedtime. If you've been at work all day and haven't seen the baby, enjoy evening playtime, then help the baby quiet down to get ready to go to bed.

Reduce or Eliminate Caffeine, Alcohol, and Cigarette Smoking

Just as exercise promotes sleep, caffeine, alcohol, and cigarette smoking interfere with sleep. If you can't decaffeinate, at least try not to consume caffeine within eight to ten hours of your usual bedtime. Read labels for caffeine. Caffeine is present not only in coffee, many teas, and cola beverages but also in a number of noncola beverages, chocolate, and many prescription and over-the-counter medications. Check with your pharmacist to learn whether any medications you are taking are known to alter sleep and, if so, change or stop taking the medications if possible. If you are breastfeeding, remember that a breast-fed baby will get some of whatever mom takes in and can therefore be affected by caffeine, nicotine, and alcohol—which will then interfere with your sleep. Remember that all these practices take teamwork. If only one of you changes your behavior, your partner will sabotage your efforts.

Establish a Bedtime Routine

Children and adults alike benefit from a bedtime routine. Establishing and following a bedtime routine promotes sleep. Establish a relaxing bedtime routine for the thirty minutes or so before going to bed. You might try such things as a warm bath, slow stretching or relaxation exercises, yoga, meditation, prayer, soothing music, or reading nonstimulating materials.

It can be very tempting to use the time after the baby is put to bed to deal with issues and solve problems. These stimulating activities are likely to interfere with sleep. Move them to an earlier hour and reserve the pre-bedtime hours for friendship and relaxation. Bedtime can be a great time for sensual and sexual activities if they leave you satisfied and relaxed and are what you both want to do rather than something that feels like a "must do."

Begin early to establish a bedtime routine for your baby. The structure added through routines provides security and predictability for infants and children. Your baby's activity pattern will eventually follow yours, so the baby will learn to be awake when you are awake and to sleep when you sleep.

Craig began a bedtime routine when his daughter, Julia, was three weeks old. After Julia nursed, Craig would change her diaper and dim the lights in the nursery. He would then carry Julia from room to room saying good night to Mommy, the cats, the fish, the plants, and so forth. He and Julia would then return to the rocking chair in the nursery, where they would snuggle while listening to a sleepytime tape. When Julia was drowsy and snuggled on his shoulder, Craig would put her in her crib with his hand on her tummy. When she nodded off to sleep, Craig would quietly leave the room, closing the door behind him.

As Julia grew, she learned that this routine meant it was time to go to bed to sleep. Going to bed was positive, not a form of punishment or something to fight about. She is now two; she still has the same bedtime routine and has never had difficulty going to bed and to sleep. Craig and his wife found this routine helped them as well. It signaled the beginning of some couple time, which they had come to treasure. Routines are predictable and make the world feel safe. Using these techniques to promote your baby's sleep benefits you directly. If your baby sleeps well, you sleep well.

Create an Environment That Supports Sleep

Your sleep environment can significantly affect the quantity and quality of your sleep. Sleep experts recommend room temperatures between sixty and sixty-five degrees Fahrenheit for sleeping. Both high and low temperatures can interfere with sleep. What's most important, however, is finding the temperature that works for the two of you. Jon and Sally worked out sleeping with the window open so that she could have a cold nose, and used a dual-control electric blanket so that Sally could be warm and Jon could roast. Even these kinds of challenges can be dealt with creatively if you put your minds to it and work together.

Temperature is also an issue for your baby's sleep. The room should be sixty to sixty-five degrees, with no drafts. You might think this is too cold for a baby, but most parents tend to overdress their babies and keep the room too warm—both of which interfere with your baby's sleep (and therefore yours).

No lights should be on in the bedroom during sleep time—in your room or the baby's. Light tells you it's time to be awake. If you use a night-light, it should be no brighter than a Christmas tree light. If outside light is a problem, use room-darkening shades or cover the windows with foil. If you wake during the night to use the bathroom or when you get up to take care of the baby, avoid turning on lights. Many parents find it helpful to install a dimmer switch so that they can see to tend to the baby at night without stimulating the baby too much.

Also try to make your bedroom as quiet as possible for sleep. This means no TV or radio on during sleep. If you are particularly sensitive to sounds while sleeping, try wearing earplugs or using a machine that generates white noise. Air cleaners also serve this function well. These recommendations also help if your baby is a light sleeper or is very sensitive to sound. Contrary to popular opinion, you don't need to tiptoe around when your baby is sleeping. It does help to close the door and minimize any sudden, loud noises, however.

When Abby was three weeks old, her parents were totally exhausted and at their wits' end. They had tried everything to help Abby sleep and had run out of ideas. At two o'clock one morning, they called their closest friends who were also parents of a young child. Although they found their friends' recommendation strange, they tried it, and it worked. They took Abby's blanket and put it in the dryer for five minutes. Then they swaddled Abby in the warm blanket and laid her on another blanket on top of the dryer. Then they turned on the dryer and stood by to make sure Abby didn't fall off. After fifteen minutes, Abby was deeply asleep, and they moved her to her crib and immediately fell into their own bed and fell asleep. It seems the combination of the sound and vibration of the dryer did the trick.

You often see parents driving their baby around the block in the car in the evening to accomplish the same thing. Repetitive, monotonous sound, such as quiet singing, or movement, such as swaying or rocking, is soothing to babies and helps them settle down to sleep. Varying sound or motion is stimulating to babies and wakes them up rather than helps them quiet to sleep.

Your bedroom should be used only for sleep and intimacy. It is *not* for such activities as work, school, balancing the checkbook, and so forth, unless balancing the checkbook is a sensual experience for the two of you. We've heard just about everything over the years!

Have an Appropriate Bedtime Snack

If you must eat something prior to bedtime, eat a snack containing protein and carbohydrate, such as warm milk or a banana. Snacks should be light and low in fat. Going to bed with a full stomach usually interferes with sleep, so plan meals well before bedtime. Sometimes this is difficult with a baby, when you may be lucky to grab a meal at all or when you wait until the baby is in bed to have an adult meal.

You might think these recommendations for good sleep habits are common sense. Some sleep experts believe that the majority of people have poor sleep habits and slog through life chronically tired. Getting enough sleep as new parents will be essential for your survival. Being exhausted and short tempered can be deadly to your marriage.

Decide Where the Baby Will Sleep

Another factor that will affect how you sleep is where the baby will sleep. Some parents want the baby in the same room; others want the baby in another room. Discuss this with each other. You will probably find that this discussion reveals values, beliefs, expectations, issues, and hidden issues, so you might want to use the Speaker-Listener Technique for good discussion of the problem and then follow the steps of the Problem-Solving Process.

Like many new parents, Ethan and Rebecca decided to have the baby in bed with them. When the baby woke up to eat, Rebecca could just roll onto her side, put the baby to breast, and go back to sleep. Ethan liked this arrangement as well, appreciating the closeness to the baby and the minimal disruption of his sleep. For Rebecca, Ethan, and baby Timothy, the family bed worked well. Other couples don't want the baby in bed with them. Every family is unique, and the decision about where the baby sleeps needs to be one you make jointly and can both live with.

Babies make noises in their sleep. Some parents are so sensitive that they awaken with every squeak or whimper. If this is the case, put the baby in another room. Put a closed door between you if necessary. Bob and Carol put the baby in another room but made the mistake of keeping a baby monitor—which amplified all the baby sounds—on the bedside table! Your baby will be sure to let you know when you are needed. You may have been able to sleep through just about anything before, but once you become a parent, you develop "baby radar."

DEVELOP STRATEGIES SO YOU AND YOUR PARTNER GET ADEQUATE SLEEP

After the baby comes, you'll need a plan to maximize sleep for *both* of you, and this will take teamwork. It's better to discuss strategies *before* the baby is born. You don't want to be starting from scratch on this issue when you are both exhausted. Talk to other new parents. What has or hasn't worked for them? Parents come up with very creative methods of getting sleep, such as the technique used with Abby. These are true survival strategies. Draw on parents' ideas as well as your own. You'll need to decide what will work for you as a unique family, based on your particular situation and preferences.

Who Gets Up with the Baby

It will probably be months before your baby sleeps for an extended period of time or through the night. This situation creates the major issue of who will get up with the baby at night. At first, Cara and Carlos got up together to tend to the baby at night. After a few nights of this, they were both bleary eyed and irritable. They went back to brainstorming and decided they would take turns getting up with the baby on alternate nights. This way, neither missed that special middle-of-the-night closeness with the baby, and both got more sleep. Other couples take half the night based on who is the night owl and who is the early bird in the couple.

Cameron found he just couldn't sleep with the baby nearby. His job as an air traffic controller demanded that he be alert. After discussing the problem, he and Trish decided he would sleep in a separate room on nights when he had to work the next day. On his days off he would "pay back" Trish by taking care of the baby so she could nap. He looked forward to this time alone with the baby. Some men feel guilty for trying to get a good night's sleep when their partner can't. This isn't the time to put yourself on a guilt trip.

There are many ways to resolve the issue of sleep. Coming to a successful plan takes good discussions, teamwork, and revision of the plan as necessary. When your baby starts sleeping through the night, you'll have to develop a plan for who will get up at night with a sick child or for nightmares. Later you'll be deciding who waits up for your child to come home from a date. There are likely to be some issues around sleep throughout your parenting career and marriage!

Hints for Getting Sleep During Pregnancy

Both early and late pregnancy present particular challenges to sleep. In early pregnancy, the growing uterus crowds the bladder in the pelvis, resulting in mom's awakening frequently to urinate. To keep these interruptions to a minimum, moms should spread their daily fluid intake over the entire day and keep fluid intake to a minimum in the hours before bedtime. This problem goes away when the uterus grows large enough to move up out of the pelvis into the abdomen, usually about the third month of pregnancy.

In late pregnancy, this problem often returns. Sometimes it is due to the baby-filled uterus dropping back down into the pelvis. The previous recommendation should help again here. More often, at this stage, the need to wake up to urinate at night is due to the accumulation of fluid in the legs during the day while mom is standing or sitting. Once she lays down to sleep, the pressure is off her legs, and the fluid moves back into her bloodstream and needs to be eliminated. In order to minimize awakenings, mom should lie down, preferably with her feet up, for at least one hour, two to three hours before bedtime. This will allow the fluid to be reabsorbed and eliminated before mom goes to bed, reducing trips to the bathroom during the night. This helps mom and dad get a better night's sleep.

Like most women, Caitlin had a difficult time sleeping in the last weeks of pregnancy. As her abdomen got larger, it became progressively more difficult to find a comfortable position for sleep. She couldn't lay on her back because she'd feel uncomfortable or lightheaded. The generous use of pillows helped some, especially between her legs to keep them from resting directly on top of one another. Caitlin would also lean against one or more pillows scrunched behind her, or forward with a pillow hugged in front of her. She used a pillow, folded towel, or blanket to support her baby-filled belly. When she reached the point at which she couldn't get comfortable even using these techniques, she took the advice of a friend and slept in the recliner. Caitlin and Michael prevented this from being a source of conflict by discussing their mutual need for sleep and developing a plan that worked for both of them.

Fathers need to examine the effects of their partner's sleep disruptions during pregnancy on their own sleep. When mom is up and down all night or just can't get comfortable, it's likely that dad's sleep is not too great. You may need to sleep separately in order to sleep. This issue can be very sensitive, and it needs to be discussed. Sleeping separately can awaken hidden issues of rejection or set off alarms that the marriage is in trouble. Remember, the goal is for *both* of you to get as much sleep as possible. Temporarily sleeping apart to accomplish this goal doesn't have to indicate problems in your relationship. It's a survival technique.

Fatigue is one of the greatest challenges of being a parent. When you're tired, both your marriage and your parenting are at risk. Being tired opens the door to conflict, increases your stress level, and can ignite anger. There are things other than not getting enough sleep that can cause fatigue. If you are following the recommendations in this chapter and are still really tired, or if you are *unable* to sleep, consult your health care provider. In the next chapter, we'll explore techniques for identifying and managing stress. Stress can contribute to fatigue, so managing stress may be one way to feel more rested and energetic.

EXERCISES

The goal is for *both* you and your partner to be as well rested as possible before and after the baby is born. Together you can form a plan to achieve this goal. Making the effort to do so is well worth the time and energy.

Reviewing Your Current Sleep Status

First, you need to examine your current sleep status. Jot down your answers to the following questions.

- What is your current sleep pattern?

- When do you go to bed to sleep?

- When do you get up?

- How many hours do you typically sleep each night?

- Do you feel rested or tired?

- Do you feel you are getting an adequate amount of sleep?

Review the basics of good sleep outlined in this chapter. Are there changes you need to make *now* to sleep better and manage fatigue? If so, use the Problem-Solving Process with your partner to develop a strategy to promote sleep and manage fatigue.

Promoting Sleep for New Parents

The goal after the baby is born is for *both* of you to get adequate sleep. How will you do that? Take the time now to use the Problem-Solving Process to discuss strategies and develop a plan. This way you will have methods to try when the baby is born and will not be trying to develop a strategy from scratch when you are both exhausted. Be sure you consider the following questions in your discussion.

- What expectations do you have of your baby's sleep pattern? How long do you think your baby will sleep at night? During the day?

- Where will the baby sleep?

- How might this affect your sleep?

- Who will get up to take care of the baby at night?

- How will your baby be fed? Breast-fed? Formula-fed?

- How might this affect your getting enough sleep?

- If you will be breast-feeding, what can you and your partner do so mom gets enough sleep?

- If you will be using formula, how will you manage nighttime feedings?

These are questions that are likely to get into values, beliefs, expectations, issues, and hidden issues. Be sensitive. We recommend you use the structure and safety of the Speaker-Listener Technique for these discussions. You will likely need some very good discussions before you are able to move into Problem Solution.

Promoting Sleep in Late Pregnancy

Typically women are run down and very fatigued by the time the baby is born. Jot down your responses to the following questions.

- How can mom get as much rest as possible during late pregnancy so that she's in the best shape for the baby to be born?

- Which suggestions from this chapter can you follow?

- Can mom reduce her work effort at home and out of the home during the last weeks of pregnancy?

- How can you and your partner work as a team to have a rested mother and father to welcome your baby into the family?

Review your responses together and use the Problem-Solving Process to formulate a plan together that will work for both of you.

14

Managing Stress

We live in stressful times—filled with financial pressures, dead-lines, work or school concerns, performance anxiety, rela-tionship issues, and so forth. Add one or more babies, exhaustion, and the reality that your partner is now in love with someone besides you, and you have a recipe for being pushed to the limits of your coping.

As we said in the last chapter, fatigue is a universal complaint of new parents. Stress and fatigue are often related. When you're tired, you are more susceptible to stress and have a short fuse. And stress can sap your energy and exhaust you. Fatigue and stress feed into each other and, when you are new parents, can leave you hang-ing on by your fingertips. In this chapter, we'll help you identify your reactions to stress, understand the effects of stress on your couple relationship and family, and manage stress more effectively to pre-vent its potentially damaging effects on your marriage and family.

Some of the information in this chapter is adapted from the Stop Anger and Violence Escalation (SAVE) program developed by Peter Neidig and colleagues to teach couples techniques to man-age stress and anger and to prevent aggression.

STRESS AT WORK AND AT HOME

Although stress is a normal part of life that often promotes growth, excessive stress and the mismanagement of stress can affect the quality and length of your life. It can also affect your relationships with others, especially those closest to you—your partner and children. Let's look deeper.

Understanding Your Reactions to Stress

Each person has his or her unique way of responding to stress. When under stress, we are not at our best. Stress usually affects our emotions, behavior, mood, thinking, and ability to function. When stressed, people often have knots in their stomach, headaches, tension in their neck and shoulders, clenched fists, panic attacks; they are forgetful, impatient with others, and so forth. Think about what you're like when you're under stress. What are your most common stress symptoms?

Think of your stress symptoms as early warning signs that you need to take some sort of action to protect both yourself and your relationship. When you are stressed, you're more likely to experience stress in your couple relationship. Stress adds to the filters that get in the way of good communication. When stressed, you probably are more self-centered and have a shorter fuse. You may be less able to tolerate little hassles and less likely to use the communication skills you have learned. All this means you are a more difficult person to live with—yes, you—when you are under greater stress or when you aren't handling the normal stresses of your life very well.

Whatever other stresses you deal with in life, the transition to parenthood adds its own stresses. There are the challenges, fears, and, sometimes, complications of pregnancy; anxieties about money; concerns about the health of the baby; and all the planning. If you are adopting, you may be stressed about all the factors that may come between you and your goal of parenthood. This is usually a positive time of life, but it is likely to raise the stress level for you and your partner.

HOW STRESS AFFECTS THE FAMILY

When a family member is stressed and not managing that stress effectively, it is very likely to affect other family members and therefore the family as a whole. Here is an example.

Like most new parents, Nate and Cindy found the time after the arrival of their son pretty stressful. Nate was struggling with being the sole breadwinner for the family while Cindy was on maternity leave. His stress was often magnified by how his day went at work. He would often come home with a headache and pain in his neck and shoulders.

Cindy was grappling with the challenges of being a new mom and being isolated from friends and the stimulation of work. Most days she would have a knot in her stomach from wondering whether she could ever be a good mother and if she could really leave the baby to return to her career.

It's not that any one thing was really wrong. The changes they were going through made life more difficult, and they were showing the wear and tear. They each pulled in a bit, and their sense of being connected to one another suffered.

Their stress affected Nate, Cindy, and the baby in fairly typical ways. When Nate came home from work he would say a quick hello to Cindy and the baby, grab the mail, and retreat to the den. At the same time, Cindy would be following him trying to tell him about the baby and the challenges of her day. Although this might look like the pursuer-withdrawer pattern, each was really just trying to deal with his or her stress, though not in very productive ways.

Both Nate and Cindy felt like pressure cookers as their stress levels increased. They also began to feel distant from each other and presumed their partner didn't really care. They were short tempered and irritable. It almost seemed the baby was the only link between them.

After a few weeks and some real humdinger fights, Nate and Cindy could easily recognize each other's signs of stress but tended to overlook their own. Cindy would see Nate's jaw was set and that he "had no ears," meaning his neck and shoulders were tight and drawn up. Nate would hear the urgency in Cindy's voice as she talked a mile a minute. Their reactions to stress began to have broader effects on each other, their relationship, and the family as a whole.

There are four common effects of stress on couples and families: keeping score, living in a small world, resenting the intrusion of outside pressures and activities, and losing perspective. We'll discuss each of these and continue with the example of Nate and Cindy.

Keeping Score

When people are under stress, they are more likely to keep score. That is, they compare how hard they feel they're working with how hard it seems their partner is working. As we noted earlier, score-keeping is also a sign of hidden issues, especially the desire for recognition. When people are stressed, it's common for partners to lose sight of what the other does, seeing their partner's contribution as less than what they are personally doing for the relationship and the family. As they work harder, they perceive their partner as doing less and less. Each partner becomes convinced he or she contributes more to the welfare of the family than the other does. Although keeping score is a natural tendency, it's important to keep it to yourself and not attempt to convince your partner that you're the harder worker.

Nate saw Cindy as having the cushy job of staying home and playing with the baby all day. Cindy resented that Nate only had to work eight to ten hours a day while she worked twenty-four taking care of the baby. As their partner's perceived score fell farther and farther behind, each became resentful, angry, and far away. It's important to recognize how biased you will be in your perception when you start to keep score. You will see everything you do but fewer things your partner does—if for no other reason than that you are always with yourself and *not* always with your partner.

If you find you have started keeping score, avoid announcing the score and bargaining: "I did it last time," "It's your turn," "You owe me," "You *never* do it." Instead, acknowledge the positive contributions your partner makes. Don't complain about what your partner *isn't* doing. Support each other's day-to-day efforts and assume that over the long run, the score is likely to even out.

Living in a Small World

People under stress often start living in a small world. They develop a very narrow focus and reduce the scope of their activities and interests so that one thing begins to dominate their lives. Typically this is work, the baby—or work at home—or a personal interest or hobby.

Nate's focus became almost entirely limited to his work. His world shrank, and there was no longer any balance between work and family. It seemed to Nate that all he did was go to work, come home exhausted and stressed out, fall asleep, get up, and return to work the next day. Cindy, the baby, hobbies, personal interests, and pleasurable activities all got pushed to the back burner. Nate became so preoccupied with work he could no longer enjoy his time off. He wasn't able to downshift into a more relaxed mode or turn off thoughts about work. His entire world seemed to consist of work—being at work, thinking about work, worrying about work. He continually felt rushed and guilty about "wasting time" doing anything but work. He stopped seeing work as only a part of his life and started to see it as just about all of life or all that was really important in life. Needless to say, this did little for his relationships with Cindy and the baby.

People under a lot of stress come up with a number of reasons—excuses—for the shift to a small world. For example, "I don't have time or energy," "It's not worth the effort to do fun things," and so forth. People may decide to wait until they have more time and energy before they spend time with their partner or baby or try to have fun. You have to try to pull yourself up out of this when you see yourself moving into it. And it can be difficult to see you have reached this point. Your living in a small world is often obvious to your partner long before it is noticeable to you.

You and your partner might want to agree to a gentle way of notifying each other if you have moved into small-world mode. We emphasize that this be a joint plan and a *gentle* reminder, because the person in the small world is already highly stressed and probably sensitive and irritable. This type of gentle reminder can often help people see how narrow their focus has become. When they stand back and try to look at their life objectively, they may be able to see how stress has caused their world to shrink.

There are a number of consequences of living in a small world. Productivity declines, even if more hours are spent on the activity, such as working. Relationships suffer because people in a small world have little fun themselves and aren't much fun to be around. We've discussed how important friendship and fun time are to your relationship. When people aren't having fun, they have trouble staying motivated and often experience burnout. They invest lots of time and energy with little to show for it and little satisfaction or feeling of accomplishment.

Resenting the Intrusion of Outside Pressures and Activities

As people under high stress begin to live in a small world dominated by one main concern, such as work, and as they have less time and energy to devote to their couple relationship, their partner begins to resent the intrusion of the main concern into the life of the family. As Nate's world shrank to consist almost entirely of work, he spent minimal time with the baby and no longer took time with Cindy—for friendship, fun, or intimacy. This didn't happen overnight; it took time for things to disintegrate to this point.

Cindy began to resent how much Nate's work had intruded into all the good things in their relationship and family. At the same time, Nate resented what he saw as Cindy trying to intrude on his responsibilities and time for work. This is a lose-lose situation that can become explosive. It's ripe for escalation, negative interpretations, and the activation of hidden issues. When Cindy would try to raise with Nate the issue of his physical and mental absence, the discussion would quickly escalate. Nate began to see Cindy's efforts at making contact as negative no matter how well intentioned she actually was. He felt Cindy was not appreciating how hard he was working to support the family—his "monumental" contribution was going unrecognized.

If you find this happening in your relationship and your partner expresses feelings of resentment, you can respond in ways that make the situation better or worse. Try to validate your partner's feelings rather than defend yourself. If you are the one feeling resentment, be gentle in how you express it. And try to look at the situation objectively. Are you living in a small world?

Loss of Perspective

Yet another way stress affects the family is through loss of perspective. As is common with people experiencing high levels of stress, Nate felt "everything" was wrong. He couldn't see the specific factors related to his work that were creating the high levels of stress. He started to see problems with the baby, Cindy, his mother-in-law, the neighbor. He seemed unable to tolerate even the most minor hassles, blowing them out of proportion. His negative interpretations became more widespread. He was no longer able to see much of anything in a positive light. He began to see Cindy as lazy and irresponsible, because she *only* took care of the baby and house. Cindy's behavior hadn't changed, but Nate's perception of Cindy had.

As you think about these four common effects of stress on families, it's important to realize that the source of the stress can vary. Although Nate's stress came from work, the stress can just as easily come from the baby and parenting or from involvement in a hobby or other type of personal interest.

Effect on the Baby

Stress in one or both parents often affects the baby. Babies tend to be barometers in families; they can sense increasing tension and conflict. Then they often act out the stress and tensions in the family by becoming more irritable or by developing eating or sleeping problems. As if things weren't bad enough with one or both parents being stressed, the baby kicks in to make the situation even worse. Too often parents try to "fix" the baby's problem rather than realize that *they* might be the problem. This doesn't mean it's your fault if the baby is fussy or has problems. What we are trying to emphasize is that *stress that is not being managed well by any family member will affect the other family members and the family as a whole*. If you start seeing any of the effects we have just discussed—keeping score, living in a small world, resenting the intrusion of outside pressures and activities, loss of perspective, or changes in the baby's behavior—consider that they may be signs of stress—your partner's or your own.

TRANSITIONS AS TIMES OF STRESS

Times of transition are typically times of stress. We will address two types of transitions: major life transitions, such as becoming parents, and daily transitions, such as those from work to home.

Major Life Transitions

You are experiencing what is believed to be the most significant of all life transitions: becoming a parent. As your childfree years draw to a close, you are entering a new era in your life—one that comes with a major new role and significant changes in your responsibilities and relationships.

Although becoming parents is typically viewed as positive, the loss of your old self and way of life can cause feelings of grief and sadness. As you make this transition you can also expect to have feelings of disenchantment and discomfort. Such feelings are normal. Consider them growing pains. Use them as reminders to take extra good care of yourself and your couple relationship.

You will probably feel more vulnerable during this time. Your feelings will act as filters and are likely to distort communication between you and your partner. You will also be more susceptible to escalation, invalidation, negative interpretations, and withdrawal and avoidance—all those things we said could be harmful to your relationship. Therefore, making the effort to be clear with your partner and really listen to and hear your partner is particularly important during this time. This is an important time to use all the techniques we taught earlier in the book. And keep in mind that although you and your partner are making the same transition, your journey is likely to be along different timelines. Your job is to help your partner understand your feelings and experience and to make the effort to understand your partner's feelings and experience.

Daily Transitions

The many transitions you make each day can also be stressful. For Nate, as for most people, making the work-to-home transition was often pretty stressful. He was already stressed by being the sole wage earner for the family, on top of the demands of his job. After a hectic day at work and fighting traffic, he wanted home to be an oasis. Instead, he was often greeted by Cindy wanting to recount her day and pass the baby off like a football so she could finish making dinner. In response, Nate started to retreat more and more to the den to be alone.

It's helpful to develop ground rules specifically for these daily transitions. These will be even more specific than those we recommended earlier—which we hope you are putting to use. Here we're suggesting specific agreements about how to manage the often stressful transition times in your days, such as morning, coming home from work, dinnertime, and bedtime.

When Nate and Cindy finally got around to using the Problem-Solving Process to deal with their stress, one of their solutions was a work-to-home ritual for Nate. They agreed that when Nate arrived home, he would greet and hug Cindy and the baby and then have twenty minutes to change, look at the mail, and unwind. Afterwards he would take the baby so that Cindy could finish preparing dinner without interruption. After dinner they would take time to discuss their days, getting validation and support in the process. They also planned for Cindy to have some focused personal time away from the baby each evening while Nate cared for the baby. With teamwork they were able to create a win-win situation.

DEALING WITH STRESS EFFECTIVELY

Now that we've talked about reactions to stress and the effects of stress on you and your family, we turn our attention to dealing with stress. Effectively managing stress includes dealing with stress as an individual and as a team. Let's start with what you can do as an individual.

Improving Your Individual Coping

There are any number of ways to manage stress effectively. What is most important is finding a technique that works for you and that you will actually use. We've already talked about how exercise can help you manage fatigue. Exercise is also one of the best ways to manage stress because it dissipates pent-up tension and makes you feel better in general. The world just seems better when you're exercising regularly.

Other common stress management techniques include progressive relaxation, breathing exercises, listening to relaxation audiotapes, meditation, yoga, visualization, and biofeedback. You'll find excellent resources at your local library or bookstore that provide overviews or specific directions on a variety of stress management techniques. There are also stress management consultants, or you can talk with your health care provider for guidance.

Your approach to stress management will be most effective as part of a broader effort to take more personal control of your life. Those efforts might also include a nutritious diet, regular exercise, adequate rest, quiet time alone, keeping up personal interests and hobbies, spending time with friends, and taking good care of your couple relationship.

It is *your* responsibility to identify your reactions to stress, control your behavior when stressed, and develop ways to deal more effectively with stress. Your stress affects not only you but those around you. Your partner and family can also be sources of stress. *The key to managing stress effectively as new parents is to work as an individual and as a team.*

Improving Your Couple Coping

Rather than something that pushes you apart, coping with stress can bring you together. Your partner can help you with your stress, just as your partner can help you manage fatigue, as we discussed in the last chapter. In order to do so, the two of you need to be aware of each other's signs of stress and know what to do to help relieve that stress. There's an exercise at the end of the chapter that will help you do this.

By now this should sound pretty familiar. Working together means opening the dialogue around expectations, issues, hidden issues, and feelings. We recommend you use the Problem-Solving Process we introduced in Chapter Three to help you discuss your situation constructively and formulate a plan for dealing with stress.

Nate and Cindy were able to develop a plan that worked for them as individuals and as a couple, but it took teamwork. They began walking together every morning. At first it was a hassle getting up forty-five minutes earlier and packing the baby into the walking stroller, but after three weeks, they both felt so much better they couldn't imagine how they coped without it. Nate added listening to a fifteen-minute relaxation audiotape to his work-to-home transition ritual, and Cindy practiced progressive relaxation for thirty minutes during the day while the baby napped.

Once Nate and Cindy had established these new habits, they began to add other relaxing activities. Cindy took care of the baby while Nate played ball with the guys once a week, and Nate took care of the baby while Cindy took a leisurely bubble bath or read a book. Working together, they were able to change their whole outlook on life by making some key changes in their routines. They were no longer like two porcupines pricking each other. Working together to develop and carry out solutions brought them to a new level of connection and opened the door to renewed intimacy.

Another important way to work together to manage stress is to use Time Out—when you need time to pull yourself together and calm down or to prevent or manage escalation with your partner.

Using Time Outs

We've already talked about using Time Out when you want to stop a discussion that is escalating or derailing, or when you or your partner decide it isn't a good time to have or continue a discussion. Here we'd like to talk about using Time Out as part of your approach to stress management. If you haven't been using Time Outs to this point, you might want to start now as you develop ways to manage stress effectively.

You need to monitor your own stress level and take responsibility for instituting a Time Out when you need to. *Tell your partner you need to take a Time Out.* You might do this by saying something like, "I'm beginning to feel upset. I need to take a Time Out." This clearly communicates that you are recognizing your feelings and taking responsibility for your response to the situation. You are controlling your behavior by taking time and space to get yourself back together.

Leave the situation, but not necessarily the house, unless you feel unsafe. Go to another room. Separate yourself from your partner. If you leave, let your partner know where you are going and when you'll return. If you don't do this, your partner may feel abandoned, which may complicate things when you return. Better yet, if one or both of you tend to have problems with stress or anger, agree ahead of time on a couple of basic options so that you can do what's necessary when you need to calm down.

Both Don and Carla have volatile tempers, which flared regularly in early pregnancy when Carla was nauseated and tired and couldn't hold up her end of household responsibilities. They agreed that either one could call a Time Out, and the one calling it would say, "Plan A" or "Plan B." Plan A was their agreed-on term for a basic thirty-minute, give-each-other-some-space Time Out. Plan B meant one or the other was aroused enough that getting more separation made sense. They agreed that this meant Don would take a walk for thirty minutes or so, and when he returned they couldn't be in the same room or talk for two hours. This plan worked well because they developed it together and agreed to honor it. That's the key: having a plan you both agree to follow to help you manage difficult emotions.

During a Time Out, *mentally calm yourself*. Mentally reviewing the situation or, if the situation involved your partner, thinking about who was right and who was wrong, will only escalate things. Instead, you might try taking slow deep breaths and at the same time saying to yourself something like, "I can calm down. I am calming down now. I can take control of my feelings and behavior and handle stress well." Bring to mind relaxing images, picture yourself in a comforting place, or try some of your regular stress management techniques. You might also do some nonaggressive exercise, such as walking.

Return and check in with your partner after the Time Out period has elapsed. This is a vital part of this technique. It demonstrates responsibility. If you both want to talk, you can try again. If you get upset again, take another Time Out. Sometimes it's not that you are having a difficult discussion, it's that you are having a very stressful day and really need to be alone to get yourself back together. You may need Time Out away from your partner and the baby.

There are several things to *avoid* when taking a Time Out. *Using drugs or alcohol* usually alters your ability to think clearly and take good care of yourself, often escalates anger, and may lead to physical aggression and substance abuse problems. *Aggressive activities,* such as hitting a punching bag or chopping wood, are too close to violent behavior and may actually increase anger. *Driving* when upset is extremely dangerous to yourself and others. Contacting your partner before the Time Out is over or before you have calmed down will only increase the stress or reignite the anger.

As with the other skills and techniques we've been teaching you, the Time Out technique may feel artificial at first. It's essential to practice so you have it to use when you need it. If you fail to manage severe stress and anger constructively, you are likely to experience the most destructive form of communication: physical aggression.

We can pretty much guarantee you will experience more stress as you become parents. You can choose to manage it more effectively as an individual and as a couple. You can work together to manage stress just as you can work together to manage fatigue. But you don't need to rely only on yourself and your partner. In the next chapter, we'll discuss how to create a support system that works for you. We all need support, especially as we become parents. With adequate support it is much easier to keep stress under control.

EXERCISES

There are several exercises for this chapter that will help you identify and manage stress so that you can control your stress rather than allow stress to control you and your couple relationship as you become parents.

Identifying Stress

Jot down your answers to the following questions. When you and your partner have done so, compare and discuss your responses.

> When I'm stressed, I tend to . . .
>
> When my partner is stressed, he or she tends to . . .
>
> My partner could help me with my stress by . . .
>
> I could help my partner with her or his stress by . . .

Which of the effects of stress have you noticed in your couple relationship?

- Keeping score

- Living in a small world

- Resenting the intrusion of outside pressures and activities

- Losing perspective

If your baby has already joined the family, what effects of stress have you noticed in the baby?

Doing Transitions

Which times of the day are most stressful to you? How can you deal more effectively with the stress of daily transitions? How can your partner help you with this? Develop some ground rules to make these times less stressful.

Managing Your Stress

Make an agreement as a couple to take charge of the stress in your lives by developing ways to deal with it more effectively. You might decide to do some individual thinking and work before you begin couple work, or you may want to move right into the Problem-Solving Process with your partner.

Explore some different stress management techniques you think might be a good fit for you. Choose at least one. Be sure to give the approach a fair trial of at least one month. If you aren't satisfied, try another technique. You will be able to find an approach to stress management that will be effective and doable for you.

The difference that managing stress can make in your life is well worth the effort. It is a gift not only to yourself but also to your partner and child. Take time at a couple meeting about once a month to evaluate how your stress management is working. Do you and your partner notice differences? Is there anything else your partner can do to support your stress management plan?

15

WARNING
Don't Try Parenting by Yourselves

No other event changes so many aspects of your life as does becoming a parent. This may be the first time you feel a real need for support and need to ask for help. Our goal is to help you identify your needs for support and create a network of people who can help you reduce your stress and deal more effectively with the challenges of new parenthood. The statement "It takes a village to raise a child" may be overused, but it is true nevertheless, and you don't get bonus points for trying to do it alone—especially in the early months.

Most people these days are very independent, depending on self rather than others. In addition, many people have moved away from their families and therefore no longer have this potentially important source of support nearby. Neighbors typically work and are therefore not always available, even if you know them well. In the previous chapter we emphasized that stress usually increases significantly when a baby joins the family. Creating a safety net of support is essential for keeping things manageable and preventing real damage to yourself and your couple relationship.

TWO COUPLES: ISOLATION
AND FRUSTRATION, OR TEAMWORK
AND SUPPORT

Although nearly everyone who stops to think about it can recognize the need for support during this time of transition, very few couples actively plan or take action to get the support they need. And there's a big difference between thinking you'll need support and actually getting the support you need. Some couples are fortunate enough to have a support system of friends, church members, coworkers, and so forth. But in this day of increasing social isolation and stress, many more couples don't have enough support and do nothing ahead of time to try to increase their support. If you are already dealing with high levels of stress, you may be living in a small world and unable to see or reach out to the support available to you. *The best time to work on arranging the support you need is before the baby arrives.*

Let's look at two couples as they became parents, one that didn't plan ahead and suffered for it and one that did plan ahead and reaped the benefits of doing so.

Coming Apart at the Seams

Meredith and Connor had been married three years, and both held demanding full-time jobs. Connor's parents died in an accident when he was a teen, and Meredith's parents lived on the other side of the country. Although Meredith and Connor had friends and neighbors with whom they did things, they all worked full-time and were childfree. Both Meredith and Connor were very independent and didn't like to rely on others. In addition, they preferred to take a "wait and see" approach to life rather than to plan ahead. Other than taking childbirth preparation classes, Meredith and Connor did little to prepare for parenthood. They thought that because just about everybody did it, "How hard could it be?"

Labor was a lot worse than Meredith had expected. Although her husband's presence and support were helpful, she really wished she had her mom or some women friends with her. Once their baby arrived, both were in awe. They named him Abe. Abe was beautiful, and, having never been around babies, they were fascinated by every part of his tiny body, his jerky movements, and his cute little sounds. Both Meredith and Connor appreciated how helpful the nurses were, especially considering that breast-feeding was more challenging than Meredith had expected. Didn't babies just know what to do when they were born?

The new family was home twenty-three hours after Abe entered the world. Mom and Dad were exhausted, and it seemed scary to be home alone with the baby after all the help in the hospital. Like most first-time parents, they thought, "Wow. They just let us take this baby home from the hospital with us!"

The next day Connor picked up Meredith's parents at the airport. Grandma immediately took over caring for Abe. Because Grandpa wasn't very interested in babies, he began making a list of sights to see before they had to return home. On Abe's third day of life, Meredith and Connor became tour guides, dragging the baby with them as they showed Meredith's parents the sights.

By the fourth day of running around, Meredith and Connor felt like zombies. They had chauffeured, cooked, and done everything to keep Abe quiet at night so Meredith's parents could sleep. In fact, they did everything but get to know and enjoy their new son.

Tensions mounted between Meredith and Connor; bickering and frustration became most of what they experienced together.

MEREDITH: (in tears) This is not what I expected. I thought Mom and Dad would help. I never dreamed we'd be chauffeuring them around sightseeing. And Mom has just about taken over the baby.

CONNOR: (disgusted) They're your parents. Why don't you talk to them or, better yet, just tell them to leave.

MEREDITH: *(raising her voice)* I can't do that. It would hurt their feelings.

CONNOR: Their being here is hurting us! This is *our* home. Tell them to go, or I will.

You can probably hear the escalation and invalidation. This is not a productive way to handle the situation.

By the time the grandparents left, Connor had to return to work, leaving Meredith feeling deserted. To make matters worse, Abe was a fussy baby. Meredith struggled through each day trying to take care of the house as well as the baby. She missed adult conversation with her coworkers and began to feel isolated from the rest of the world. Because her friends were childfree, they didn't understand, and, though they brought dinner a couple of nights, Meredith needed much more help. She continued to have difficulty with breast-feeding and, without anyone to turn to for help, began to think, "What's the matter with me? I've had a successful career and managed countless crises at work. Why can't I take care of this little baby and get a shower all in one day?"

Connor came home each evening angry to find the house a mess, the baby crying, and Meredith still in her robe. He moved to the couch so that he could get some sleep and stayed at work late to avoid the chaos at home. When Abe was two months old, Meredith was diagnosed with postpartum depression. Connor needed to cut back his work hours to be more involved at home and, despite their tight budget, had to hire someone to help Meredith with the house and baby. More and more he thought the baby was a mistake and wondered whether their marriage would survive.

Teamwork

Like Meredith and Connor, Rudy and Alecia had been married three years. The major difference between the two couples was that Rudy and Alecia liked to plan ahead because it gave them a sense of having some control in their lives.

Before the baby was born, they discussed how they could get the help they thought they would need. They asked for advice from parenting friends and neighbors, and even took care of someone's baby for a day for experience. They listed all their friends' names on a piece of paper and talked together about how each might be able to help them out. After all, these were true friends whom Rudy and Alecia had often helped during times of need in their lives.

Alecia and Rudy wrote a letter to Alecia's mom, who would be staying to help out for a week after the baby was born. They wanted to spell out what would be most helpful to them. They had heard some real horror stories from friends about what happened when their parents came to "help."

Dear Mom,

We're so glad you can come stay for a week after the baby arrives. We've thought and talked a lot about what will be helpful to us during that time and wanted to share this with you.

As new parents, we think it will be most important for us to "nest" and get to know the baby. Although we've never done this before, we believe it will be important for us to find our own way. Of course it will be great to have you here to answer questions or give advice when we ask.

What we'd like you to do is cook your delicious meals, run errands, do laundry, clean, and take care of the baby when we need a break. With this being your first grandchild, you'd probably just as soon take care of the baby all the time. But we have a lot to learn, and the sooner we do it, the better. We have no doubt you'll get lots of time with the baby— what we hope will be the beginning of a special relationship between the two of you.

We'll talk to you next week. Thank you so much for being willing to come share this momentous time with us. We really need your help.

A few days after they knew the letter would be received, Alecia phoned her mom. Her mother said she had been a bit put off when she first read the letter, because she had looked forward to taking care of the baby to give them a break. Alecia's family was not too different from most: people aren't very used to having other family members be so clear about expectations. In this case, Rudy and Alecia had thought that the clearer the expectations were now, the less the stress later.

This was a good phone call between mother and daughter, and Alecia's mother really came to understand what Alecia and Rudy thought they needed most from her. Grandma began to plan ways to "spoil" them as they nested.

On the advice of friends, Alecia and Rudy had several discussions about their expectations of labor and birth and their expectations of each other during that time. Though they had taken childbirth preparation classes, they decided each would have a good friend as their "special" support person. They spoke with these friends together to make their expectations clear. Both friends were honored to be invited to help them out. Lisa understood she and Rudy would work together to support Alecia. And, having become a father only a few months earlier, Alan had lots of ideas for supporting Rudy—including making sure Rudy ate and drank, got bathroom breaks, had periodic shoulder rubs, and had someone to vent and share with. Alan understood that he would wait in the hall if Alecia became uncomfortable with his presence.

Rudy was relieved to know Alecia wouldn't be depending solely on him and felt secure knowing he would have his own support person. Alecia felt she would be able to relax more knowing that she had Rudy and her friend to help her and that Rudy had someone who would be specifically looking out for him. Though some of their friends teased them about it, they took a breast-feeding class and had the phone numbers for a La Leche League member and a lactation consultant in case they needed help.

Although they were nervous when they arrived home with baby Alfredo, they had several friends they could call. Neighbors brought meals the first two days and collected Alecia's mom from the airport. Grandma spoiled the new parents for the first two days and then started to take over the care of Alfredo. Alecia was able to gently remind her mom of what they really needed from her. Although no new grandma is going to love that kind of reminder, she handled it well. They even let Grandma call their friends to request specific help. Because the couple had made their expectations clear beforehand, Grandma's visit turned out to be a big help rather than a big hassle.

Both these couples were having a first baby, but their experiences were quite different. Meredith and Connor let things unfold as they would, without much discussion or planning. They paid a high price for not planning ahead to accommodate their support needs. Labor was not what they would have wanted, and they seemed to be constantly angry with each other; considering that Abe was a newborn for only a short while, they cheated themselves out of that special time.

Alecia and Rudy gathered information, had discussions, worked as a team, and as much as possible planned how they wanted things to be. It wasn't all smooth sailing, but their active planning greatly reduced the amount of stress they felt as new parents. That left them better able to take good care of each other and their new son.

Of course there is danger in planning too much or naively expecting things will go exactly as planned. No matter how well you plan ahead or how much support you have, *you can never fully appreciate what it is to be a parent until you are one*. The key point here is the importance of working together to anticipate your needs, to plan ahead as much as possible to ensure those needs are met, and to ask for and accept help from others.

IDENTIFYING YOUR SUPPORT NEEDS

Think about your own situation in relation to the couples we have described here. What kinds of support can you imagine wanting or needing as you become parents? Keep in mind that you will probably be home within twenty-four to forty-eight hours after a vaginal birth and about seventy-two hours after a cesarean birth, which is major abdominal surgery. During labor and birth you will likely be surrounded by more professional support than you are likely to experience again unless you are faced with a life-threatening illness. That experience is in sharp contrast to going home alone. Newborns eat about every two hours around the clock and usually don't sleep for more than a few of hours at a stretch. As we've discussed in previous chapters, you and your partner will probably be exhausted and stressed. What would you like people to do for you?

Losing Contact and Losing Self

With the addition of a baby to the family, the world of the primary caregiver shrinks. Whereas you may be accustomed to regular interaction with coworkers, friends, and family, you may find yourself home alone with a totally dependent and needy infant. At a time when you might benefit most from contact with others, you may feel most isolated. It doesn't have to be this way. You can arrange to have adult contact and adult time.

Many new parents complain they feel they have "lost their self." This is particularly a problem for mothers. They are so busy being a partner and parent, and often a worker as well, there seems to be no time for them as a unique individual. This loss of self became apparent to Andrea when her daughter was about three months old and she went to the mall alone. "I realized that when people looked at me they just saw *me—a woman*. I wasn't with my husband, so they didn't see me as a wife. The baby was at home, so they didn't see me as a mother. They just saw a woman shopping in the mall. I suddenly realized there was a part of me, the core of me, who isn't a partner or a parent or a worker. It was scary to think I had lost touch with my real self."

Women can easily lose touch with themselves during this time, in part because they tend to lose contact with many of their typical supportive relationships. For example, if you work outside the home before the baby and plan to take maternity leave or remain at home after the baby comes, you'll have far less time with coworkers. The time and energy demands of parenting can result in less time with friends, particularly childfree friends who may not appreciate time with your baby.

When you lose contact with your network of friends, you are prone to lose some sense of self because the sum of all your relationships with others plays a major role in how you see yourself. So you may increasingly see yourself as "only" your baby's parent and your partner's spouse. This same thing can happen for fathers as the demands of work and parenting compete with time with friends.

As you deal with the many changes of being a new parent, you need to be able to continue to do the things that "recharge your batteries." *If you don't take care of yourself, you really can't take care of anyone else or be in a truly healthy relationship.* It is very appropriate to ask for help from others so that you can take care of yourself.

Supporting One Another

All these dynamics are even more important in the relationship between the two of you. That's why we included an entire chapter on preserving your friendship. It is that important and far too easily lost in the hubbub of life. Here we add to those recommendations by suggesting you talk very specifically together about how you can support each other better as you become parents. What do you want your partner to do that will give you the greatest sense of support? Be open and honest with yourself and your partner and stay current with what will really help.

Looking Beyond the Two of You

Remember, both you *and* your partner are making a major life change, and certainly there is no more important support during this time than that which you give to one another. No matter how good you are at supporting each other, though, it's important that both of you have support beyond each other. When you are both feeling overwhelmed, which is a normal experience for new parents, it's hard to be there for each other. Each of you will need someone outside the situation to talk to and spend time with. Who might that be for you?

Luke and Angie followed their good friends Carl and Samantha into parenthood. Their babies were born five months apart. Angie and Samantha spent a lot of time together with their babies or on the phone. They felt comfortable discussing the realities of being new moms. Although they got a lot of support from each other, Angie felt she got the better deal because Samantha was always one step ahead and shared her victories as well as what she would do differently. They were essential supports to each other as new mothers.

Luke and Carl shared a similar connection. They were able to support each other and truly understand the experiences of new fatherhood. Such relationships with good same-sex friends bolster the support partners give to each other.

Often support for new parents is directed toward the mother. Through their good intentions, people may push the father aside. This can have negative and long-term consequences. Remind others that you are *both* new parents and that you *both* need support as you get to know each other and "gel" as a family. Mothers set a powerful example. Be sure you are sending the right messages to others.

CREATING A SUPPORT NETWORK

Once you've given some thought to your support needs, you need to identify who can provide the help you need. Usually a support network consists of both a personal network of friends, neighbors, family, church family, and coworkers, and a professional and community network. Support can take tangible forms, such as providing meals, money, baby-sitting, or other material help. Emotional support includes listening and caring.

Using support is *not* a sign of weakness. If you have trouble asking people who care about you for help when you need it, this is a great time to get over it. Asking for help is an important way to take care of your family and yourself. As entertainer Dinah Shore said, "[Challenge] is a part of your life, and if you don't share it, you don't give the person who loves you enough chance to love you enough." Allowing those who care about you to do things for you is a gift to them. Typically those who care will offer support. If you can specify what will be most helpful and use their support, everyone benefits. If you aren't an organizer, you might ask someone to help you with this or even to take charge of coordinating helpers.

Before Myron and Elaina's baby was due, their friends gave them a "casserole shower." Myron thought this was about the dumbest thing he'd ever heard of. How could intelligent people do such a thing? Myron was later blown away by what turned out to be the best gifts anyone gave them. He and Elaina were typical exhausted new parents, too tired to plan meals and almost too tired to eat. But, thanks to the thoughtfulness and generosity of their friends, they had weeks of delicious, easy-to-prepare frozen meals. Each meal was clearly labeled and included instructions for preparation. These weren't tuna casseroles—they were complete nutritious meals. Myron is now a convert, and he and Elaina organize casserole showers for any friends adding a new member to their families. Sometimes pretty simple ideas can have a huge impact on your life.

Evaluating Your Support Network

As we said at the beginning of the chapter, this might be the first time you really need support from others. You can benefit, therefore, from identifying who might be available to help you and in what ways. You can do this by listing the names of people you can count on to help you and your family as you become parents. Note what type of help each person gives or could give, such as listening, providing information and advice, baby-sitting, doing household tasks, running errands, preparing meals, and so forth. Review your list with your partner's; you may come up with additional names. It's good to discuss how helpful each person on the lists has been in the past.

Help and support are great, but they often come with "strings attached." You and your partner need to be aware of both the positives and negatives of support from each of the people on the lists. For example, you may have a friend on your list who could be a great help but has some very strong opinions about parenting. You will have to weigh the value of the help against the likelihood of a critique of your parenting. This is often an issue with new grandparents. They may be willing and able to help but tend to come with issues from your own parent-child relationships with them. Only you and your partner can decide whether the costs are too great.

Also consider and list community and professional resources, such as agencies, professionals, church or social organizations, and self-help groups: sources of health care, child care, financial assistance, recreation, social services, transportation, housing, and food. Discuss with your partner how helpful each resource has been or could be and what concerns you have or negatives there might be in using this resource for help. If your baby will be breast-fed, be sure to identify resources to answer your questions or provide help if needed.

After you and your partner have compiled and discussed your lists of potential help, you will need to decide whether these supports seem adequate for your family. If not, take time before the baby arrives to identify and recruit additional support.

Creating a Help List

As we've said previously, after the baby comes you and your partner will likely be exhausted and stressed. You won't be functioning at peak levels. If you take the time before the baby arrives to make a list of what you believe will be most helpful to you, you can refer to it when someone wants to help. If you don't tell people what will *really* be helpful to you, they will use their own best judgment. You might end up with six tuna casseroles, when you think the only place a tuna casserole belongs is in the garbage. People can be really helpful if you provide some guidance. Periodically review and update your help list to keep it current.

Identify one or two people to be your emergency contacts. At some time almost every new parent reaches the end of his or her rope and needs someone to take over care of the baby on an emergency basis to keep parent and baby safe and sane. Ideally you should be able to call this person any time of the day or night. If you make sure you have an adequate support network and actually ask for and use help, you will be much less likely to need to use your emergency contact.

Remember, this is *not* the time to go it alone. Using help creates a win-win situation. You get the help you need, and people who care about you get the satisfaction of helping you in a time of need. Parenting, whether it's taking care of a newborn or dealing with a feisty adolescent, shouldn't be done in isolation. You aren't the first person to become a parent, nor will you be the last. There is knowledge and support available to you. It's your choice whether or not to use it.

In the next chapter, we'll examine who will do what in your family and your household after the baby comes—how you determine who fills what roles and who does what tasks. Who does what becomes a much more important and sensitive issue once you become parents.

EXERCISES

The exercises for this chapter will help you explore your support needs and support network. They will help you identify what supports you have available and any gaps in the support you might want or need as you become parents. Take the opportunity to plan ahead and use the time before the baby arrives to evaluate and bolster your support network.

A Typical Day

Think about your typical day from the time you wake up until you go to bed. Jot down your typical activities and responsibilities. Now rethink that day with a baby in it. For this exercise, assume your baby eats every two to three hours around the clock and sleeps only two to three hours at a stretch. Keep in mind that if the baby takes about thirty minutes to eat and get a clean diaper, you have even less time to do anything else between feedings.

Go back over the activities and responsibilities of that typical day. How will you manage the day with the baby? Be sure to think of the mundane things. Where will the baby be while you bathe? How will you manage household chores with the baby? Cooking, cleaning, laundry, grocery shopping—can you get to the store, buy what you need, and get back home and put the ice cream in the freezer before it's time to feed the baby again?—errands, yard work, house maintenance, paying bills, and doing other paperwork. Where will you fit in self-care? Where will you get the couple time to maintain your relationship? Put a check mark next to the things you might want some assistance with.

Jot down who or what might be helpful to you for those things. You might want to do this exercise twice: once for a typical weekday and again for a typical weekend day.

When you and your partner have both completed this exercise, review it together. Discuss the new insights you have gained into life with baby. Share your ideas on when you might benefit from some help, and discuss who might provide such help. The next exercise will help you evaluate your support network and identify gaps you might want to fill before the baby arrives.

Evaluating Your Support Network

For the next two exercises you might want to refer back to the information in the chapter sections with the same titles. Both you and your partner take a piece of paper and make a list of the names of people you can count on to help you and your family as you become parents. Follow the guidelines in the chapter for identifying who might help, how they might help, and whether or not there might be a downside to their helping you. Use what you learned from the Typical Day exercise to identify some of your help needs.

Review your lists a second time, discussing what concerns you have or what strings might be attached to using each person for help. Discuss whether the benefit of the help from this person will outweigh the cost of this person's help.

Now do the same thing with community and professional resources, such as agencies, professionals, and self-help groups. Again, when you have each completed your lists, review them with each other, discussing how helpful each resource has been and what concerns you have or negatives there might be in using this resource for help.

If you are planning to breast-feed, be sure you have someone to help should you need it. Also, be sure you have someone you can call in if you need to escape from parenting on an emergency basis. Keep this person's name and number near your telephone.

As you look back over your lists, do you and your partner believe these supports will be adequate for your family? If not, how might you strengthen your support network before the baby is born?

Creating a Help List

People care about you and will want to help after your baby is born. For most families the help list would include things like meals, errands, grocery shopping, laundry, baby-sitting, and house cleaning. What will *really* help you? Put your list by the phone so that when people call to ask what they can do, you can tell them the next thing on your list. This way, you get the support you need, and people who care about you can get the satisfaction of knowing they helped. This is a win-win situation!

What If Things Go Wrong

Although it's not pleasant to dwell on negatives, it's important to consider what you would do if complications develop in the pregnancy, if the baby is born early or with health problems that require staying in the hospital, if you have a cesarean birth, if the adoption falls through—you get the idea. If you don't even think about these possibilities, you are likely to be blindsided if they occur. Go back over the exercises for this chapter and work as a team to form a plan for what you'll do if things don't happen as expected.

16

Roles and Tasks
Who Does What?

There's a whole lot to do in life, and there will be even more when your baby comes. So "Who does what?" is no minor question. The focus of this chapter is not only the nitty-gritty of who does the chores but also the big picture of who will fulfill the major roles of parenting and of financial support of the family. Conflicts in these areas can be very intense, uncovering expectations, beliefs, and issues that may not have been apparent until now. You may find that becoming parents brings out strong expectations of what men and women should do in families.

Even if you don't plan on any big changes in who does what in your family as you become parents, it is wise to think about and discuss these issues before the baby comes. Most couples find they are rethinking and renegotiating who does what throughout their parenting careers. If you and your partner are satisfied with your division of work and family responsibilities, you are more likely to be happy with yourself, your marriage, and your relationship with your child.

REEVALUATING YOUR LIFE

Expectant and new parents typically reevaluate their lives in a number of ways. For example, the beginning of a child's life can lead you as parents to a new appreciation of your own mortality. In turn, this can lead you to think about where you are in your life, where you are going, what's really important, what you are living for, and, therefore, how you spend your time. What roles you spend major amounts of your time performing will have a great impact on your sense of identity—who you are, what defines you as a person, and what mark you will leave when you are gone.

Becoming parents pushes you to think about what's most important to you in life. One major part of this evaluation for many new parents is in the realm of work and career. You may consider whether you enjoy and are fulfilled by your work; make enough money; have opportunities for growth and advancement; have enough time off to be with your family; and have good benefits, especially those affecting your child—such as health care coverage and child-care resources. Both men and women ask themselves, Is this really what I want to be doing? You will probably find yourself wondering whether it's work or family roles that you want to be most important in your life.

Growing Together

Although a good part of this reflection occurs within you, it's important to share your thoughts with your partner. If you don't share these thoughts, preferences, hopes, and dreams, you not only increase the potential for conflicts but also miss a great opportunity to deepen your friendship. After all, what is having a true friend really about but sharing your innermost wonderings about who you are and who you want to be?

Scott and Emily had been married seven years when they became parents. They had both completed their educations and worked in fairly satisfying jobs. As they thought about being parents and about the importance of their baby, they decided they wanted to make some changes in their lives. They wanted to have as much time together and with the baby as possible and were willing to sacrifice some material things and a higher standard of living to do so. They didn't take a vow of poverty, just realigned their priorities.

After a good deal of thought and discussion, they decided they would assume traditional roles. Scott's job was satisfying and allowed flexible hours. Both Scott and Emily had strong feelings about their child having a stay-at-home parent. Emily would be able to pick up some work hours during peak times, which would help her stay connected and supplement Scott's income. She planned to increase her work hours when the baby started school.

Emily and Scott decided to find a church they liked so that they could further develop their spirituality and be better able to give the baby a foundation of values and beliefs. They also looked at this as a way to connect with other parents for support and socializing. Both believed there was more to life than earning money and raising children.

Becoming parents prompted many deeper discussions between Emily and Scott. They talked about expectations, values, and beliefs in depth, as they had never done before. Out of this grew a deeper connection and level of intimacy, and, for the first time, they set individual and family goals. Each had a renewed sense of purpose and dedication to their marriage and their child. This renewal was possible because they made the time for it, and they used enough structure—such as the Speaker-Listener Technique and the Problem-Solving Process—to help them through some of the more sensitive issues. Emily and Scott were able to develop a plan they believed would work for them. To ensure they both continued to be satisfied, they made a note on the family calendar to review how things were going every three months—and, more remarkable, they did it.

We don't want to give you the impression such work is easy. This is tough stuff, and as things change you need to revise your approach. Even though Emily and Scott did all the right things in their discussions and planning, it doesn't mean they lived happily ever after. Emily had difficulty making the transition from working outside the home and earning a good income to being a stay-at-home mom. She had to make an effort to remain connected to the adult world and to see how important she was to the baby's growth and development. Scott found he enjoyed being a father far more than he thought he would and was jealous of the time Emily had with the baby. Because they valued their relationship and their family, they made the effort to discuss their feelings and work together to get their needs met.

Deciding Who Does What in Your Family

For most couples, who does what becomes a significant issue as they become parents, whether or not it's been an issue for them before. If you and your partner don't take the time to negotiate who does what, you will probably fall into a division of duties similar to what you observed in your family of origin. For most couples, that pattern tends to be male as the breadwinner and female as the homemaker. If you and your partner experienced similar divisions of labor in your families growing up and that is what you both are planning on and agree on for your own family, you may not have to work through as many issues. But if you want a division of labor different from what you observed growing up or if you experienced different models in your respective families, you'll need to take action to develop a plan that will meet your unique individual and couple needs. As we've stressed elsewhere, the key is for the two of you to decide how adding a baby to the family will change who does what.

There are three major areas to address when considering who does what: financial support of the family, care of the baby, and household chores. As you consider these issues, you may want to go back to the exercises in Chapters Six and Seven. Your expectations, values, and beliefs will strongly influence your preferences for who does what. To remind you of a key point, *when you have different expectations for how things are going to be, your opportunities for conflict are greatly increased.* By working through such issues in advance, you can do a lot to prevent some problems from developing in the first place.

WORK AND CHILD CARE

There are probably no more important matters for the two of you to discuss and agree on than who will support the family financially and who will take care of the baby. These two issues are so intertwined that we recommend you consider them together. This is a great place to use the Problem-Solving Process we described earlier. But first, take the time to discuss in depth what you each think and feel about these issues. A lot of how you see yourselves may be tied to these roles, so take your time working on this.

Don't limit your brainstorming to "mom takes care of the baby and dad works," or vice versa; any number of arrangements can work well. There are endless possibilities from which to select the arrangement that is right for your family. It also helps to realize you don't have to make final decisions now to last forever. How you divide work and family responsibilities will continue to evolve as your child grows or you add other children to the family.

Divisions of Labor

Each family is unique in terms of what division of labor is best for them. Here are some examples. As we discussed earlier, Emily and Scott decided to assume traditional roles. Knowing she would lose her sense of connection from daily contact with people at work, Emily set up a schedule of regular social contact with friends and coworkers. She also made the effort to search out other new moms to maintain adult contact and have support for parenting. Because she planned ahead, Emily didn't feel the isolation and loneliness many women experience when they make the transition from working outside the home to parenting at home. And this way Emily didn't put an unfair burden on Scott to keep her connected to the world outside their family.

A different division of labor worked for Bill and Karen. Although Bill is the primary breadwinner in the family, Karen's income is necessary to meet basic expenses. Both wanted to have as much time as possible with their daughter and minimize her time being cared for by others. They were both able to rearrange their work schedules; Bill works during the day, and Karen works from noon until eight. During the hours neither is home, Karen's mom takes care of the baby in their home. This way the family is able to meet their financial obligations, both parents get time alone with the baby and still have some couple time, and the baby is cared for and gets to know her loving grandma. Although this arrangement is satisfactory for now, Bill and Karen miss the friendship time of dinner and evenings together. They view this arrangement as temporary because both are considering career changes.

Yet another couple negotiated a very different division of labor. About the time their baby was due, Julio decided his job was less than satisfying and the opportunities for promotion limited. Marta enjoyed a high-paying job with excellent benefits. Although both parents wanted to stay home with the baby, they decided it was economically prudent for Marta to continue working full-time while Julio cared for the baby. Although this arrangement worked well financially, it had a downside.

Julio really enjoyed his time with the baby, and they became very attached to one another. Whenever they went on outings, Julio found himself the only male with a baby. He struck up friendships with several mothers he saw regularly at the park. They said it was so nice to see a father with his baby but repeatedly asked when he would be returning to work. Julio also took a lot of grief from his parents, who asked what kind of man lets his wife support him.

At the same time, Marta found herself feeling jealous and resentful of the special relationship between Julio and the baby. Her coworkers frequently asked how she coped with being away from her baby, and her mother pointedly questioned her putting her work ahead of her child. Although their division of labor worked well financially, they had little support. By the time the baby was a year old, Julio had a new job, and Marta had cut back to part-time work. They had to be much more careful with their budget, but they were both happier.

There tends to be a strong basic assumption that parenting is women's work and breadwinning is men's work. It can be extremely difficult to go against the grain of expectations from your family, the broader society, and within yourself. Unlike Julio and Marta, Ben and Beth Ann have been able to make such an arrangement work for them. Beth Ann is a securities analyst. She took two months off to be with the baby and then returned to her high-powered and lucrative job. She is a professional dynamo and the primary bread-winner. Ben is domestic, loves being home with the baby, and works from home part-time as a technical writer. They have a circle of friends who are supportive of their division of labor, which helps make this arrangement work.

Child-Care Options

If you and your partner will both work after the baby comes, or if one of you will be a stay-at-home parent and may need periodic breaks from parenting, it's never too soon to start thinking about child care. It may take weeks to months to find suitable care for your child, regardless of the number of hours of care you need or the age of your child. As you consider this important issue, you'll want to keep in mind how important the early months and years of your baby's life are when it comes to both intellectual and emotional development. You are the most important people in your baby's life. No matter what decisions the two of you make about roles and child care, you want to be comfortable together that you are doing the best possible job for your child.

Being in a loving environment is important. So are talking, reading, and singing to your baby, introducing your baby to the wonders of the big world outside the womb, and stimulating and supporting your baby's development. You need to make sure your baby has these opportunities regardless of who the caregiver is—you and your partner or someone else in whom you have great trust.

There are a number of options for child care: care in your home by a relative or nonrelative; care in the home of a relative or non-relative; family child care or taking the baby to a home providing care for several children; or taking the baby to a child-care center. If anyone else will be providing care for your baby, you and your partner need to discuss your feelings about this and about all the options available to you.

There is a good deal of information that you should gather in order to have productive discussions. First, you need to decide whose decision this will be: yours, your partner's, or yours together. Then you need to know what your choices are. Find out which of the options listed earlier are available in your area. Many communities have child-care referral services that provide lists of child-care options. As you consider options, you need to know the relevant laws and regulations for child-care providers in your area. These can be obtained from your local or state department of human or social services.

Other parents are excellent resources on child-care options. Ask what choices they have made, why they made them, whether they would make the same choices again, and what recommendations they have for you. Be sure to check with your employer to see if there is on-site or employer-subsidized child care. Which of these options do you and your partner feel might be acceptable for your child? These questions are important to answer first.

Child-Care Costs

What can you afford to pay for child care? Some families are fortunate to have relatives or friends who will care for their child for free or through bartering of knowledge or services. Most new parents are shocked when they learn what child care costs. Don't assume you know. You need to get information from your own community. Typically the better the child care, the higher the price tag. One of the exercises for this chapter will help you evaluate costs of child care versus lost income. You can begin to work together now by dividing up who will gather what pieces of information you will need to make arrangements that are the way you want them to be.

Something you should think about as you consider options and calculate costs is the possibility of sharing child care with another family. Shortly after they learned they were pregnant, Patrick and Laurie discovered that their neighbors were expecting as well. After a number of discussions, they decided they had similar standards and expectations and wanted to hire a nanny. Before the babies were born, they learned about different options for hiring a nanny. They decided on a particular company that, for a fee, would find a nanny meeting their requirements, provide complete background and reference checks, and, if within the first year the original nanny did not work out for any reason, would find them another nanny.

A few months after the babies came, both couples began to interview potential nannies. By the time the mothers' maternity leaves ended, they had hired someone who both families thought would be an excellent caregiver for their babies. Both couples wanted the benefits of child care in their own homes, so they arranged that one week the nanny and babies would be at Patrick and Laurie's home and the next week at the neighbors'. Through discussions and creative problem solving Patrick and Laurie ended up with high-quality child care at an affordable price.

Tyson and Latisha found another solution to their child-care needs. Tyson's sister had two children of her own and agreed to take care of her nephew in her home for a small fee. When Mark reached one year of age, Tyson's sister was pregnant and found it too difficult to keep up with three active youngsters. In the meantime, Tyson and Latisha had met a couple in their neighborhood who provided child care in their home and were highly recommended by other parents. When Tyson and Latisha visited the home, they were pleasantly surprised by the loving and stimulating environment. The three other children there were busy and happy. Tyson and Latisha were pleased to find convenient, affordable, quality care for their son, Mark.

Bernard and Dee found yet another solution to their child-care needs. After carefully evaluating options in their community, they decided to take their baby to a day-care center located between their home and Bernard's office. In addition to being convenient, the location provided the opportunity for Bernard to have more time alone with Emma. He loved to pack her up in the morning and sing to her as they drove. Emma's glee at seeing her daddy at the end of the day made Bernard's heart soar and reminded him what was really important in life.

Even if your baby will be cared for at home by you and your partner, you will still need some breaks for self- and couple care. You can start looking into things like "Parent's Day Out" programs, which exist in most communities. You will also want to begin to think about and line up child care or baby trades so you and your partner can go out on dates.

Remaining Flexible

Every family is unique. Deciding how to meet your family's financial needs and how best to care for your children is important and challenging. Your satisfaction will depend on how carefully you have made these decisions and will influence your happiness and well-being as individuals, a couple, and a family. If you are satisfied with arrangements, your family is likely to thrive. If you are dissatisfied, everyone is likely to suffer.

Be open to change. Many couples make thoughtful plans before the baby is born, then change their minds after having the baby at home. Julie held a responsible and high-paying job. She always assumed she would return to work when her maternity leave ended. In fact, she and her husband were so sure of this that they never considered other options. It came as a shock when Julie decided she couldn't bear to leave the baby and return to work. This happens more often than you might imagine. As you and your partner discuss the division of work and family responsibilities, make sure to give yourselves options. You never know what's going to happen or how you will respond.

Just as Julie never considered staying at home, Taylor never considered returning to work. When her baby was born three months
early and had to remain in the hospital, Taylor had to return to
work so that she and her husband could pay the medical bills.

Adopting parents face the unique challenge of not knowing
exactly when their baby will arrive. Plans for a particular baby often
fall through, so you can never be sure when parenting will begin.
Making the appropriate arrangements requires careful planning and
open communication with your employer.

Whatever the situation, you need to be prepared to be flexible—
don't make the mistake of thinking that your plan is carved in
stone. Even if you are able to carry out your original plan, plans usually need to change as time goes by, your baby grows, or you add
another child to the family. You should revisit key decisions regularly, following up on plans and solutions and tweaking things to
make them work as well as they can.

GETTING THE CHORES DONE: NEGOTIATING HOUSEHOLD DUTIES

In addition to deciding who will earn the household income and
who will take care of the baby, you will need to make decisions
about who does what at home. You will need to decide what needs
doing, what your respective expectations are regarding those tasks,
who will actually do what, and how this may need to change before and after the baby comes. If you don't work these matters
out directly and with care, you risk lots of conflict in the months
ahead.

The first step is to make a list of all that needs doing. You'll be
guided through this in one of the exercises at the end of the chapter.
The next step is to discuss your expectations about each of these
tasks. Most couples don't take the time to talk about these things
until they're forced to. Although you may think you can put this off

until the baby comes, you will probably find that these issues must be dealt with earlier.

Early in pregnancy, many women are exhausted, nauseated, or both, which can limit their ability to complete chores. Most women find it difficult to bend or do physical chores late in pregnancy. It's better to start discussions about household tasks earlier rather than later. Don't wait until the baby comes, or you may be trying to deal with this division of household duties when you are exhausted and needing to focus on mastering basic parenting skills.

Adjusting Your Expectations

You may be surprised by the expectations the two of you have attached to various chores. Commonly held expectations include that men should pay the bills, take care of the car, and mow the lawn, and that women should cook, clean, do the laundry, and change diapers. Only open discussion of your respective expectations will reveal who you believe should do what in your family. Again, conflict can easily erupt during such discussions, so be respectful of each other and head off conflict by adding structure and safety. You will probably find issues and hidden issues lurking in these discussions. You may have figured out by now that deciding who will do what at home is not going to be quick and dirty, especially if you want to end up with a division of duties that you both can agree on and be satisfied with.

An expectation you are likely to bump into is that men believe women have innate parenting knowledge and skills. If they are honest, most women will confess this isn't true. They are usually able to "fake it" because they usually have more time with the baby early on to figure out which part of the diaper goes in front and how to get the baby's rubbery arms through sleeves. They are usually able to fumble along without an audience until they are fairly competent. Fathers, in contrast, are usually learning these skills under the critical eyes of mothers and grandmothers, and positive reinforcement can be scarce. Be sure to include these expectations in your discussions.

Whose Standards Must Be Met

Negotiating who does what at home includes another important consideration: Whose standards must be met? There are different expectations of what constitutes a job well done. A clean house can mean anything from a clear path between rooms to passing the white glove test. An adequate dinner can range from fast-food take-out fare to a six-course gourmet meal. One person's idea of a clean toilet can be very different from another's! Remember, when expectations and reality don't match, someone will be upset or dissatisfied.

Ginna and Bob bought their first home in anticipation of becoming parents. They were proud of their investment and wanted to make everything perfect. Ginna kept the house spotless. In fact, Bob often commented that the floors were clean enough to eat off of. The yard was Bob's pride and joy. Everything was always weeded and neatly trimmed. When the baby came, they tried to maintain their high standards. Their inability to do so led to some nasty fights. When they finally took the time to discuss the situation, they agreed that the priority was to spend time with each other and the baby. It took some effort and strong support from each other, but they were able to lower their standards to maintain a reasonably clean home and tidy yard, which allowed them to raise their standards for their relationships with each other and the baby.

Kelly and Drew had issues around standards even before their baby came. Kelly worked from their home. Drew always complained that her office looked like it had been hit by a tornado. They argued frequently about this, and things blew up completely when the baby was about two months old. They took a two-day Time Out to distance themselves from the big fight and gather their thoughts and ideas about this problem. They finally sat down to talk and were amazed by what surfaced as they used the Speaker-Listener Technique.

Kelly learned that Drew's intolerance of her mess came from his having grown up as the child of alcoholic parents whose home was always a disaster. Drew learned that Kelly heard his criticism as a lack of acceptance of her and a lack of recognition of her financial contribution to the family. After two good discussions, they were able to move through productive problem solving. In the end, they decided that the door to the office would remain closed. That way, Kelly could keep her workplace to her own standards, and Drew wouldn't have to see it and become upset. This was a relatively simple solution to a very volatile problem.

Many couples lower their house cleanliness standards when they become parents. They accept that things will get dirtier and more messed up with a child in the house and decide that time with the baby is the priority.

MAKING THE MOST OUT OF YOUR TIME

As you decide who will do what and to whose standards, you want to be sure you are using your time effectively. One of the most common comments made by new parents is, "What on earth did we do with all that time we had before the baby came?" Everyone has the same twenty-four hours in their day. It's how you decide to use those hours that really counts.

Putting a Value on Your Time

The key question here is, How much do you value your time? Forget how much money you earn. Put a dollar value on one hour of your time, and use this time value to guide your decisions about how you use your time. If your time value is $30, is it worth driving fifteen minutes out of your way to save $5 on a sale item or taking thirty minutes to cut coupons in order to save $3?

Jake takes pride in stretching every penny. Through careful investigation he found the lowest gasoline prices in the city. It's a forty-minute drive from his home to the gas station. Sure, he saves a few bucks, but he's spending precious family time to do so.

Once the baby came, Luci joined a membership warehouse store to save money. The place was thirty minutes from home, and because it overstimulated the baby she would hire a baby-sitter so she could make her monthly trip. If she had stopped to think about it, she would have realized she spent more on the baby-sitter than she saved at the warehouse store. Putting a dollar value on your time may shed new light on how you spend your time.

Another way to manage your time effectively is to divide chores into two categories: those that don't require much concentration or mental ability, such as washing dishes, which can be done when you're tired or when the baby is awake; and those tasks that need concentration, such as paying bills, and are better done when you are rested and the baby is asleep. Parents tend to become quite skilled at juggling more than one task at a time. You need to separate out the things that need your full and alert attention.

Another question to ask yourself is, What if it doesn't get done today? Sometimes we get caught up in "shoulds" and "musts." Does it really matter whether you clean the house today or tomorrow? If you put something off until tomorrow, will the sky fall? Will someone die? Learn to discern which things are life-or-death matters or have absolute deadlines, and be flexible with the rest. For some of us, drawing these distinctions is a real challenge.

Consider your time value and the multiple demands on your time. Separate tasks that absolutely require your skill or expertise from those you can hire someone to do. When money is an issue, you can barter services (that is, exchange skills or expertise with someone else).

Personal time, couple time, and family time need to be part of your time management plan. If you don't schedule time for yourself, your couple relationship, and your family, you just won't have it. Having regular times blocked out for these important activities will go a long way toward ensuring that your time isn't eaten up by mundane things like chores. Through the exercises in previous chapters, you have already thought and talked about how to maintain your couple

time for friendship, fun, and intimacy and your own time to recharge your batteries. As you work on the bigger picture of work
and family and household chores, don't forget to include those previous plans.

EXERCISES

The following exercises will help you think through work and family issues and decide who will do what in your family. Most couples
reconsider their decisions as their baby grows. As you move through
the exercises, develop a schedule for periodically reconsidering your
plan. Issues of who does what tend to be very sensitive, so you will
probably want to use the safety and structure of the Speaker-Listener
Technique for the more sensitive parts of these discussions.

Role Job Descriptions

Your expectations and core beliefs influence your expectations of
yourself and your partner for the roles you each enact in your relationship. We typically assume that our partner understands, without
discussion, what he or she is to do as a partner and parent—an assumption that typically results in disappointment and dissatisfaction.

First think about and then jot down your expectations of *yourself* as a *partner* (wife or husband) and *parent* (mother or father).
What is your job description for each of these roles? Then think
about and jot down *your* expectations of *your partner* as a *partner*
(wife or husband) and *parent* (mother or father). What is the job
description you expect your partner to fulfill for each of these roles?
It is very helpful to complete this exercise before your baby joins
the family. It will give you a sound foundation to build on and revise
as your baby grows.

When you and your partner have completed your individual
work, exchange the job descriptions. Use them as a basis for discussing the similarities and differences in your expectations of each
other. What values and beliefs do you become aware of in this

process? Are your expectations of yourself and your partner reasonable? Can they be met?

Use the Speaker-Listener Technique and the Problem-Solving Process to come to some agreement on how you will each enact the roles of partner and parent in a way that will work for you as a couple. Reaching agreement may take several discussions. In fact, this topic should be revisited regularly in your couple business meetings.

Who Will Support the Family Financially?

In order to determine who will support the family financially, use all the steps of the Problem-Solving Process. As part of Problem Discussion, you might want to review the exercises on expectations in Chapter Six and on core values and beliefs in Chapter Seven. You'll want to have any issues about the breadwinning and parenting roles on the table as you formulate a plan. When you are brainstorming, be creative. Consider *all* the possible ways your family's financial needs can be met.

You might want to come up with a list of the top three solutions and then consider each as you work through the next exercise. As you discuss these financial issues, be sure to include how you are currently spending your money, your standard of living, and where you live.

When becoming parents, many couples believe they "should" or "must" live in a house rather than an apartment, and in a particular neighborhood or part of town. They believe they *must* have certain "things." Consider and discuss where these expectations are coming from. Be sure you are discussing the realities and needs of your own unique family. Do what is best for you and what will work for you.

Financial Considerations of Working

As you work toward deciding how your family will be supported financially, you'll need to think through the financial impact of various alternatives. Many people today telecommute or work from their homes. If this is your situation, don't make the mistake of thinking you can work at home and take care of the baby at the same time. Even though young infants sleep a lot, they require a lot of attention. And it usually isn't considered appropriate to have business interactions interrupted by a crying baby.

Monthly Income

What is or would be your income from working full- or part-time? Consider all of the following:

- Salary
- Benefits

    Health and dental insurance coverage

    Social security benefits

    Retirement funds

    Child-care subsidy from your employer

    Child-care tax benefits

    Any other benefits that actually augment income or reduce your expenses

Monthly Costs of Working

Whether you work from your home or outside your home, what are the costs of your working? Keep in mind that hours devoted to work eat up hours that could be used in other ways. Consider all of the following. It might help to think through a workday from the time you get up until the time you go to bed, to be sure you have considered all expenses related to working.

- Child care
- Additional taxes from being in a higher tax bracket than if you don't work

- Commuting costs

    Public transportation

    Your own vehicle

    Need for a second vehicle if both parents are working

    Gas

    Vehicle maintenance

    Insurance

- Costs of meals at work (brown bag or restaurant)

- Clothing for work (this may include uniforms or business or professional clothes)

- Professional or union dues associated with working

- Frozen, prepared, or fast foods versus home cooking

- Costs of home and yard maintenance that is hired out—or the costs of the stress of not taking care of this maintenance

    Housecleaning

    Lawn and garden maintenance

    Home repairs or remodeling that you hire out rather than do yourself

- One-stop shopping rather than chasing bargains and sales

- Store-bought clothing and gifts rather than homemade

- Other costs

When you have calculated both income and the costs of working, subtract the costs of working from income to get the potential financial gain or loss from working. Most couples find this exercise quite revealing; they realize they have not fully considered the costs of working or not working.

Who Does What at Home?

A satisfying division of household duties won't happen by itself: you will need to invest time and effort to develop a plan that will work *for both of you*. You'll need to use all the skills you've learned so far to discuss the issues, problem-solve, and formulate a plan. The goal should be to create a division of labor that feels fair to each of you. Be sure to take into consideration work-for-pay responsibilities that will influence your availability for home chores.

- Together make a list of all the things that need to be done, including food chores (shopping, cooking), clothes chores (buying, doing laundry), baby care (all the basics plus arranging for appointments and activities), home maintenance (mowing lawn, repairs, car), and paper management (bills, taxes).

- Review the list and indicate who is currently doing each task. You will no doubt gain insights into the current division of labor in your household.

- What changes will make these chores more manageable? Can any be eliminated? Can any be delegated, hired out, or bartered out?

- Individually review the list again, indicating the chores you like to do or *don't mind* doing and those you *dislike* doing. Discuss together whether there are chores you can trade so as to be more satisfied.

- Develop a plan for who will do what starting now. Agree on a set time period after which you will evaluate how the plan is working. You will need to revise your plan over time. Before the baby comes, begin your discussions of how your plan may need to be revised *after* the baby arrives. Remember, the closer your expectations are to reality, the less dissatisfaction you will experience. It may help to use a calendar to schedule regular chores. Be sure also to schedule in your self-care time, couple time for fun and friendship (and perhaps even intimacy), and special mom and baby and dad and baby time. If at any time you are not satisfied with the division of labor, it is your responsibility to raise your concern with your partner.

Some Final Words

Becoming parents together is an exciting adventure that provides incredible opportunities for growth. You could think of this book as one of recipes for a solid and satisfying relationship as you move into parenthood together. We've reviewed what is damaging to relationships and have taught you specific skills and techniques to prevent, overcome, or manage such assaults on your future together. Now it's up to you. You can choose to invest the time and effort to do what it takes to have a great relationship, or, like too many parents, you can let your relationship fall by the wayside. We hope you'll choose to keep your relationship strong and growing while you share the adventure of parenthood.

IT TAKES SOME WORK

It's not easy to change habits. If you choose to use these techniques and skills, you will need to practice until they become second nature. Bill Coffin, a colleague and U.S. Navy specialist in the prevention of marital and family distress, recommends couples think about relationship fitness as they would physical fitness. Just as you might exercise for at least thirty minutes four times a week, you should devote at least that much time to relationship fitness.

If your partner isn't as motivated to learn and use these techniques, you can have an impact on your relationship just by changing your own behavior. You might also encourage your partner to try some of the relationship-enhancement techniques related to friendship, fun, and intimacy, which don't necessarily depend on knowing or using the other information in this book.

But here's a word of warning. Even if you and your partner are gung ho—you read this book together, do all the exercises, practice, and change your behaviors and interaction style, you can expect to fall back into some of your old patterns at some point. That's normal. Just as your baby will need booster shots to bolster the original immunizations, you and your partner will need periodically to reread some or all of this book and to work through exercises. We encourage you to make a pact to do this on a schedule that will help you stay on the right path.

WHEN YOU NEED MORE HELP

There will probably be times when you and your partner feel stuck or when you aren't able to handle an issue or situation by yourselves. We hope you will value your relationship enough to get professional help when you need it. If your car slid off the road into a ditch and you couldn't push it out yourself, you would probably call a tow truck. Your relationship can slide off the road, too. A skilled and caring therapist or clergy member can help you get back on the road and rolling again. If you decide you could use some help, get it sooner rather than later. Research suggests that most couples who are struggling wait far too long before they reach out for some help—waiting until significant damage has been done to their relationship.

If you do seek help, make sure you choose someone who works with and respects the importance of your relationship as a couple. Sometimes individual-oriented therapists can do more harm than good for a relationship. So make sure you check out the views of any helper to be sure they are compatible with your values and goals.

At some point you or your partner may have personal problems or issues—such as depression, unresolved issues around childhood abuse, or substance abuse—that are affecting your couple relationship. Again, cherish yourself and your marriage enough to get the help you need. Healthy relationships are made up of healthy people who take care of themselves and their relationship. Give yourself and your relationship the tender loving care you give your child.

IN CLOSING

Again, congratulations on your growing family! Your life and your relationship will continue to change as your child grows and develops. We hope you will find the information and techniques presented in this book helpful as you journey into and through parenthood— may your marriage and parenting together be even better than you hoped they could be.

FOR MORE INFORMATION

We conduct workshops for couples and train people as leaders to offer the Becoming Parents Program, the Prevention and Relationship Enhancement Program (PREP), and Christian PREP. We maintain a directory of people who have been trained in each of these programs and who offer workshops or counseling using these programs. You can obtain a directory by writing us requesting a referral directory or by visiting our Web site.

We also have *Fighting for Your Marriage* audiotapes—a six-hour set covering the basic PREP content—and a four-videotape series that covers the key communication and conflict management information. We plan to continue creating new ways to help couples learn this material.

You can contact us at

PREP, Inc.
P.O. Box 102530
Denver, CO 80250
(303) 759–9931

You can also e-mail us (info@PREPinc.com) or visit our Web site (http://members.aol.com/prepinc).

For more information on the Stop Anger and Violence Escalation Program (SAVE) and the Domestic Conflict Containment Program (DCCP), please contact

Behavioral Sciences Associates, Inc.
16 Knox Avenue
Stony Brook, NY 11790
(516) 689–6114

Some Thoughts on Domestic Violence

Because this book deals with communication and conflict between partners, sometimes questions arise about domestic violence. Domestic violence is a complex topic and is not the subject of this book. Nevertheless, we would like to stress some important points.

- This book is *not* a treatment program for domestic violence.

- Some couples can reduce their chances of becoming physically aggressive by using techniques such as those taught in this book. This would be most likely for couples at risk of crossing the line because they have difficulty managing conflict well. These techniques are *not* applicable to couples in which a controlling male uses physical aggression to dominate or subjugate his partner. In the latter case, women may only become safe by removing themselves from the presence of the aggressive partner.

- Although jealousy, anger, and conflict are normal elements of family life, physical aggression within the family is *never* justified. Domestic violence of any sort is unacceptable and wrong and dangerous, whether engaged in by the male, the female, or both.

- An alarming amount of domestic violence is taking place in families in our society.

• Domestic violence often starts or escalates during pregnancy and early parenthood, making this a time for couples to be especially attentive to patterns of escalation and anger.

• No matter what the nature of the violence, when males strike females, females are in greater danger and will likely suffer more long-lasting and negative aftereffects. Females also strike males, which is just as unacceptable.

• *When there is any kind of domestic violence, the primary concern should be safety.* Use whatever resources are necessary to ensure that neither the baby nor either partner is in danger, including taking the baby and leaving the house, calling 911, receiving counseling from a therapist who has experience in this area, or getting help from a community shelter for battered women.

Recommended Reading

There are countless books on pregnancy and various aspects of parenting. The content may be similar, so we encourage you to choose those that best meet your needs and have the format you prefer. The following are resources we *highly* recommend as you become parents. Books marked with an asterisk (*) may be difficult to find but should be available through your local library.

Dave and Claudia Arp. (1998). *Love life for parents: How to have kids and a sex life too*. Grand Rapids, MI: Zondervan. This outstanding resource contains countless suggestions for maintaining your couple relationship—friendship, fun, and intimacy—as you parent. Filled with practical advice, humor, and great wisdom.

Jay Belsky and John Kelly. (1994). *The transition to parenthood: How a first child changes marriage*. New York: Delacorte Press. Based on Belsky's large landmark study, this book explores why some couples grow closer and others apart as they become parents. Uses couples to exemplify key points.

T. Berry Brazelton. (1994). *Touchpoints: Your child's emotional and behavioral development*. Reading, MA: Addison-Wesley. Touchpoints are the universal, predictable times just before a surge of rapid growth and development (motor, cognitive, or emotional) when, for a short time, the child's behavior falls apart. Parents can anticipate these times and therefore deal with their challenges more effectively while continuing to promote their child's development.

Armin Brott. (1997). *The new father: A dad's guide to the first year.* New York: Abbeville. A very practical month-by-month guide for new fathers. Each chapter includes information on what's going on with the baby, what the dad is going through, and you and your baby—all the tools needed to understand and create the deepest, closest father-child relationship. Also included is information on issues that will affect not only dad but also the family as a whole.

Armin Brott and Jennifer Ash. (1995). *The expectant father: Facts, tips, and advice for dads-to-be.* New York: Abbeville. A very practical guide for expectant fathers. Each chapter, organized by the months of pregnancy, includes information on what the mom is going through, what's going on with the baby, what the dad is going through, and how the dad can stay involved.

Carolyn Pape Cowan and Phillip A. Cowan. (1992). *When partners become parents: The big life change for couples.* New York: Basic Books.* These authors, both psychologists, use data derived from their landmark study to chart the changes that greet the arrival of a first child. Drawing on the stories of a variety of men and women, the authors reveal common pitfalls and offer sound advice about navigating the troubled waters of early parenthood.

Susan Jeffers. (1990). *Opening our hearts to men.* New York: Fawcett. Prescribes specific steps women can take to explore the origins of their feelings toward men. The resulting increased awareness will allow women to relate more effectively to men personally and professionally. An important book for *all* women.

Howard Markman, Scott Stanley, and Susan L. Blumberg. (1994). *Fighting for your marriage: Positive steps for preventing divorce and preserving a lasting love*. San Francisco: Jossey-Bass. The Prevention and Relationship Enhancement Program (PREP) in a generic form that can be used by all couples.

Clifford Notarius and Howard Markman. (1994). *We can work it out: How to solve conflicts, save your marriage, and strengthen your love for each other*. New York: Berkley. The focus of this book is on how you can protect your relationship from destructive conflict, with particular attention to how you handle anger.

Brad Sachs. (1992). *Things just haven't been the same: Making the transition from marriage to parenthood*. New York: Morrow.* This outstanding book zeroes in on the key issues of becoming parents, including all the issues of each parent's family of origin. The author presents not only the issues and where they come from but also very helpful exercises on how to deal with them.

Jerrold Lee Shapiro. (1995). *The measure of a man: Becoming the father you wish your father had been*. New York: Delacorte Press. The author describes what fatherhood has traditionally meant and why it is so difficult to break free from the negative elements of this traditional role. He also explores women's influences on the father's role and how traditional motherhood hinders change in men's fathering. The heart of this book is an examination of the effect of a man's experience of having been fathered on his behavior as a father.

Gary Smalley. (1996). *Making love last forever*. Dallas, TX: Word. The author uses wit and humor, stories and metaphors to inspire couples to reach toward expressing honor and love so as to protect and deepen marital quality.

Scott Stanley. (1998). *The heart of commitment*. Nashville, TN: Nelson. Based on scripture and research on marital success and failure, this book offers specific and practical advice on how to build true commitment in your marriage. The focus is on how to develop the kind of commitment that moves you beyond merely staying together to being together in the fullest measure for life.

Scott Stanley, Daniel Trathen, Savanna McCain, and Milt Bryan. (1998). *A lasting promise: A Christian guide to fighting for your marriage*. San Francisco: Jossey-Bass. The Christian version of the Prevention and Relationship Enhancement Program (CPREP).

Deborah Tannen. (1991). *You just don't understand: Women and men in conversation*. New York: Morrow. Using powerful evidence from her research, the author shows that men and women live in different worlds, even under the same roof, so conversation between them is like cross-cultural communication. This book can help men and women find a common language with which to communicate and to build deeper bonds with each other through mutual understanding.

Carolyn Webster-Stratton. (1992). *The incredible years: A troubleshooting guide for parents of children aged three to eight*. Toronto: Umbrella Press. This essential resource teaches all the basics of parenting: playing with your child, praise, rewards, limit setting, discipline, dealing with anger, and so on. It is never too soon to learn these skills or too early to use them with your children.

About the Authors

Pamela L. Jordan, Ph.D., R.N., is an associate professor in the Department of Family and Child Nursing at the University of Washington in Seattle. She is an expert on the transition to parenthood, especially expectant and new fatherhood, and has authored research articles on becoming parents for the first time. She has developed the Becoming Parents Program, which is a modified and expanded version of PREP (the Prevention and Relationship Enhancement Program). She contributes regularly to print media on the topics of expectant and new parenthood and of maintaining your marriage as you become parents.

Scott M. Stanley, Ph.D., is codirector of the Center for Marital and Family Studies at the University of Denver in Colorado. He has authored numerous research articles on relationships and is an expert on marital commitment. He has worked with Howard Markman on the research and development of PREP for over twenty years. Stanley has coauthored the best-selling book *Fighting for Your Marriage* and has developed audio- and videotapes by the same title. He is also the coauthor of *A Lasting Promise* and author of *The Heart of Commitment*. He regularly appears in print and broadcast media as an expert on marriage, marital commitment, and the prevention of divorce.

Howard J. Markman, Ph.D., is a professor of psychology and co-director of the Center for Marital and Family Studies at the University of Denver. He is widely published and internationally known for his work on the prediction and prevention of marital distress and divorce. He has often appeared in broadcast and print media, including segments about PREP on *20/20, Oprah,* and *48 Hours.* Along with his colleagues, he has coauthored the books *We Can Work It Out: Making Sense of Marital Conflict* and the best-seller *Fighting for Your Marriage.*

Index